Connecting

Connecting

How We Form Social Bonds
and
Communities in the Internet Age

Mary Chayko

State University of New York Press

Published by
State University of New York Press, Albany

© 2002 State University of New York

All rights reserved

Printed in the United States of America

For information, address State University of New York Press,
90 State Street, Suite 700, Albany, NY 12207

Production by Michael Haggett
Marketing by Michael Campochiaro

Library of Congress Cataloging-in-Publication Data

Chayko, Mary, 1960–
    Connecting : how we form social bonds and communities in the Internet
age/Mary Chayko.
        p.cm.
    Includes index.
    ISBN 0-7914-5433-9 (alk. paper)—ISBN 0-7914-5434-7 (pbk. : alk. paper)
    1. Interpersonal relations. 2. Internet—Social aspects. I. Title.

HM1106. C488 2002
302—dc21   2002019099

10 9 8 7 6 5 4 3 2 1

To Glenn, Ryan, and Morgan, to whom I am so lovingly connected

Contents

Preface   ix

1 A Meeting of the Minds   1

2 From Cave Paintings to Chat Rooms: The Sociomental
   Foundation of Connectedness   7

3 Making the Connection . . . Across Time, Space,
   and Cyberspace   39

4 Till Death Do We Disconnect? Keeping Connections Alive   79

5 How Real Does It Get? Properties of Sociomental Bonds   101

6 The Social "Fallout" of Connecting at a Distance   127

Appendix 1   Investigating the Sociomental: The Face-to-Face
   Interview Methodology   163

Appendix 2   Cyberspace Connecting: The Online Survey
   Methodology   181

Notes   187
References   201
Index   229

Preface

When I was a young girl, I noticed that people often behaved as though they "knew" people they had never actually "met." My friends and I talked about our favorite singers, athletes, and actors as though we knew them personally. At the dinner table, my family and I compared notes on JFK and Jackie, Archie Bunker and Meathead, jazz musician Charlie Parker, and the lineup of the New York Mets in much the same way as we discussed the actions of our neighbors, classmates, and cousins. One of my grandmothers talked about her favorite soap opera characters as though they were real people; the other told me stories about her deceased husband (who had died before I was born) that were so vivid that it often seemed he was standing in the room with us. And, most interestingly, I had developed what seemed like genuine feelings of connectedness to Louisa May Alcott, the author of my favorite book, *Little Women*, and with the novel's protagonist, a girl my age, Jo March, who wanted to be a writer.

None of us, to my knowledge, were confusing reality with fantasy. We knew who we did and didn't "really know." But something still nagged at me. For I felt that in some mysterious way I *did* know these faraway "others." Feeling a sense of knowing them, of connectedness to them, mattered to me. Yet I knew it would sound ridiculous to say so aloud, so of course I never did; I thought what I thought and felt what I felt solitarily.

Why did I feel something for these distant, absent others? Why did these connections feel so real? And why, I wondered, didn't people ever talk about things like this? I became more and more intrigued. Years later, when I discovered the ease and allure of contacting like-minded others a world away on the Internet, I realized that plenty of other people had to be engaged in some of these same processes. In invisible—but meaningful—ways, we were *connecting*. But how, in the absence of face-to-face interaction, did we make and maintain these kinds of connections?

I found a "home" for my questions, a place to articulate and explore them, at Rutgers University in the graduate department of sociology. I was fortunate to have arrived at Rutgers when the field of cognitive sociology was emerging as a specialization within the discipline and to have had the opportunity to meet and study with some of the very best in the field. I also took some highly stimulating classes with faculty who epitomize original thinking and demand the same of their students. With their encouragement, I developed the ideas and designed the research upon which this book is based.

Eviatar Zerubavel, in particular, "opened" my mind with his innovative approach to sociology and academia. He meticulously helped me sort through, articulate, and stretch and extend my ideas. He was satisfied only with my very best efforts, unfailingly detecting laziness, redundancy, and irrelevance in my work and always suggesting a useful path for improvement. And I'll never forget his heartfelt concern for my well-being when that was what I needed most. More than anyone, Eviatar saw what my work, and what I, as a scholar, could be, and for helping me see these things, too, I will be forever grateful to him.

I have been influenced by other fine scholars as well. Karen Cerulo has been the consummate teacher, colleague, co-author, and friend— smart, imaginative, tough, honest, and caring. Judy Gerson, Deirdre Kramer, Randy Smith, Carl Couch, Sarah Thompson, Jim and Greta Pennell, Geoff Curran, Jill Roper, Tracy Budd, Greg Metz, Nicky Isaacson, Christena Nippert-Eng, and Dan Ryan have each made a special mark on my life and on this work. And perhaps no one has ever been more supportive of me than Ira Cohen. Though his analyses of my work always overflowed with invaluable ideas and suggestions, it was, most of all, his genuine compassion and our long, illuminating talks that sustained me through the ups and downs of my life during the span of this project.

Eddie Manning, my boss at the Livingston College Educational Opportunity Fund, where I worked full time during the research for this book, gave me many types of assistance and support, and never made me feel as though I had to choose from among my professional or personal commitments. Several of my co-workers were particularly helpful with regard to the writing of the book and gave me many useful suggestions and ideas. They include: Jennifer Agosto, Milagros Arroyo, Natasha Datta, Eileen Faherty, Terri Goda, Mahasti Hashemi, and Paula Van Riper. Barry Lipinski gave me much-needed library assistance. Ron Helfrich, my editor at SUNY Press, has been a source of support and encouragement since we first "met" electronically. And this book benefitted greatly from the thoughtful, intelligent editing of Michele Lansing and Michael Haggett at SUNY Press.

To the College of Saint Elizabeth in Morristown, New Jersey, which welcomed me so warmly as I completed this project, I offer sincere thanks. I look forward to many wonderful times and exciting projects to come. I especially want to note the kindness and guidance (both scholarly and spiritual) of Sister Ellen Desmond, Sister Francis Raftery and Dean Johanna Glazewski.

To those who consented to interviews with me, I thank you for your time, your candor, and your willingness to share your stories.

Without a loving family, work such as this must be so much more difficult to do. My parents, Bob and Terri Chayko, have always believed in me and been there for me. My brother John, sister Cathy, and brother-in-law Gary have done the same, always helping and teaching me. But in the end, it is my son Ryan, daughter Morgan, and husband, Glenn Crooks, who give the deepest meaning to everything in my life. Because of them, I have learned to commit to work and to relationships, to set and reach goals, to trust, to recognize and appreciate goodness, and most of all, to love. This is for them—for *us*.

1

A Meeting of the Minds

When Diana, Princess of Wales, lost her life in a car crash in the summer of 1997, many of us felt a sense of grief and loss—or, at the very least, sadness at the tragedy of a life cut so terribly short. Of course, this was not the only time we mourned the loss of someone we had never actually "met." JFK, his brother Bobby, and his son John, Martin Luther King Jr., Elvis Presley, John Lennon, Kurt Cobain, Marilyn Monroe—we felt that we knew them, in a way, and we experienced a flood of genuine emotions upon their untimely deaths.

It is not only in death that we can come to feel that we have gotten to know, and have come to care about, someone whom we have never "met" in a face-to-face sense. It is, in fact, a common occurrence.[1] From the child who establishes a relationship with a pen pal to the old man who considers Walter Cronkite a kind of trusted friend, from the cancer patient who finds companionship in an online group of cancer survivors to the lover of literature who feels a sense of like-mindedness with a favorite author (or even, possibly, with a favorite character in a novel), there are as many examples of connecting with others at a distance as there are people seeking social connection.

These are bonds that exist primarily in a mental realm, a space that is not created solely in the imagination of one individual but requires two or more minds—a "meeting of the minds"—to make possible, to "activate." These bonds are *sociomental*.[2] But they are no less real for being located in a mental realm.[3] They are the manifestation of an absolutely genuine and often deeply felt sense that despite physical separation, a closeness among

1

people, a nearness, exists; that while the physical distance separating people may be great, the social distance between them may be very small indeed. They represent an experience of communion with another person, one that does not depend on face-to-face meetings to be initiated or maintained.

Sociomental bonds—bonds between people who cannot or do not meet face-to-face—have never been more prevalent, more central to people's lives, and more critical to an understanding of the times and of the social order. But they are still, for the most part, an underground, understudied phenomenon.[4] They can seem strange—even a little shameful. We do not talk about them much, let alone consider their contribution to and impact on our societies, our communities, and ourselves. The implication is that they are not normal, not authentic, or that they exist on the fringe of the social world—odd, false, and inconsequential.

But that is not the case. Connecting with people across distances and even across time is a rather ordinary part of the human experience. A social environment saturated with technology virtually ensures that we will all have extensive knowledge of a whole host of people who are not part of any face-to-face social circle of ours—celebrities, heads of state, historical figures, influential writers and thinkers, pen pals (or phone pals, or e-mail pals), even our own faraway or deceased family members and friends. Through television, radio, books, magazines, and, increasingly, on the Internet, it is likely that we will come to feel that we have "gotten to know" plenty of people in this way. We will probably respond to and resonate with at least some of these people mentally and emotionally. We may even come to care about them—possibly quite deeply—and feel that we have bonded in some way with them. And as all bonds do, these touch and affect us, as they inspire us to view different perspectives on the world, to take on new roles, and to learn subtle but important lessons about "the other." According to John Caughey, each of us makes several hundred connections—some weak, some strong—with others whom we have never met and may never meet (1984: 22).

This book explores exactly how, under what conditions, and with what effect social connectedness takes place in the absence of face-to-face contact. I unfold a theoretical and historical framework for understanding the phenomenon, look at the ways these connections are made and maintained, discuss some of their properties, and look at the benefits, hazards, and implications—the social "fallout"—of the role they play in the Internet age. I examine strong, long-lasting *sociomental bonds*, weaker and perhaps more fleeting *sociomental connections*, and clusters and groupings of such connections and bonds into what I call *communities of the mind*.[5] And I illustrate these concepts and ideas with dozens of the personal, real-life accounts of

sociomental connecting that emerged in the fifty in-depth, face-to-face interviews and the 143 online surveys that I conducted.[6] The result is a look
at a type of social bonding that is rarely recorded: the bonds and communities that form among people who never meet face-to-face but still feel undeniably, if sometimes unexpectedly, connected.

Even in face-to-face interaction it is by no means guaranteed that
a true social connection will emerge when two people spend time
together. "Very frequently," Emile Durkheim reminds us, "those closely
knit by ties of blood are morally and legally strangers to one another"
(1984 [1893]: xliv). What looks to the observer like a strong social bond (a
seemingly "happy" marriage, an ostensibly "close" parent-child relationship) may in reality be weak, neutral, or, for all intents and purposes,
nonexistent. Conversely, what may seem *not* to be a bond (a connection
that is felt with a deceased person or with a favorite author or actor) may
in reality be a strong and meaningful one in the connector's eyes. The assumption that social connections must satisfy certain narrowly determined
criteria (such as "containing" a face-to-face component) in order to be
truly authentic greatly oversimplifies the phenomenon of social bonding.

For one of the strongest and most compelling components of social
connecting is the perception of a connection in a person's *mind*. Even social connections initiated in face-to-face interaction endure periods of
separation—often long periods—in which the connectors are physically
apart (with an exception being conjoined twins). In fact, though we do
not usually think of them this way, the terms *social connection, social bond,*
and *social tie* are, in virtually all situations, merely metaphors for the "getting together" of people who are separated from one another. People are
not (usually!) physically connected, bound or tied together; rather, we call
them "connected," "bonded," or "tied" when we intuit that their relationship is sufficiently strong to warrant the metaphor.[7]

We maintain social connections mentally as a matter of course; we
"carry" absent others with us in our minds and hearts. Social connections
that are formed when people are *frequently* separated from one another
have quite a lot in common with those that form when people are *always*
separated from one another. Sociomental connections are "layered," in a
sense, above, underneath, and around face-to-face connections—intersecting with and overlapping them to a large extent. Since we all have had
the experience of maintaining social connections mentally, it only requires
taking the next logical step to consider how we might initiate and then
sustain social connections *solely* in our minds.

This book takes that step. It shines a spotlight on otherwise invisible
forms of social connectedness. And it proposes that there is great value in

such visibility. Children tend to accept rather easily the premise that imaginary friends have a degree of social reality, that characters in books are known by us, and that a pen pal is, indeed, a bona fide friend. But as we grow older, we learn to officially discount such feelings, to push them into the dark corners of our minds. In time, they become disavowed, enjoyed only secretly (as "guilty pleasures") or all but expunged from our consciousness. It is no wonder that they take on the quality of strangeness or, when they visibly erupt, to cause us no small measure of embarrassment.

In the end, though, a greater harm than embarrassment lurks. When we fail to acknowledge (and study) a form of human sociation, we devalue that sociation—and with it, a large portion of existence, a big chunk of everyday life. We devalue our own experiences and emotions. Unwittingly, but inevitably, we end up diminishing important and legitimate parts of ourselves. Yet even as we deny them, we continue to form sociomental connections. In an age in which technology continuously "brings" absent others into our social spheres, our tendency to connect in this way will only increase.

Perhaps this is why, when given the opportunity to speak at length about the connections they had formed with distant or absent others, the people I interviewed seemed happy to do so; indeed, many found it downright cathartic. As I explained the concept of the sociomental bond to them and prompted them to think and talk about such connections, it was as if I was giving them permission to speak openly (and *legitimately*) about such things. Once the floodgates were opened, I often could not stop people from talking. People would contact me again and again after the interview to tell me about "just one more thing" or one more instance of sociomental connectedness that they had just remembered. Both the "high-tech" people I interviewed (twenty-five people who felt comfortable incorporating a wide range of technologies into their lives and thus did so) and those who were more "low-tech" (twenty-five who felt less comfortable with technologies such as computerization and shied away from them) told me about numerous sociomental connections that they had formed. In fact, only two individuals (one high-tech, one low-tech) told me that they did not feel they had formed any at all.[8]

The overwhelming majority of the people I spoke to related many more instances and types of such connections, and described many more emotions in response to them, than I could have imagined prior to the start of my research. A man just graduating from college described the "invisible bond" he felt with all of those who had ever attended his small, all-male high school, a young career woman told me about the special kind of kinship she felt with an established woman in her field that had developed as she read the older woman's books and articles and learned about her life, and a prospective parent movingly shared his profound sense of "already knowing" his as-yet-unborn baby. Stories such as these—and the others found in these pages—shaped, much more than reflected, my thinking, and they taught me just how important it is to give voice to such experiences.

I noticed the same thing among the people I surveyed online. In each of the six different types of online groups I looked at (groups centered around soap operas, sports, science, literature, religion, and the experience of being in an age-related grouping, "Generation X," which correlates roughly to being in one's twenties in the 1990s), I heard numerous stories about online connections that had been made and which felt absolutely genuine but about which connectors tended not to speak. People told me about connections both fleeting and long lasting, both meaningless and deeply consequential, and both narrow in scope and "multiplex" (encompassing various social spheres and arenas of social life). Again, it was as though I had opened a gate through which people's thoughts and emotions were finally free to flow. "I thought I was the only one who felt this way!" was something I heard frequently, as their stories tumbled out.

When we keep these kinds of connections and processes hidden, we not only devalue them (and ourselves), we are prevented from seeing a bigger picture. We are blinded to the "less conspicuous forms of relationship and kinds of interaction" that, Georg Simmel tells us, "produce society as we know it" (1950 [1908]: 9). In effect, we treat the tip of the iceberg— the visible, physical, face-to-face relationships among us—as the most part worthy of attention. We ignore and relegate to the realm of the insignificant that which is hidden from view. As Simmel also points out:

> [T]he whole gamut of relations that play from one person to another, and may be momentary or permanent, conscious or unconscious, ephemeral or of grave consequence . . . *all these incessantly tie men together.* . . . They account for all the toughness and elasticity, all the color and consistency of social life, that is so striking and yet so mysterious. (1950 [1908]: 10, emphasis added)

An appreciation of the hidden, inconspicuous, but very real ways in which people mentally "come together" to form bonds and communities can help us see the bigger picture of society: a more detailed social landscape revealing a wider palette of colors, more delicate shadings, and ever-changing contours.

None of this is to say that face-to-face contact is, or should be, decentered, or that connecting at a distance is somehow equivalent to or preferable to face-to-face interaction. It is not. We need face-to-face interaction. It is crucial to our intellectual and social development, it allows for the development of richer contexts between people in which more intricate details and meanings can be shared, and it provides certain satisfactions that are impossible to technologically replicate.[9] We would not want to conceive of a world in which face-to-face interaction was considered unimportant, unsatisfying, irrelevant. But that is not to say that *every* social connection requires a face-to-face component in order to become established or nurtured. A "meeting of the minds" can be just what a particular situation requires. Our individual "portfolios" of social connectedness should, ideally, consist of a healthy mix of face-to-face *and* sociomental connections in both dyadic and group forms.

This book, then, is a conceptual and an empirical examination of social connectedness and a critical component of it—the sociomental—that is frequently overlooked. Modern social forces—the speed and complexity with which our lives often move, the high rate of geographic mobility, the fast pace of technological change, the stress of combining work and home lives—often physically separate people from one another. Yet we stubbornly, inventively persist in finding ways to forge the social connections we need and desire. We have a remarkable capacity for connecting with others—for forming social bonds and communities across great distances and throughout time in the Internet age.

2

From Cave Paintings to
Chat Rooms: The Sociomental
Foundation of Connectedness

We are, all of us, social connectors. In the midst of a world that can overwhelm us with its demands and complexity, we strive nonetheless to make connections with others, whether those connections are strong or weak, enduring or fleeting, "multiplex" (maintained across a variety of settings and life spheres) or "uniplex" (confined to narrow, specific sites), and activated in face-to-face copresence or in the space of our own minds.[1] In fact, the wide variety of ways in which people can connect testifies to the strength of the human need to feel connected to others, the malleability of the social connection itself, and the mental flexibility of those who would become connected.[2]

In premodern times,[3] people relied on face-to-face contact for most of their social transactions and came to form most of their relationships with those with whom they were spatially proximate. People were in more frequent contact with comparatively fewer others than in the modern era. Together, often physically, they developed a set of values and norms; a "mechanical" solidarity, as Durkheim would put it, which sacrificed individuality to the group and connected individuals to one another and to the whole.[4] As premodern people experienced plenty of face-to-face contact with many of the same other people, the forces that would "unify" them were almost automatically activated (Davis 1973: xxii; see also Simmel 1962 [1908]).

In more modern times, social relations tend to depend more on the sharing of "common ideas, interests, sentiments, and occupations" than on the sharing of literal space (Durkheim 1984 [1893]: xlii). Technologies of communication and transportation have played a large part in the discovery and development of interpersonal commonalities across space and time. They have permitted people to "see" and know of—and thus potentially feel connected to—many more people than in premodern times. Since we do not see most of our friends or family members on a constant basis anymore, we must deliberately activate those thoughts and feelings that would keep us connected.[5] At the same time, we busily perform the specialized tasks that a complex division of labor requires; we are part of far-flung social systems that often are global in reach and impact. This interdependence on others who live great distances away and will probably never be met can be thought of as a new kind of "organic" solidarity (see Durkheim 1984 [1893]). In modern times, then, social relations are less dependent on "accidents" of proximity (Campbell 1990: 140) and emerge more often as a by-product of extensive social differentiation and specialization, the increased physical distance between us, and the capacity to choose aspects of our lives that had once been strictly proscribed.

Three basic things are required to accomplish the formation of sociomental connections: a mediator (often technological) to facilitate communication and connectedness among physically separated people, individuals whose minds are similar enough to permit the creation of a connection, and a "space" in which the connection can be said to "take root" and "grow." In this chapter, I describe these fundamental elements of sociomental connectedness. I focus on the ways in which technologies from cave paintings to chat rooms bridge the distance between absent people, I examine the role of the socially structured mind and cognition in making connections possible, and I provide a perspective with which we may envision the nonphysical realms (such as "cyberspace") in which connections at a distance form. We will then have a sturdy basis upon which our understanding of sociomental connectedness can rest.

TECHNOLOGY, THE MEDIA, AND THE DEVELOPMENT OF SOCIAL CONNECTEDNESS

Interpersonal relations and structures of social arrangement have always been influenced by the way people produce and use technologies.[6] Technologies make new modes of production and new kinds of work and leisure activities possible, they serve as mediators between people, facilitating coordinated activity among people who cannot always be in face-to-face contact, and they inspire subtle ways of thinking and behaving that would never have been possible prior to their invention and adoption. This is especially true of communication technologies for, as Marshall McLuhan argued (1964), modes of human thinking are shaped by the very media through which we communicate ideas (see also Allman 1993: 63). For our purposes, a tool or technique external to the human body that serves as an extension of that body, conducting or transmitting information among disparate individuals, shall be considered a technology.

Technology can increase our capacities to communicate, learn, think, and act, irrevocably changing the world that we inhabit. One significant technological change, Neil Postman writes, "generates total change" (1993: 18). For

> [a] new technology does not add or subtract something. It changes everything. In the year 1500, fifty years after the printing press was developed, we did not have old Europe plus the printing press. We had a different Europe. After television, the United States was not America plus television; television gave a new colorization to every political campaign, to every home, to every school, to every church, to every industry. . . . New technologies alter the structure of our interests: the things we think *about*. They alter the character of our symbols: the things we think *with*. And they alter the nature of community: the arena in which thoughts develop. (18–20; emphasis in original)

Technology makes possible new ways for us to think and form connections and communities. As new technologies of communication continue to emerge, new social environments are constantly created (see Meyrowitz 1985: 19) in which new ways of apprehending one another develop. It is in these new environments that sociomental connections are established.

The first, simplest systems of interpersonal communication and language—gestures, grunts, cries, and the crude technologies of drawing and picture writing—marked the first moments in human history that people could label concepts and then communicate those concepts to someone else. For it was then possible for something or someone external to an individual to *mediate* between the thoughts of that individual and another—to carry a concept or an idea to a third person who was spatially separated from the first, with the potential result a *realized* and *communicated* point of commonality. Anthropologist Richard Leakey considers how this may have occurred in the Upper Paleolithic Ice Age:

> It requires little imagination to think of Upper Paleolithic people chanting incantations in front of cave paintings.... When one stands in front of an Ice Age creation now, as I did with the bison in the cave of Le Tuc d'Audoubert, the ancient voices force themselves on one's mind. (1995: 83)

For the first time a connection could be formed across space and time.

In predominantly oral, preliterate societies, in which written language was either unknown or extremely crude, knowledge had to be contextualized verbally to be passed along to future generations. "Language," McLuhan writes, invoking Henri Bergson, "does for intelligence what the wheel does for the feet and the body" (1964: 83). It enables the intellect to "move from thing to thing," even when those things are not located in one's immediate line of sight (ibid.); it permits knowledge of distant things and distant others. Through the use of mnemonic devices and formal rituals, information such as king lists, genealogies, clan names, stories, legal precedents, and the like was given oral textual form with the intent that it be fixed in individual memories and in the social memory of groups (Fentress and Wickham 1992: 79). Specific situational information, as opposed to the abstract concept, was most easily memorized and passed along this way (Ong 1982: 49–57; Luria 1976).

People who lived at this time were thus limited to learning specific, fairly concrete things about their predecessors. They could not, for example, know much about the subtleties of character of a long-dead king, and as such they likely had no sense that it might be desirable, or even possible, to know such a thing. People in oral societies could not and did not develop the ability, the need, or the will to connect across time and space in any kind of sophisticated fashion. Their minds (and their lives) were not so structured.

As picture writing and the spoken word became codified into written languages somewhere in the range of 5,000 to 6,000 years ago, they both influenced and reflected an increasing desire among humans to communicate with greater specificity and at a higher level of abstraction than systems of picture writing and memory permitted. Correspondingly, our ancestors gained the related abilities to think in more abstract ways and to communicate these abstract concepts to one another. As they increased in sophistication, written languages liberated communication from the restrictions of orality. Writing began to connect more people, in a more meaningful way, across time. And with this increasing linguistic capability came no less than a restructuring of human consciousness and connectedness.

Someone in a different place and time could now read another person's words and gain access to the actual thoughts, the precise words, of that absent person. People could mark the past in a specific, detailed way and produce ideas and information that might be used to bring about change in the future (Schramm and Porter 1982). People's lives—and minds—became structured to accept and create more abstract phenomena and to consider experience in a more linear fashion, with an eye toward knowing things and doing things related to the past and the future. For as people came to *want* to look to the past and to the future, they slowly came to *desire* connections with people from the past and the future—a huge conceptual leap from preliterate connectedness. People could feel, in a more direct way than ever before, connected to someone who had passed away before he or she was born, in a way that was probably not too different from that which my interview subject Maria describes:

> My grandfather. I didn't know him. And I do feel connected to him. And I wanted to meet him and share with him the grandfather-granddaughter thing. I heard stories. But he died before I was born.

It is in talking about people of the past and people *projected* to live in the future, my interviewee Ling told me, that people of different generations become and "feel connected, just in passing information from one person to another."

Of course, it was still a long, slow journey from then to now. Premodern people spent much of their time in face-to-face contact with small, contained groups of others—groups that constituted the bulk of their social relationships. The spoken word had prominence in human life (as it still does today). But in combination with writing and drawing, speaking began to take on the role of connecting distant others, and at this point in history technologies began to be used in combination with one another and with face-to-face interaction to connect people. People could, in effect, create individualized "portfolios" of connections "containing" both face-to-face and sociomental connections.

When stone tablets, paper and ink, hand-copied books, and early newspapers—our first mass media—appeared in the early centuries A.D., another revolution in social connectedness followed. For Gutenberg would adapt existing printing technologies in the mid-fifteenth century to create multiple copies of the Bible with his printing press and ensure that ever afterward information could be "passed" from one person to another in an entirely new, large-scale way. This extended almost indefinitely people's ability to share information about themselves and the world around them (Schramm and Porter 1982: 12). A lot of people, or a "mass" of them, could now connect to a single individual or to one another across space and time. As people's brains began to internalize these capabilities and as technology continued to advance (though probably not without the fear and resistance that tend to accompany the introduction of any technology to a society), more and more opportunities for making sociomental connections began to emerge. People began to become adept at making such connections.

People also could at this point begin to develop and extend their thoughts with an eye toward mass publication—for personal, ideological, or financial satisfaction or gain. Intellectual activity in general burgeoned as ideas became more plentiful, precise, and commodifiable. The technological mediation of human thought became an industry or, more accurately, multiple industries. Numerous businesses, organizations, universities, libraries, and specialized religious sects and political parties were born as people discovered what could be gained by pooling their ideas and resources via the written word if not always by face-to-face interaction.

In short order, mass-produced books, pamphlets, newspapers, and magazines made it convenient and easy to read and learn about faraway others (and new ideas) in easily shared, preservable documents. This created the conditions for educational and political institutions to become increasingly prominent in both public and private life. The book and the newspaper accompanied and made possible the Enlightenment, just as the textbook did with organized public education. Newspapers and early magazines made it possible for ordinary citizens to become informed about and involved in government. Political and revolutionary movements from the seventeenth century on (the Protestant Reformation, the American Revolution, women's liberation) could scarcely have gathered mass strength without the organization and widespread dissemination of people's thoughts and strategies in newspapers and pamphlets. Because communication is such a fundamental social process, technologies of communication often inspire and go hand in hand with major social change.[7]

Once the mass print media became accepted parts of everyday life and people became exposed to and could learn about innumerable others, the opportunity to identify, learn about, and sociomentally connect to others increased exponentially. Any number of novelists or journalists or politicians—or any figure, public or private—could inspire a sociomental connection or a community of the mind. Now my interview subject, Nicole, can say of a woman in her field whose books and articles she has read:

> I feel like I know her . . . like she's a friend telling me something new, that makes sense and rings true.

And Cindy can feel connected to a woman whose books she has read:

> I've never met her, but I feel like I could probably co-write a book with her. It's just a feeling I have about her.

For Tonya, feeling connected to the author of a book or a character in the book is

> the only thing that can get me through a book. If I can't make that connection, I can't finish the book.

E. J., who writes for a newsletter, shares his view on the ability of print to connect those people who constitute a publication's readership:

> Just the idea of print publications being out there somewhere where people can have them—they're always available to read. It's not like a television where you have to program a VCR to catch something if you're not present. It's always available. It's as if it's constantly communicating, but it needs a human presence to activate itself . . . and unless [other readers] are really divided along political or ideological lines, you've got that common bond. Of literacy. And accessability.

His vision of print as "constantly communicating" neatly corresponds to the print media's potential to engender sociomental connections easily and almost continuously.

Each subsequent invention of communication technology has enhanced the ability of people to discover and explore commonalities with one another, even when they are very distant in space or time. Technological advances in transportation systems, such as the railroad and automobile, increased the opportunities for spatially separated people to know about one another. And the establishment of the postal system created a large market for information, as news of other people became widely available and convenient, thus increasing, again, the number of potential connections that could be formed (John 1997; Febvre and Martin 1976).

> I've seen my cousin in Jamaica maybe four times in my life. We write letters—I probably mail him three letters a month. . . . I was born in Jamaica and I left when I was four and came to America and didn't go back until I was fourteen. And that was the first time I saw him. And I've seen him two or three times after that. . . . But thanks to the letters, he's like my best friend. (Jessica)

> (Letters are) one way to get to know them (her faraway family members). It makes me remember who they were, and who they are, and even though I left, to know they are there. It brings back all the memories we had together. (Tapashi)

In recent decades, it has become common for schoolchildren to write letters to faraway "pen pals."

> Often times, schools, when you're in the fifth grade, contact another school and you got a pen pal. Of course, you may never, ever meet them. But through what they say . . . you get an idea of what they're like. (Bruce)

That many teachers still arrange such assignments (though sometimes updating them by using e-mail) is an implied testament to the importance of getting to know distant others, and to the ability of the written word to facilitate such connections.

The modern world has seen electronic technology bring *simultaneity* to communication across distances and with it another revolution in social connectedness. Now people who are spatially separated can actually share an experience at the same time, which makes the connection even more direct, more vivid, and, as we shall see, more *resonant*. The instantaneous linking of faraway people began with the invention of the telegraph and the telephone, the latter of which is now so ubiquitous that we are rarely aware of the role it frequently plays in bringing us together (see Fischer 1992).

> My district manager at my job, I never met her. She calls me every night at work, every day, and it's like she knows what I do, what time I leave, things like that, but I never met her. And it's just like we have this connection. . . . It's real eerie, because I don't even know what she looks like. [How well do you feel you can know

her under circumstances like these? I mean, do you feel like you know her fairly well?] Yes, I do. (Rashima)

In many of my jobs, the people I spoke with were across the country, or overseas, and there was no way of meeting them, but there was still a rapport, a connection. [Can you describe for me how you can feel connected to somebody like that, whom you've not met?] Besides doing your daily business with these people, you have interpersonal conversation about their health, their children, their spouse, or whatever, and by getting to know them, that's how you get a connection. [Does it feel real to you, even though you've never met them?] Oh yeah. [Do you get the feeling that you know what they're like?] If I've spoken to them enough times, yes. Even without ever having met them. (Janice)

The telephone is a prime example of the way a technology can come to play a key role in connecting people yet be nearly "invisible" while doing so. The people I spoke with did not find the telephone an impediment in "getting to know others." They felt that they could know people with whom they only had telephone contact rather well. Similarly, people have come to be linked through the often invisible but quietly reliable technological mediation provided by cameras, film projectors, phonographs, and CD players, various types of tape and digital recorders, radio, television, computers, answering machines, fax machines, beepers and cell phones, and video gaming and conferencing.

Even as they connect us, electronic media have numerous other effects. They contribute to people's perceptions of events and the world around them, set agendas and shape public discourse, and even alter the very social boundaries by which we divide public from private, child from adult, male from female, leader from follower, and physical from psychological location (Altheide 1997, 1995; Meyrowitz 1993: 63; 1985). Some people argue that with computerization, the "shackles" of linearity and the "tyranny of writer over reader" are being shed, ushering in an era unprecedented in its potential both for individual, democratic participation in the production of culture and an increasingly abstract mode of human thought (Newhagen and Rafaeli 1996). Of course, delusions and dangers accompany media use as well (see Chapter 6). It is a safe bet that technologies that are being developed, refined, and disseminated as this is written will lead to currently unimaginable changes in our society, in the nature of connectedness and in thinking itself (again, see Chapter 6 for a more extensive treatment of the consequences of connecting via technological mediation).

As the convenience, speed, and ease of use of communication and mass media technologies have made them central to modern life, people have come to use them to make sociomental connections in increasingly creative ways. For example, one interview subject, Cindy, told me about leaving a message on her boyfriend's answering machine:

> One time I called and sang part of this song I'd heard on the radio . . . I left it on his answering machine, and thought, "Gee that's kind of romantic." That technology allowed me to be romantic in ways I couldn't otherwise, especially long distance.

The willingness of people to use technologies in new and changing ways—to work, play games, plan vacations, and give and receive social support—demonstrates our increasing ability to blur the boundaries between information and entertainment and between work and home (Flanagin and Metzger 2001: 159; Nippert-Eng 1995). To devise different uses for technologies and adapt them to our needs, thus changing the ways in which we live and work and relate to one another, has become a hallmark of modern life (see Marvin 1988).

The mass media give us exposure to a range of others unprecedented in size and scope. This includes

> all those beings with which the individual is "familiar" through television, movies, books, newspapers, and other forms of the media. The beings in this media world—the movie stars and politicians, the talk show hosts and soap opera characters, the sports figures and comic strip characters—are typically more numerous than the persons in anyone's actual social world. . . . [They] play important roles in the individual's subjective social experience . . . *they take the individual into a system of social relationships.* (Caughey 1984: 21; emphasis added)

The mass media—through which endless "cultures of interest" thrive—open up a world of others to us. Though these others are far away from us, they "enter" our homes and our most private spaces, making possible what can be at times an extremely personal sense of knowing them.[8] Alicia learned so much about the life of Jacqueline Kennedy Onassis that in time she felt she had developed a full-fledged sociomental bond with her:

> You know all these things about another person you've never met, and you feel like you know them because you're grown up with

them. I heard about her and her family my entire life . . . I would like, of course, to have met her.

Roy, who participates in a fantasy football league (in which participants compile a fantasy team from among the players on the NFL roster and compare its statistical chances of success against those of other participants, who form their own such teams), describes this sense of knowing distant others:

> The funny thing is, I've started to feel like I'm getting to know the guys on my team a little bit—like they're my guys. You know? Like last week, one of them made this ridiculous play—really bad—and I got a lot of grief about it. Everybody had something to say about it. And I started to feel bad, like, hey, that's my guy! Like I'm responsible for how he does or something.

Thinking about these NFL football players in a personal way—for he chose them as members of "his team"—he began to feel connected to them. Forty-five of my fifty interview subjects reported having made connections with celebrities who became "known" to them through some form of mass media:

> I've never met Nelson Mandela and of course I don't have any contact with him but I'm in total awe of him . . . and when I read about him, and when I learn or hear people talk about him I just feel like . . . how can you not feel a connection to him? (Jessica)

> When Magic Johnson revealed that he had AIDS, I was very upset. People were calling me up, saying, hey, are you OK? Because I felt like he was one of my friends. (Joe)

> He [television "painting instructor" Bob Ross] is my friend. Such a gentle, kind man. And the best teacher one could have. He passed away last year. But I think he'll live on forever. All his videos are on sale. . . . In my heart I feel he's still around; in my head I know he isn't. (Sally)

Fan "worlds" that surround popular cultural products (such as TV shows) and are perpetuated and represented by magazines, Web sites, and all types of entertainment programming can be a rich source of connections between and among viewers:

> I would like to thank [soap opera] *Days of Our Lives* for giving me a common bond with my older brother. Since he is a college

student and I am in junior high, there is a huge age gap. Whenever he comes home on the weekends, we spend a lot of time talking about what happened on *Days*. (letter sent to *Soap Opera Digest*, June 4, 1996, p. 140)

I credit GL [*Guiding Light*] and other soaps like it for keeping the lines of communication open between the generations. Even when we fought over boys in my teenage years, my mom and I could always sit together and have pleasant discussions about storylines and actors. . . . My husband does it with me now . . . and my kids. (letter sent to *Soap Opera Weekly*, March 18, 1997, p. 36)

As we shall see, the shared viewing of TV shows and the enjoyment of other mass mediated cultural products help sociomental connections and communities form and cohere.

Computers facilitate a particularly direct type of sociomental connection through communication both asynchronous (e-mail, message boards) and synchronous (chat sessions, games, conferencing). Along with the telephone (and still in conjunction with face-to-face interaction), we use computers to fulfill a variety of needs, including the need for conversation, social bonding, and relationship maintenance (see Flanagin and Metzger 2001; Walther, Slovacek, and Tidwell 2001: 106–7).

I just met this girl on an Internet forum. We share interests and things we have in common. And it's strange, we both log on almost daily. And I want to call it a friendship that we've formed. (Rhonda)

I think that what's gained is access to a whole bunch of different people that I would never have a chance of contacting [face-to-face]. The Internet is a place where a lot of different people come . . . so the good part is, I get to meet, or I get to interact with, a bunch of other people that I never would. (Bruce)

I really enjoy chatting online. It's a lot of fun. Meeting other people. I think it's just like any interaction. (Mabel)

The idea that I'm talking to someone I would not otherwise talk to, interacting with someone I would otherwise not have the opportunity to interact with, finding similar likes and dislikes, especially on something like music. A lot of what people talk about are different performers as well as different instruments. Here's a whole new world of people that I would never talk to. That I can now interact with. That is very interesting. (Tom)

An online connector from the message group dedicated to literature summed up the experience well when she stated that, "It's interesting to find unexpected bonds with people I've never met."

Technology now even blurs the boundary between life and death, further complicating the nature of connectedness. Medical technologies have advanced to the point that people can exist for long periods of time in liminal states of "aliveness"—as on life support, for example, but without higher brain functioning. Even more commonly, the dead can be effectively brought into the "lifespace" of the living through such technological means as viewing videotapes of the deceased, the audio mixing of dead people's vocal tracks with live ones (a la the deceased Nat King Cole and his daughter Natalie in "Unforgettable"), the visual editing of "real world" individuals into existing film frames (as in the movies *Forrest Gump* and *Zelig*), and so on.[9] With medical life support and communication technologies such as film, tape, and computerization, we can now create and experience situations that can help us feel more vividly and tangibly connected to people who are not alive. So connectedness itself continues to "expand."

Throughout history, people have gained the ever-increasing capacity to move away from the "here" and "now" and to still form connections with one another. As it becomes less and less feasible to maintain social relationships with face-to-face interaction alone, more and more mental activity is required to form and sustain connections. Put another way, all social connectedness requires some degree of mental activity, which increases as the individuals involved become progressively removed from one another in space or time. To understand the way in which mental activity can generate sociomental connections, we must consider the foundation for connectedness that develops as the mind becomes socioculturally structured and thus able to relate to others.

THE ROLE OF THE MIND

Social connectedness is rooted in the mind. To form a connection, we must be able to grasp the properties of the world (and of ourselves) through the cognitive processes of perception and sensation, and we must be able to communicate these properties to one another. We also must learn to classify phenomena and construct and interpret categorical distinctions. As we do so, our mind becomes structured in ways similar to some other, but not *all* other, people.

It is in groups and communities that our minds become structured in a manner similar to others. We learn to sense, perceive, classify, interpret, model, and think about the world in groups, and what we learn determines whether and how and with whom we will be able to form a connection with an absent "other." Tracing the process by which this occurs, then, is critical to the understanding of sociomental connectedness, for *it is the similarity of mind that two or more individuals may come to share—their similarly structured minds—that "paves the way" for social connections to be formed.* When minds are structured similarly—at least in some way—they can conceive of phenomena in an analogous fashion, create an intersubjectively understood reality, and utilize categories and mental models similarly enough that their interpretations of the world and of their relationship are consonant. They can feel that they understand one another and feel as though they are like-minded. They can mentally approach various phenomena from a common perspective and thus be brought experientially together, even from different spatial and temporal vantage points.

We spend a great deal of our lives engaged in mental activity, and we spend, on average, half our mental activity on some kind of daydreaming. Daydreaming, in fact, appears to be a prerequisite for normal cognitive and intellectual development and can produce vibrant mental environments complete with people, places, and things.[10] (We mentally produce such environments in our dreams at night as well.) It is not only inevitable but necessary for optimal mental functioning and for the development of intellectual maturity for us to construct mental environments and to populate them with "others" (Mead 1934), and we do so in the following manner.

We have evolved two systems of mentally representing and understanding the world: sensation (representations of stimuli that help one understand "what is happening to oneself") and perception (representations of stimuli that help one understand "what is happening out there in the world"—Humphrey 1992: 191). For example, when eating an apple, we learn something about ourselves as our senses respond: whether or not we enjoy this particular type of apple, whether or not we are able to digest it, or even whether we think it pretty (to paint in a still life, perhaps?). When I gave my daughter Morgan new and different foods to eat during her infant years, I was given a rare, pure glimpse of the information-gathering system of sensation, for as she tasted bits of food for the first time she could not help but react to the information it provided to her in a completely uninhibited fashion (clearly exhibited by the response—not to mention all of the food—on her face). Her startled, indignant response to her first sip of grapefruit juice left no doubt as to the sensations she was experiencing.

Along with sensation, we perform the process of perception in order to obtain information about the nature of things: is this apple sour or sweet, red, green, or yellow, ripe or not? As we taste it, we make judgments about the apple, about the properties of apples, and about a world in which apples are found. We combine our findings with those gathered in the process of sensation, and slowly and gradually piece together our views, our meaning, of the world around us. Then we locate ourselves in that world and try to figure out where and how we fit into it.

But we do not perform these processes solely as individuals, "in a vacuum," as it were. We perform them as people who have been exposed to various sociocultural backgrounds. Even our prenatal experiences and our very sensorimotor capacities are embedded in a cultural context and influenced by the groups of which we and our caregivers are a part.[11] Neuropsychologist Roger Sperry has gone so far as to state a theory of "emergent mentalism" in which the culturally shaped mind "drives" the brain: "We should not expect to find that a single neuron or isolated patch of neurons, or even a cortical center, could sense, feel, experience, or think anything in isolation," he claims (1952: 311). Or, according to George Herbert Mead, "we must regard mind . . . as arising and developing within the social process" (1934: 133).

It is, after all, as members of groups that we learn to interpret, classify, and "feel" many sensations. We can be influenced by other group members, for example, to try, and to try to learn, to enjoy sensations that we might have initially found unpleasant. People often dislike the experience of smoking their first cigarettes, or taking their first sips of, say, coffee, beer, or scotch. Children may try to identify with the adult world by drinking coffee, even though it has an initially bitter, unappealing taste to them (Nippert-Eng 1995: 129), while adolescents may do the same by drinking beer and other alcoholic drinks, or by doing drugs. In identifying with a community of others that enjoys such substances (or in rejecting a community that does not use them), people can, in time, come to truly enjoy those things. Initially unpleasant sensations, then, can be "learned" to be sensed as pleasant—due in large part to the influence of others.

We also learn to perceive, organize information, and make decisions as members of groups.[12] As Eviatar Zerubavel explains in his "invitation" to the field of cognitive sociology (1997), to think is neither a haphazardly individual nor strictly universal phenomenon; rather, people have different capacities to think, and they do so in different ways, because they are members of different social configurations. Karl Mannheim's formulation of this fundamental proposition has become a classic:

> Only in a quite limited sense does the single individual create out of himself the mode of speech and thought we attribute to him. He speaks the language of his group; he thinks in the manner his group thinks. . . . Strictly speaking, it is incorrect to say the individual thinks. Rather, it is more correct to insist that he participates in thinking further what other men have thought before him. (Mannheim 1936: 29)

Individual thought is a process emerging from social life. Even a seemingly original thought is conditioned and shaped by all of those individuals who have contributed somehow to the development of the concepts and linguistic and symbol systems that the individual must use in order to formulate the thought (see Whorf 1956 [1940])—a grouping of individuals mutually exchanging ideas and "intellectual interaction" in what Ludwik Fleck calls a "thought collective" (1981 [1935]: 39). In his example of the scientific thought collective, Fleck points out that it is, for all practical purposes, impossible to say where one person's idea begins and another person's ends, as "a set of findings meander through the community, becoming polished, transformed, reinforced, or attenuated, while influencing other findings, concept formation, opinions, and habits of thought" (ibid., 42). It is impossible, therefore, to completely isolate individual contributions to a culture or subculture, for we are all enmeshed in a sort of endless cycle of influencing one another's thoughts and ideas.

We learn to use the words, ideas, and categorical distinctions of groups of others to perceive and classify—and, hence, to be able to think about—the world around us. In a sense, we "dip into" the common stock of knowledge of a group (in Durkheimian terms, the cognitions, emotions, and moral judgments that constitute a group's *conscience collective*) and take its categories and concepts into our individual minds.[13] In each group of which we are a part, we learn to "see" the world through a sort of "mental lens," which results in our gaining a perspective, worldview, or thought style similar to all those others—but only those others—who use the same lens (Zerubavel 1991: 61–80). Such a lens, of course, is not something we "look through" as much as something we "think with."

Thought collectives of all types (e.g., Catholics, Yankee fans, Democrats, accountants, single parents, terrorist groups) develop distinct mental "lenses" and interpretive frameworks that members "borrow" and use in order to develop outlooks toward the world. "Once one has incorporated a particular outlook from his group," Tamotsu Shibutani explains, "it becomes his orientation toward the world, and he brings this frame of reference to bear on all new situations" (1955: 565). We can think of these thought collectives as mental reference groups (see Shibutani 1955; Chayko 1993a). With regard to their reference groups, individuals make countless decisions every day, such as which portions of the body are to be publicly exposed and which to be covered, what is appropriate to eat and what is to be considered inedible and disgusting, and with whom it is socially acceptable to have sex (see Zerubavel 1991; Douglas 1966). As members of groups and categories make such distinctions, classificatory boundaries are drawn that have very real consequences: they shape the ways we think about and act toward each other and even touch off some of the greatest debates and ethical dilemmas of our time (Nippert-Eng 1995: xi–xii; see also Foucault 1973 [1966]):

> This is because placing lines here or there has definite implications for how we treat each other and the world around us. Depending on which category she or he belongs to, someone will or will not receive medical insurance coverage; will or will not be taken from the caretakers they've known all their lives and placed with a stranger having similar DNA; will or will not be subjected to hard prison time, the military draft, or parental notification for medical procedures; will or will not be formally or informally entitled to live, vote, work, buy a house, and/or go to school in a certain place; will or will not be slaughtered, resuscitated, and so forth. (Nippert-Eng 1995: xii)

As we use various mental lenses and "think within" the interpretive frameworks of the thought collectives of which we are a part, then, we begin to make the distinctions—whether minor, life changing, or somewhere in between—that frame our lives.

Mental lenses can be "wide angle" or more narrow. We can share them with members of large categories (people who share general "status characteristics," such as sex, race, ethnicity, age, religion, nation, sexual orientation, education or income level, occupation) and with people who share more specific commonalities (followers of a sport or a team, people who hail from one's region or alma mater, people with a shared cultural taste).[14] In any grouping of people, from the very large to the very small, a way of seeing the world can emerge, as members are encouraged to "think alike" (and, it often follows, to act alike) along some particular dimension or set of dimensions.[15] Thus we are able to connect with others in ways that range from the general and more diffuse (with large throngs of people) to the particular and more specific (with comparatively fewer others).

The mental lenses that emerge as most prominent in our lives—sometimes "provided to us" in our youth, sometimes adopted later on—become deeply internalized and serve to shape, constrain, and enable our individualized cognitions. We tend to view our thought processes as derived from nature and our particular cognitions as wholly original. But they are largely influenced by the way we learn to see the world, through the lenses we come to internalize. If, for example, a person has learned to view life through the mental "lens" of a fundamentalist Christian group, that person would probably have learned to view Jesus Christ as the son of God, to see a fetus as a life, and to consider homosexuality a sin. Conversely, the adoption of a more "liberal" lens might render one's views quite opposite to those of the fundamentalist's. These views could come to seem so "natural" and right to the individual and become internalized so deeply that they would be very resistant to change. Yet even if a person ended up rejecting such views, he or she would still have learned to think within the categories of a thought collective. As Lee Thayer puts it,

> People do not learn to take the world into account through their experiences with it, but through the minds they have to do so with. And these minds, of whatever culture, are not a function of the world, but of that culture, or subculture. (1990: 323)

In short, *as distinctions that emerge in cultures and various communities of the mind transcend any one person's ability to construct them, and as they are internalized by the individual, they strongly influence that person to develop ways of thinking and behaving and his or her overall perspectives on the world.*

An individual's thoughts and perspectives are influenced by *all* of the groupings and thought collectives that have meaning for and relevance to him or her. People must sift through, evaluate, and somehow balance the various group perspectives to which they have been exposed. They can do this in a rigid way (making sure that all perspectives they have been exposed to "line up" neatly) or more flexibly (allowing themselves to consider different types of views, some of which compete with one another, simultaneously). In the modern era—in which each of us is a part of so many groups—this is a rather constant, though rarely conscious, process, as we juggle and make choices within a tangle of roles, obligations, and perspectives. Having to decide (though tacitly) which lenses to use and which ones to reject at any given time is a uniquely modern task (on mental rigidity and flexibility, see Zerubavel 1991: 33–80; 1995; 1997).

We often assume that long-held distinctions and "rules" we learn in this way represent the "truth"—that they are factual and, for that matter, morally correct. We may fail to question whether these rules derive from nature and may be fixed and immutable, or whether they have been culturally constructed and thus subject to reinterpretation. Groups—with their identities at stake—often draw distinctions and defend boundaries sharply, using rigidly formulated "lenses." This can lead to polarized clashes in which people in different groups find it virtually impossible to find common ground, see one another's viewpoints, or even really hear one another. In order to question such things, one must adjust or discard established "rigid lenses"—a difficult thing to do, for these lenses are deeply internalized and often seem completely "natural."

This is why it is so difficult for some people to change their views (their lenses)—to "walk a mile in another's shoes" and to see the world from another's perspective (i.e., to "try on" a different lens). It may be difficult for a bigot to see the value in other races, for an elderly person to appreciate the music that teenagers love, for a technophobe to appreciate what life online must be like, and for a pro-life advocate to see a week-old fetus as anything but a human being. It is indeed a challenge (though not an insurmountable one) to productively communicate and form meaningful relationships with people who approach issues from vastly different viewpoints than our own. Members of different groups, Mannheim teaches us, learn to think so differently from one another that in attempting to communicate they unwittingly "talk past" one another (rather than directly "to" one another), so great are the gulfs in their understanding of the world (1936: 277–80). Yet they tend to treat differences between them as though they are confined to a particular problem at hand rather than this difference in worldview. In general, people are quite unaware of just how deep and fundamental differences in groups' perspectives can be.

How, then, do people from different groups and backgrounds—participating in different communities of the mind—manage to communicate meaningfully and have an opportunity to form social bonds? Alfred Schutz provides insight into how "the problem of intersubjectivity" is resolved in everyday life—that is, exactly how, given that the subjective experiences and "inner life" of individuals are essentially inaccessible to others, people can share common experiences and understandings and communicate about them. He makes the important observation that unless they are given reason to believe differently, people tend to *assume* similarity among their inner states and thus to *act* as though others experience things more or less as they do ("the idealization of the interchangeability of standpoints"). Furthermore, although we all know that we are different from others, we tend to assume that if we were to change places, we might see things similarly to others, and that such "biographical" differences in our perspectives are irrelevant for most practical purposes ("the idealization of the congruency of the system of relevances"). Thus we establish a "common world" (or "common worlds"), which we *believe* we see in similar ways and which we maintain by constantly and routinely performing these two basic "idealizations" (Schutz 1962: 11–12; see also Heritage 1984: 54–61). It is indeed a fundamental part of being human to relate "subjective" experiences to others and to evaluate others' responses to us; in doing so, we become aware of the meaning of our private experiences, which is necessary for the normal development of the mind (Mead 1934). Unless and until we are given reason to believe otherwise, we assume intersubjectivity in our dealings with others. We are able to relate to others and form connections to them.

Intersubjectivity presupposes sufficient similarity of mind and thought in individuals to enable them to share a common stock of knowledge and to communicate with one another about their "common world." Stocks of knowledge, culturally given and constructed, reified in systems of language and symbols, strongly constrain our ability to move beyond them (as do the mental structures and "lenses" that develop). Thinking, then, is not so individualized that we cannot understand one another, nor so universal that we can *all* understand one another—it is a phenomenon by which some of us, but not all of us, share the products of our minds and go on to form connections with one another.

To aid us in perceiving a world of otherwise undifferentiated phenomena and trying to organize it so that we can live in it together, we construct and use categories. The formation of categories is fundamental to survival and to connectedness, for if we did not classify phenomena into categories, we would have to treat every sensation as unique, we would not learn to perceive general "types" of things (Dunbar 1989: 48; Lakoff 1987), and the world would appear to us as an undifferentiated, chaotic stream of sights, sounds, odors, and so on (see Zerubavel 1991: 1–20). We could not coordinate our functioning and communication with others. Since we must function continuously (and communicate nearly as continuously),

> every time we see something as a *kind* of a thing, for example, a tree, we are categorizing. Whenever we reason about *kinds* of things—chairs, nations, illnesses, emotions, any kind of thing at all—we are employing categories. Whenever we intentionally perform any *kind* of action, say something as mundane as writing with a pencil, hammering with a hammer, or ironing clothes, we

are using categories. . . . And any time we either produce or understand any utterance of reasonable length, we are employing dozens if not hundreds of categories: categories of speech sounds, of words, of phrases and clauses, as well as conceptual categories. Without the ability to categorize, we could not function at all, either in the physical world or in our social and intellectual lives. (Lakoff 1987: 5–6)

Because we categorize, we are able to order our world and understand it, and we can become social participants and connectors in it.

We learn the all-important rules of classification that aid us in categorization in the cultures and communities of which we are a part. Classification is a process of concept formation, of forcing reality into supposedly discrete compartments, rather than of "discovering" categories that "already" exist.[16] No natural divides separate, for example, masculine from feminine, childhood from adulthood, black from white, the middle class from the poor, hot from cold, alto from soprano, one language (or season, or time zone) from another, or even one day from the next. We learn to make these distinctions based on the mental "fine lines" we learn to draw as members of groups and societies, and in doing so we learn "rules" of relevance and irrelevance for the countless situations of classification that we will encounter.[17] We learn to attend to certain features of things (e.g., that the presence of lace makes an item of clothing "feminine") while ignoring others (that the presence or absence of sleeves, however, is irrelevant to the "gendering" of clothing). The mental lenses that we absorb from various communities help us learn how to "filter out" what is irrelevant and disattend to it, and to "see" or "sense" what is relevant and attend to only that. We learn the rules as to what "counts" as relevant or irrelevant, then, in group life.[18]

Members of different cultures and groups create and use different categories, rules of relevance, and classification. In doing so, the minds of the people in these groups become differently structured. This is a complicated process, because most social categories do not have precisely defined criteria of membership but a continuum of grades of membership, so the rules are both difficult to learn, *and* they are constantly changing. The categories, for example, of "beautiful women," "tall men," or "all real numbers which are much greater than one" are not discretely bounded—they are what Lofti Zadeh calls "fuzzy sets" (1965: 338–39)—which means that there will be disagreement about what is to be included or excluded in the category, especially at the borders.[19] Most categories of phenomena, especially social phenomena, are not discretely bounded and do not exist "out there" in the world to be recovered.[20] They must be discerned and created by people who are all sensing and perceiving things in their own cultural contexts. In other words, the same physical evidence does not lead all of us to a similar picture of the universe, because we can only interpret the world within the categories we have learned.

People in cultures, subcultures, and groups construct mental models together. Assuming some rationality, some regularity, to life,[21] we create these models (also called mental schemata) to help us represent and understand relevant phenomena and the relationships that exist among these phenomena.[22] As we encounter various situations, we activate and use our mental models to give us the "shortcuts" we need to make the world seem simple and predictable enough so that we can make decisions, reason, understand concepts and categories, and take action.[23] In using similar mental models in generally similar ways, people in a group or a thought collective or a culture go on to construct a world together that comes to be seen as a "natural fact" (Shore 1991: 16). Modeling the world "together" further facilitates group identity and a sense of community as it structures our minds in ways that are roughly similar to others in our group.

So critical are these mental models to our thinking and acting that we work hard to protect them from disconfirmation: we try to make ambiguous things conform to previously existing models to keep social reality as orderly as possible (Douglas 1966). Still, mental models are not permanently fixed; we can override and adjust them when necessary, as when a problem presents itself, when we are dissatisfied with the status quo, or when existing models fail to account adequately for new evidence. For example, while some groups have developed mental models that contain elements of racism or sexism, individuals in those groups can override those models by developing and demonstrating open-mindedness, awareness, and reflexivity. Though people may initially form perceptions on the basis of stereotypes, they can override such perceptions when faced with strong, inconsistent evidence.[24] Schematic (modeling) theory respects the agency of the social actor and his or her ability to structure his or her social action (see Giddens 1979, 1984). It acknowledges, though, that the process of overriding deeply held models and schemas takes great mental effort, for in doing so one must break with a deeply internalized, seemingly "natural" perspective on how the world works.

The sharing of a common language is critical to the development of a mental model. Rather than simply representing a way of thinking about the world, language shapes it, and shapes it differently for each group of people that creates and uses a language or dialect.[25] As words come to represent specific things to a group, it follows that only those who learn those words can ever form and understand those representations. For

> the world is presented in a kaleidoscopic flux of impressions which has to be organized by our minds—and this means largely by the linguistic systems in our minds. We cut nature up (into categories). . . largely because we are parties to an agreement to organize it in this way—an agreement that . . . is codified in the patterns of our language. (Whorf 1956 [1940]: 213–14)

As cultural symbols (such as words) and their referents become fused in our minds, they do so similarly for others in our group. They help people identify and use the appropriate models for a particular situation. A common language, then, both contributes to and reflects the mental similarity of a people.

Helping us structure, order, and process our thoughts, mental models can be thought of as *defining* the groups who use them in a way very important for our purposes here: they serve as a *representation* of the "mental life" or "mental existence" of a group. Individual brains "contain" both unique characteristics and those shared by groups of others. And when several groups think similarly about something, mental models can aggregate into *thought styles*: the converging ideas, logics, and paradigms employed by a number of groups or a culture.[26] For we think in ways we share with groups, subcultures, and entire cultures.

It is in thinking similarly to others in this structured and modeled way that we can mentally connect with them without the absolute necessity of face-to-face copresence. Our brains develop so similarly to certain others in certain ways that we are able to feel connected or bonded to them simply as a function of discovering or "activating" or "hooking into" that similarity. It can produce the feelings of like-mindedness and resonance so critical to the development of social connectedness (see Chapter 3). Because each of us is a member of so many groups and subcultures, we share commonalities and points of reference with many others. This is why sociomental connectedness is such a common experience, especially in this "other-oriented" Internet age.

Modern people are exposed to a multitude of "others"—public figures, fictional characters, and ordinary people—in a multitude of "places." Their similarly structured minds enable physically separated people to mentally "come together" (see Chapter 3 for more on exactly how mental connections are made). If a "meeting of the minds" does take place, though, where can we think of this meeting as being located? Indeed, where is cyberspace? We can conceptualize a mental meeting place to help us understand sociomental connectedness as fully as possible. I therefore put forth a conception of the space in which sociomental connections are made and maintained that I call *sociomental space*.[27]

WHERE MINDS MEET: SOCIOMENTAL SPACE

It is necessary for us to represent social contexts and spaces mentally so that our cognitions can become clearly envisioned and organized (Jackendoff 1994). With the "erosion of territory" as the preeminent marker of community, our societal need to conceptualize nongeographic forms of social space is great (Jacobson 1997: 127). In order to envision complex social systems and thus feel more "grounded" and secure, people often use topological imagery, "locating" one another on various geographic, social, stratifying, economic, cultural, and interpersonal coordinates (Davis 1973: 96). We routinely use topological constructs such as metaphors to evaluate the comparability of phenomena—to determine, for example, who or what is nearer or farther away from oneself, or better or worse in some way. For it is only in a topological network that everything has a distinct relationship to everything else (Palombo and Bruch 1964: 253).

It is important to keep in mind that the social world—people in some relation to one another bound by a common culture or language—is neither synonymous with nor directly analogous to the physical world. People are distributed within a social world and differentiated from one another in it based upon those factors that they deem relevant. Within a social world, we tend to collectively assign individuals to various "positions," "locations," "classes," and "regions" (e.g., "the elite," "the working class," "a leader," "a fourth grader," etc.). These designations help form the contours of the social world and delineate its space—a space that could not be envisioned in the inner space of any one person's mind, and yet could not be envisioned similarly in the minds of *all* people. I therefore conceive of the space in which certain groups of people jointly form connections, bonds, and communities and share an intersubjectively understood set of ideas and mental activities—employing a shared mental model—as sociomental space.

Such a space must be considered the *social* approximation of the psychological construct of the "inner space" of one's own mind (see Lewin 1936). Regions of this space correspond to the overlap or *mental intersection* of two or more minds, as when one person thinks about another, or two or more people jointly think about or "fix upon" something external to them. As two or more minds "meet," the connection that may then form can be envisioned as mentally "placed" or existing in this space. "In order to have society it is evidently necessary that persons should get together *somewhere*," Charles Cooley points out, "*and they get together only as personal ideas in the mind*" (1964 [1922]: 19; emphasis added).

The shared mental models of people who form connections within social worlds can be envisioned as converging in a kind of giant mental field. The "points" in the field would be represented by connectors. Lines, or "pathways," might represent the connections. For Kurt Lewin, a path that connects any two points in "topological space" so that certain regions *influence* other regions is a conduit for the connectedness of those points (1936: 54). The mental paths that connect people can form various patterns throughout space and coalesce in webs of connectedness that can be envisioned as emanating from and surrounding each individual. Alexander Solzhenitsyn likens connections to threads, and his metaphor provides a splendid means with which to visualize this space:

> There are . . . hundreds of little threads radiating from every man, millions of threads in all. If those threads were suddenly to become visible, the whole sky would look like a spider's web. . . . They are not visible, they are not material, but every man is constantly aware of their existence. (in Beniger 1986: 390)

As such "threads" can be visualized as representing sociomental connections, the set of all such threads would constitute a map, the topology in its entirety, of sociomental space.

This "space" is more than just a construct. As people feel that they are *in* it, that they are in some invisible but tangible and real way connecting with another person, they come to feel a sense of presence with or proximity to the "other." They feel a nearness that belies the physical distance involved. This is not unusual. In fact, proximity is generally perceived as multi-dimensional and is ordinarily influenced by much more than physical closeness or distance. Proximity can most accurately be thought of as the extent to which one can be exposed to information and to others—to those who "bring" information—in a social system.[28] Presence, too, is often defined in a way that transcends the physical; as the sense of being in a specified "understood" environment; as a state of consciousness in which sensed stimuli are broadly attributed to some environment or place that is vaguely "outside" the self yet not necessarily physically

circumscribed.[29] Sociomental connections, and especially strong sociomental bonds, have this sort of presence: a "there-ness," a sensed tangibility, that persists despite the lack of spatial copresence. They seem to be
situated *somewhere*, in an environment or a habitat of some sort, a space
that takes on certain qualities and may come to feel quite tangible. "Does
anyone else have the sense that people in this group are becoming closer
to one another?" a member of the online literature group I looked at asked
the others one day. This tangible sense of presence or nearness may be a
kind of psychological residue of the experience of sharing sociomental
space.

When people sociomentally connect, they share an "understood" environment that can be neither imagined nor created by a single individual
acting alone. This is the "place" where one might "go" when one's mind
focuses on, thinks about, and understands things "in concert" with at least
one other person—where a sense of proximity with another person might
come to feel especially strong, or where a distant loved one might feel or
seem to be "near." The technology that assists in "bringing" people "together" lends a certain texture to the sociomental space that is created.
The oral tradition of early storytelling tended to "transport" listeners mentally to the time and place in which the events occurred (Lombard and
Ditton 1997; Biocca and Levy 1995). Written narratives can give readers
the same sense of "transportedness."[30] Electronic media bring "information and experience from everyplace to everyplace," as Joshua Meyrowitz
observes (1985: 118), for as people watch and listen to electronically disseminated material—television and radio programs, Web sites, movies—
they have access to the same images, often at the exact same time, and
they can feel as though they have been transported to the very same (mental) "place."[31] When they watch the same television show, for example,
viewers "go" to a "place"—in their collective minds—that has been
"beamed" identically to all of them and, depending on cultural background and the mental models employed, may very likely be conceived of
similarly. Cable television executive Rich Cronin provides a neat illustration of the sociomental "place" called "TV Land":

> We believe that in every person's brain there's this lobe where TV
> land exists. It's this town where the Cleaver family from *Leave it
> to Beaver* lives down the street from the Douglasses from *My
> Three Sons* and the Douglasses live next door to the Posts from
> *Mr. Ed*. It's all tongue-in-cheek, of course, but we really try to
> believe that such a place exists. And everything we do . . . flows
> from that belief. (in Svetkey 1990: 52)

Cronin's colorful example may help us envision one particularly vibrant sector of sociomental space. People in the space he describes do seem somehow proximal to one another (as the metaphor of "living on the same street" implies). But this is a mental street in a mental place. It is sensed rather than visibly marked. As they experience some of the same things in the same way, the creators, actors, crew, viewers, and marketers of a television show collectively create a mental space. This place only exists in their collective minds, in their shared mental experience of the show. But in its seeming tangibility and presence, people can actually feel that they have "visited" it—mentally—and they can more easily make connections "within" it.

Fans of any cultural product (from a TV show to a novel to a sporting event to a Web site) acquire common experiences that they filter through their culturally constructed mental lenses. They can then envision various "sectors" of sociomental space in a manner similar to others whose minds are similarly structured. Others whose experiences are different and come from different backgrounds—using different cultural categories to see and understand the world—cannot visualize those specific "places" and cannot mentally "go there." They do not share a mental model or a sector of sociomental space. Children who view the popular PBS series *Mister Rogers' Neighborhood*, for example, are given a sense of "visiting" people and places in a fictional neighborhood that may be comparable to places with which they are familiar, yet is actually situated "nowhere in particular," and therefore takes place "anywhere." As they join Mr. Rogers on excursions through this unidentified (but very accessible) neighborhood, "meeting" people who are defined as "neighbors," a strong sense of proximity and presence is constructed—and is constructed similarly among those who view and experience it. The same sense of a collectively envisioned space is constructed among people who listen to Garrison Keillor's radio tales of the people and places that make up "Lake Wobegon Days." These programs—and other communal cultural experiences—promulgate, quite literally, the idea that audience members and media figures can be technologically brought together to create social bonds in a "neighborhood" that has meaning for them, but that exists only in their collective mental activity.

The portion of sociomental space in which people are brought together via computer has been termed *cyberspace* by writer William Gibson (see Jones 1995: 118). Cyberspace can be thought of as a subset—an Internet-bound, computerized sector—of sociomental space. In cyberspace, inhabitants act "as if they inhabited common social territory" (Stone 1992: 621)—a territory that one interview subject, Mabel, described as so social as to be downright "neighborly." Cyberspace connectors also have a sense of mobility—a sense that they can "move" from place to place—and a sense of location, of "being somewhere,"[32] as the emphasized portions of the following quotes indicate:

> I've gotten to meet and *hang out with,* via [the] Internet, famous folks who I never would have gotten in contact with, because they're far away or they're too famous. (Bruce)

> A message board like this is an excellent place for those who hold the same interest to *meet* and talk. (from the online science group)

> I'm so glad to *be around* other people who feel the same way! (from the online soap opera group)

> I think this is a great *place* to share our thoughts about our favorite soap and look forward to getting to know you all better. (from the online soap opera group)

In fact, the structure and composition of cyberspace connecting are indebted to spatial imagery. When online, people "surf" a "'Net" composed of Web "sites," "home" pages, chat "rooms," and discussion "groups." Microsoft's "Windows" system of organizing data relies on the visible, iconic representation of things traditionally located in literal spaces, as "windows" of "files" and "folders" on a "desktop" are "opened," "closed," and "saved." People "have sex" on the phone or online, thereby having an affair "behind" a partner's "back." Cyberspace, then, is commonly constructed and thought of as a kind of "place."

Such is the experience in *all* sociomental space. Whether one moves from Web site to chat room to message board or from daydream to fictional novel to face-to-face conversation, one has a sense of moving among "places." When my interviewee Louise told me about a project that she had undertaken, transferring family photos to videotape, she described the satisfaction of the project in sociomental-spatial terms: "I felt like I was *with* everyone." Similarly, Gerard told me that he and his wife "think and talk about family all the time. They're never more than this far away," he said, pinching his fingers together. *How* far away? The family of which Gerard speaks lives in Ireland. Disregarding the thousands of miles that separate them in literal space as "besides the point" in describing closeness, Gerard is implicitly referring to "closeness" in a nonphysical way. In sociomental space, he and his family are never *too* far apart. Another interview subject, Anita, says of her long-distance best friend, "It's like she's near me." This sense of nearness is perhaps most poignantly illustrated by Viktor Frankl who, while in a Nazi war camp, conjured up the image, the presence, of his wife (not knowing whether she was alive or dead) in order to find the strength to survive:

> For hours I stood hacking at the icy ground. The guard passed by, insulting me, and once again I communed with my beloved. More and more I felt that she was present, that she was with me; I had the feeling that I was able to touch her, able to stretch out my hand and grasp hers. The feeling was very strong: she was *there*. (Frankl 1984 [1959]: 40; emphasis in original)

Of course, the only "place" in which Frankl could visit his wife was "in" a sociomental space.

We each carry around in our heads a "picture" of sociomental space as we conceive it. This picture is not the same as the one we have of the places we go and the people we know in the physical world. It is, rather, a kind of mental map of the social terrain, colored and constructed by our (and our cultures' and subcultures') perceptions of social class, race, ethnicity, gender, sexuality, age, and other variables upon which a society can be stratified. These perceptions give our mental maps their markers and shape. "Our whole social environment," Edmund Leach tells us, "is map-like" (1976: 51).

These maps are important tools in helping us order the information that we receive through our senses, and thus we use them all the time.[33] They represent our current knowledge of where specific people, objects, and activities exist and what they mean to us.[34] They permit us to collect, organize, store, recall, and manipulate information. They help us approximate social positions and social distance and in countless, small, subtle ways represent our social environment as we believe it to be (Downs and Stea 1977: 6). With mental maps, for example, we mentally place and locate people "above" or "below" us in, say, gender or class status (even to the extent of thinking of people "on top of" one another in a hierarchy), or at a certain social distance from us, to the extent of considering people "close" or "far away." With information depicted in these maps, we make our way in the world; we form connections, bonds, and communities with this person or that one, with these people or those.

What do these mental maps "look" like? Unlike printed maps, we cannot observe mental maps directly, and we can only speculate about the form they take in people's brains, inferring their existence from people's verbal or spatial behavior. We do know that the mechanisms of cognitive mapping are acquired very early in life (Downs and Stea 1977: 172–73). Words and images, sights, sounds, smells, tastes, and feelings can all be incorporated in a mental map and may be substituted freely for one another (ibid., 84–85). The more significant a variable is to us, the more vividly we will "map" it. The more closely two things seem to be related in our view, the more closely our minds will "place" them together on this "mental terrain." An individual's mental map of, for example, Chicago, might consist of all of these variables, somehow blended together in a system of representations:

> Your knowledge of Chicago can be equally well a series of visual images of buildings and street scenes or a series of verbal descriptions of the same buildings and street scenes. Translations from one medium of expression . . . to another are virtually instantaneous. . . . Not only can we visualize places, but we can recall their feel and their distinctive sounds and smells in highly affective, sometimes emotive terms. Not only do we have a mind's eye but a mind's ear, a mind's nose. (Downs and Stea 1977: 85)

Mental maps, as internal cognitive representations of people, objects, activities, relations, and places—virtually anything we can think about—are multifaceted, multisensory, culturally derived *processes* by which we organize our environments. They can help us visualize, think about, and understand our universe of sociomental connections just as surely as they can represent the city of Chicago.

Although these maps are very much a part of our individual minds and are pieced together by our sensory and perceptual processes, it would be incorrect to say that they are constructed by the individual alone. Just as we think in the manner that our group thinks (Mannheim 1936: 3) and create mental models that resemble those of others in our group, we map in the manner that our group maps.[35] Groupings of people whose minds are structured similarly envision environments similarly—they develop common orientations, ways of seeing the world.[36] As we associate with one another and share cultural backgrounds and experiences, we create, in effect, "collective" mental maps which represent our mental models and which we use to find our way in the social world at large, much as we use geographical maps to find our way in the literal space of the physical world.

The concept of "place" is elusive and abstract in modernity. Meyrowitz suggests that "place" be considered "a subcategory of the more inclusive notion of a perceptual field" (1990: 74). Sociomental space, I propose, *is* that perceptual field and is, therefore, a broader and potentially more explanatory and useful concept than "place." Sociomental space is a grand mental field in which an infinite number of collective mental maps are formed and intersect. It is the space in which we can say that connections and bonds form; where we can feel close to others who are physically distant; where environments and habitats wrap around us; and where we can "map" and chart connections and communities. It is the arena in which people mentally "come together."

With an understanding of the historical importance of technology, the socially structured mind, and the space in which we form and "map" connections, a foundation for understanding the mental processes underlying sociomental connecting is now in place. Sociomental connections are made possible by technological mediation and the perception of phenomena by socially structured minds that "meet" in sociomental space. Of course, life *is* lived in and through bodies. A connector occupies both a physical *and* a social trajectory in time-space (Giddens 1984; Stone 1992). In Chapter 3 I examine the ways in which connectors actually form the sociomental connections that are built upon this foundation.

3

Making the Connection . . . Across Time, Space, and Cyberspace

As people internalize the perceptions, systems of classification, mental models, and languages that they learn in group life, they gain the capability to form sociomental connections. Animals and infants are unable to make this type of connection because they cannot produce and manipulate the necessary linguistic symbols to conceive of abstract principles (Lindesmith, Strauss, and Denzin 1977: 228). They live for the most part in the here and now, denied any understanding of reality that requires a facility with language and with technology, incapable of representing their social ties in the mind with any depth or complexity and therefore denied the ability to experience the full range of social connectedness.

The rest of us easily make sociomental connections, bonds, and communities. People who share some cultural knowledge or a relevant commonality can derive a sense of interpersonal togetherness (the *social* aspect of the connection) when at least one of them is mentally oriented toward and mentally engaged with the other (the *mental* aspect), making the resulting connection truly *sociomental*. When a sociomental connection gains strength and durability, it can be considered a bond, and when it encompasses three or more people, a community of the mind can form (following Ferdinand Tonnies, for whom the *gemeinschaft* of mind is the "truly human and supreme form of community" in which "persons of a common faith feel, like members of the same craft, or rank, everywhere united by a spiritual bond . . . [which] forms a kind of invisible scene or meeting" (1963 [1887]: 42–43). Although Tonnies did not write about the wide variety of ways that people can be united mentally (and could not have imagined some of the modern technological ways), concentrating mainly on the connectedness felt by those who share a religious belief, still he notes the social significance and *preeminence* of social bonds and communities "invisibly" created in the absence of face-to-face contact. The term *community of the mind* is used here, then, to evoke this type of connectedness.

Communities in general are formed when three or more people become socially connected in a generally structured or patterned way, develop a collective identity and purpose, and share an extra-dyadic "sense" of belonging to a social entity larger than the individual or dyad.[1] It could be argued that since the mental groupings I describe do not come together physically, they should more properly be called "collectivities," "categories," "clusters," or some such term. Certainly very loosely connected groupings of people who do not meet could be considered "clusters," as I discuss later in this chapter. But other mental groupings are characterized by a definite structure, strong collective identity, and members' very real sense that they belong to a "group." I use the term *community of the mind* quite deliberately, then, without claiming that such communities are identical to, or satisfy the same human needs as, communities whose members have regular and frequent face-to-face contact.

"Community," perhaps the most sociological of all concepts (Wolfe 1989: 60), tends to be defined one of two ways: either "territorially," to depict a grouping of people relating to one another within a specific geographical area, or "emotionally," to depict the sense of belonging to such a group.[2] I favor the latter in conceiving of groups of people (including dyads, tiny "groups of two") as something other, something more, than physical, stepping on the shoulders of theorists such as George Herbert Mead, for whom even people who do not physically meet can serve as "abstract" social groups that influence people and inspire the formation of "definite" social relations among members (1934: 157); Georg Simmel, who describes groups as first and foremost having "psychological unity" that is born and perpetuated by mediating elements (1950 [1908]: 152); and Emile Durkheim, who worships group life and yet conceptualizes the "ultimate group"—the *conscience collective*—as a mental or "spiritual" entity, conceiving of *all* groups as essentially "mental" (1984 [1893]: xlii–xliv). Communities of the mind yield networks of sociomental connections and bonds that are mental rather than physical (*mental networks*) but are quite real and do indeed provide a sense of structure, identity, purpose, and belonging for their members. They are, in a word, more communal than one might think.

As with a dyadic connection, *no* modern community can realistically be characterized by continuous face-to-face contact among all members. Whether due to size, spatial dispersion, or temporal dispersion (their members live at different times in history), communities can be said to actually "exist" in their most complete form only in the minds of their members. Surely members of very large communities of the mind (nations, religions, academic disciplines) *never* meet "all together" in a face-to-face context. They maintain their connectedness mentally and may even exist without *any* of their members *ever* meeting in literal space, as in an Internet community.

How, exactly, does this happen? How do we create a "meeting of the minds"—a sociomental connection, bond, or community of the mind—in the absence of the "visible glue" of face-to-face contact? This chapter examines the processes by which a kind of "mental glue" bonds us to one another in the absence of physical copresence. I explore how people become mentally oriented toward one another, find and forge commonalities, develop a sense of resonance with one another, and form the mental networks that are so critical in keeping communities "together." For it is this "mental glue," ironically, that turns out to be indispensable in keeping even face-to-face relationships and communities strong and secure—*in between* periods of physical copresence. In investigating how we make sociomental connections and "cement" them together, then, the act of social connecting in general can become much more "visible" and better understood.

GETTING TOGETHER:
MENTAL ORIENTATION

The anticipation of the existence of another person—or becoming oriented toward an "other"—is a distinctly social act, as Max Weber explains:[3]

> Social action, which includes both failure to act and passive acquiescence, may be oriented to the past, present, or expected future behavior of others. . . . The others may be individual persons, and may be known to the actor as such, or may constitute an indefinite plurality and be entirely unknown as individuals. (1978: 22)

As we become oriented toward others, whether these others are formally "known" to us or not, we actually engage in a type of social action. "Watching is doing," Erving Goffman asserts, and the same is true of thinking: when we project ourselves mentally into a situation, we *really* experience it (1974: 381).

Technological mediators act as "bridges" between separated people, facilitating joint mental orientation. Two physically separated individuals and a technological mediator (or "mediating element," in Simmel's terms) can structurally form a three-sided social unit (a "triad") as a mediator "brings" information from one person to another (see Simmel 1950 [1908]: 118–77). Though the triad has three components or "sides" (two people and the mediator), we tend to forget or take for granted the side representing the mediator, because technological mediation occurs constantly in our society. (This would not be the case in a culture in which, for example, television had just been introduced.) The connection, then, comes to feel much more like a dyad. With the assistance of the technological mediator, two spatially separated individuals thus have a chance to learn enough about one another so that they can become oriented toward and get to know of one another.

The people to whom we become mentally oriented can be *particular others*—specific individual persons—or *typified others*[4]—those who are more generally representative of a group. For as an individual

> takes or assumes the organized social attitudes of the given social group or community [or some one section thereof] to which he belongs . . . (he) governs his own conduct accordingly. He thus enters into a special set of social relations with all the other individuals who belong to that [group or community] . . . which afford or represent unlimited possibilities for the widening and ramifying and enriching of the social relations . . . *definite social relations [however indirect]* with an almost infinite number of other individuals who also belong to or are included within one or another of these abstract social classes or subgroups. (Mead 1934: 154–57; emphasis added)

As Mead argues, we can engage in a kind of "definite social relation" with others as we mentally orient ourselves toward them. We may even begin to identify with them as a reference group (Chayko 1993a: 577; see also Shibutani 1955), allowing them to influence our thoughts, feelings, and actions.

Human beings are able to become oriented mentally toward other people because our cognitive system for forming and retrieving mental images and memories is so sophisticated and detailed. As we perform the cognitive processes of sensation and perception, we form mental impressions of other people. When we process our impressions of how we believe things and people to look, sound, feel, smell, and so forth, we do so in specific emotional states. Emotional states influence the clarity, vividness, and exact nature of these mental images and help us recall them and bring them into our conscious minds. Emotions, therefore, are critical to the creation of social bonds; they "can open or close the mental doors to a relationship," Candace Clark explains (1993: 301).[5]

The more vividly the image is created, stored, and retrieved, the more closely it will approximate an actual percept, and the more likely it is that we will respond to the image much as we might respond to the person it represents. With bits of information, images, and impressions, a would-be connector "gradually constructs a [mental] picture of the other toward which he orients himself" (Davis 1973: 94). As Jodi O'Brien notes,

> [W]hen we interact with another with whom we do not have physical contact, we proceed as if they were embodied (Stone 1992). To do so we must conjure an image of them. (1999: 100)

This "other" can be virtually any type of thing or being toward which an individual is capable of becoming oriented, including those whom we will never meet face-to-face.

In the absence of visual information, we must make inferences and guesses in order to construct impressions of them. We may use information that we obtain from observing and processing people's communication styles (word choice, linguistic cues, etc.).[6] When we think that a connection will continue over an extended period of time, we develop more detailed mental impressions. Both the breadth and intensity of interpersonal impressions can be quite well developed. Of course, these impressions can be merely stereotypes, but it has been discovered that when we are directly involved in connecting with people whom we believe will "matter" to us over time, we work to reduce this effect; in computer use, for example, we present ourselves carefully and selectively, constructing thoughtful, detailed messages that allow those involved to get to know one another much more as individuals than as types (Hancock and Dunham 2001: 329; see also Walther 1996). People who are mentally oriented toward one another over a period of time (and who anticipate continued mental orientation) tend to actively engage in constructing personalized images of one another.

Even when all we have is textual information regarding the other, we can form very detailed mental impressions, for

> [t]he sensorial parsimony of plain text tends to entice users into engaging their imaginations to fill in the missing details, while, comparatively speaking, the richness of stimuli in fancy (systems) has an opposite tendency, pushing users' imaginations into a more passive role. (Curtis 1992: 66)

As we orient ourselves toward an other and form an image in our minds, a strong *engagement* with the image takes place. It is this engagement that is so critical to the development of connectedness at a distance. Incidentally, while many people choose to post or exchange photos over the Internet to increase the visual component of a connection, pictured images do *not* necessarily encourage but can actually dampen the "getting to know one another" process over the long term (Walther, Slovacek, and Tidwell 2001). A lack of visual cues can actually aid the process of mental connecting, for it allows a connector to reallocate those cognitive resources that ordinarily would be used to manage a face-to-face interaction to the more complex cognitive task of engaging with another via mental imagery. "Freed from some of the demands and constraints" of face-to-face interaction, people often adapt surprisingly well to the challenges of nonvisual imaging (Hancock and Dunham 2001: 329, 340; see also Walther 1996), as my interview subject Tapashi does:

> [Y]ou don't get to meet the person but you know them through what you've read. Whatever you know, that's how you picture them. You don't have to see the way they are to form a picture.

Another interview subject, Bruce, offers that in reading others' written work,

> of course, you may never, ever meet them. But through what they say, you start to get an idea of what they're like.

Online connectors, such as those from the soap opera group I surveyed, describe the process of forming mental images through reading and writing messages via computer:

> We can't see each other [but] I know I've formed pictures in my mind of all of you.

I'm sure the mystery of what we look like and what our surroundings are is what makes this so much fun . . . I have definitely formed pictures in my mind of all you guys.

I picture the same things. . . . By the way, Angie, I picture you with blond hair do you have blond hair?

People form and continue to refine their mental pictures of certain others and thus become more firmly oriented toward them. These mental images or pictures then become, in effect, mental *replications* of absent others.

We can even develop mental images of *typified* absent others. When we use the mass media, the names or faces of at least *some* of the others in groups we read about or see are occasionally made known. When we are given a picture or a textual description of, say, New York Jets fans, skinheads, or gay rights activists, the people in the picture or description typify and "stand in for" the group at large. They reveal at least a sense of the others who comprise the group, as this member of the high-IQ group, "Mensa," found:

> Beginning with my first issue of the [Mensa organization's] *Bulletin*, I began to discover something very comforting nestled in its pages of letters and articles . . . there began to emerge a vision of the diversity of the membership: the different backgrounds, geography, politics, and education that have colored our individual bias. How wonderful. Now I find comfort in the discovery that many of the other members are as strange as I am. Knowledge of that sort is powerful; it can give one peace of mind. (letter sent to the *Mensa Bulletin*, December 1995, p. 9)

Without physical information, the picture or sense that we construct of others will probably not be complete or perfectly accurate. But, as Bruce points out, neither is *any* mental "picture":

> I think you're always sort of filling in the blanks of things you don't know, and making inferences like, "well if you like this, then you're probably like that." It happens, I think, in interpersonal [face-to-face] situations too.

We manage our impressions so carefully and continuously in everyday life that we are always making inferences with regard to what others are "really like," and we can very easily be wrong or inaccurate (Goffman 1959; Chayko 1993b).

Numerous forms of mass symbolic expression—from bumper stickers, T-shirts, and billboards to magazines, newspapers, newsletters, Web pages, and computer discussion groups—help people learn about one another. In such forums as letters to the editor and editorial pages, Web sites, and radio and television talk shows, members of communities—and, by extension, the communities themselves—are specifically identified and/or depicted. And at large sporting and cultural events, images of media figures *and* audience members are depicted on electronic scoreboards, video screens, and public address systems (all of which also can be seen, heard, and experienced by fans who are not in the physical arena via television— see Purcell 1997: 103). Through all of these means, people can begin to orient themselves mentally toward typified, as well as particular, others.

Internalizing the images of other people can be sufficient in and of itself to constitute a social reality and to create social connectedness itself.

My association with you evidently consists in the relation between my idea of you and the rest of my mind. If there is something in you that is wholly beyond this and makes no impression upon me, it has no social reality in this relation. The immediate social reality is the personal idea; nothing, it would seem, could be much more obvious than this. (Cooley 1964 [1922]: 119)

The mental images that people have of one another are "perhaps the most vivid things in our experience," Cooley maintains (1964 [1922]: 120)— and are as real and consequential as any physical phenomenon. Cooley considers mental life *the* most real and dominant aspect of society, for individuals, associations between individuals, and society itself are all only fully real, he contends, when they are imaginable in people's minds (ibid., 119–20). Even Goffman, who does not ascribe such primacy to mental life and generally feels that it is in everyday face-to-face interaction that social order and societies are created, allows that

at the very center of interaction life is the cognitive relation we have with those present before us, without which relationship our activity, behavioral and verbal, could not be meaningfully organized. And although this cognitive relationship can be modified during a social contract, and typically is, the relationship itself is extrasituational, consisting of the information a pair of persons have about the information each other has of the world, and the information they have (or haven't) concerning the possession of this information. (1983: 4–5)

The mental images and impressions (the "information") that we hold of one another and of the world can be seen as enabling all forms of interaction, both face-to-face and sociomental, as "one comes into relations with a thing merely by regarding it" (Durkheim 1973 [1914]: 342).

It should not be surprising, then, that mental images in general are imbued with such realness, and that images of people who are fictional, dead, or far away in literal space can have a great deal of social reality for us. As my interviewee Janice tells us, in describing her feelings of social bonding with characters in novels:

> When I finish a book, I feel very sad that I'm not going to be with these characters anymore. I know it sounds silly, but I've always felt this way. So when I put down a book I don't start another book for a while, because I almost want to say goodbye to these people.

Or, as television journalist Lesley Stahl explains:

> There ought to be a word for the way you feel when you finish a book you have loved—a word to describe the longing when these characters leave your life. Not quite grief, not quite pining— c'mon I *do* have a life—but something close to that. . . . Every time I've read [*Code of the West*] I've grieved for my lost friends. (in *O* magazine, July 2001, p. 175)

At least temporarily, characters in books become a meaningful "other" for us and take on a social reality (for more on social reality, see Chapters 5 and 6).

The "others" who influence us also can sometimes be long-deceased *real* people. After physical death, individuals may remain significant others for the living and may have a great influence on them; some widows and widowers, for example, maintain their status of "spouse" after death. The deceased can influence those who are left behind in many ways: they may inspire spouses to refuse to remarry (or, conversely, to hasten to do so), to feel sad or depressed as a consequence of their passing (or the opposite!), or to spend an inheritance in accordance with the final wishes of the deceased (or, of course, very differently). The body may be dead, but as the person associated with the body remains a significant other to some living person, his or her personality, influence, and even economic and social control can live on:

> Everyone says I'm like [my grandmother's] reincarnation. I walk like her, I talk like her. And when I listen to my mom talk about

her, which is her mother, it makes me think that I'm here for my
mother *as* my grandmother, and when she sees me, she's looking
at her mom. (Jessica)

My mother always says I'm the reincarnation of [my grand-
father]. And I hear stories about what a great man he was. He did
so many things and helped so many people. . . . The connection is
the resemblance, and it feels really good. It gives me a feeling as
though there's something big out there that's waiting for me in
life for me to accomplish, and I've got to get to it but I haven't
gotten there yet. . . . It inspires me a lot. (Ugo)

The idea that a dead person is "reincarnated" in the living is (at the very
least) a powerful metaphor for the deceased's continuing influence over
the living. One can imagine Ugo's grandfather inspiring him to live a kind
of life that might be quite different if the grandfather's influence was extinguished, so his grandfather remains a significant other for Ugo, as
Nicole's brother does for her:

I feel [my brother] Ron is still around, and I still have conversations in my head with him. And I think, what would Ron think
about this or that.

We can say that a deceased individual with such influence has had a physical death but not yet a "social death." For

when a member of a community dies, his social personality is not
immediately extinguished. His physical lifetime is ended, but his
social existence continues. It exists so long as memory of it is
felt by the living members of society. (Warner 1959; in Baker
1991: 539)

An individual, then, is not *socially* dead until his or her influence as a significant other is completely severed.[7] The same is true of absent others—
and even fictional characters—whom we cannot meet but who can
influence us in significant ways and therefore have great social reality for
us. Cooley writes of the way in which the continuing social reality of
someone who has died keeps them, in a sense, "alive" in our minds:

Would it not be absurd to deny social reality to Robert Louis
Stevenson, who is so much alive in many minds and so potently

affects important phases of thought and conduct? He is certainly more alive in this real practical sense than most of us who have not yet lost our corporeity, more alive, perhaps, than he was before he lost his own, because of his wider influence. And so. . . . Hamlet is real to the imaginative reader with the realest kind of reality, the kind that works directly upon his personal character. (1964 [1922]: 123)

As people and fictional characters become technologically "known" and mentally pictured and replicated, they can be considered socially "alive" and have a very real influence over those who connect with them. The "realest kind of reality" is, indeed, that which works directly upon our personal characters, so that our minds and hearts are affected, even changed.

The tendency of many people to believe in ghosts and reincarnation also exemplifies the influence that people can continue to have even after their deaths. Most people publicly state a disbelief in ghosts, but in a 1987 random sample survey of Americans, fully 42 percent of respondents—53 percent widowed—reported at least one believed experience of *contact* with ghosts.[8] A general *belief* in ghosts is nearly universal in societies both Eastern and Western, premodern and modern,[9] and, of course, the celebration of Halloween and the popularity of supernatural themes in movies, books, and other forms of culture perpetuate a playful mainstream acknowledgment of ghosts. It is possible that a feeling of connectedness to the dead sometimes manifests itself in the belief that actual contact with the dead has taken place.

For individuals to perceive ghostly contacts as real, they must "frame" them as actual experiences, which means that, from their perspective, connections with the dead literally have taken place (see Goffman 1974: 347). Certain technological applications—such as "psychic telephone lines" and the "channeling" of the dead by psychic mediums—encourage the sense of (and, some believe, facilitate) such connections. The phenomenon of "ghost connections" is a stark example of the definition of the situation (Thomas 1928), for regardless of whether ghosts and ghostly connections really exist, their ostensible presence and influence can certainly be quite real in their consequences. The same is true, I might add, in perceived-as-real connections to other nonphysical beings, such as gods, angels, and other spiritual figures, and to fantasized, dream-state, drug-induced, or other "imaginary friend"-type figures. Inasmuch as such beings are perceived as humanlike, our sense of being connected to them is "subjectively significant" and can be emotionally powerful (Caughey 1984: 22; Fine 1983).

Conversely, people who are legally and corporeally alive can be treated *as dead* and therefore be said to have little or no social reality. People may become unimportant to others, forgotten or ignored, and may cease to have influence *before* their physical death. We often rather casually exclude some people who are within the range of our senses from our sphere of social concern and attention, fail to orient ourselves toward them mentally, and, therefore, exclude the possibility of bonding with them (as when in particular situations we ignore the presence of children or the homeless, or carry on with our personal conversations and activities as though waiters, cleaning personnel, or cab drivers are not "really" around). At such times, despite their physical presence, they have no social presence for us. Similarly, the chronically ill can be considered socially dead when, after a period of grieving, families and friends orient their thoughts away from them and discontinue forming new mental images of them. This also happens when people are simply forgotten about. One often hears the phrase regarding some celebrity or another, "Gee, I thought so and so was dead." We tend to consider such people, for all intents and purposes, "nonpersons," forming little or no mental impression of them, even though they may have physical proximity to us (see Zerubavel 1993: 402–5). Individuals can even die and be *reborn* socially (Baker 1991: 544–8). Beyond the physical life course, then, "there is an expansion and contraction of the social self" that is technologically assisted and alternately expands and diminishes others' tendencies to form connections to that self, that "other" (ibid., 549).

Fetuses can have a social reality that *precedes* physical reality and birth (see Isaacson 1996) and begets social connectedness. Ultrasound technology, in which fetuses can be detected and "pictured" very early in the pregnancy, helped one woman establish bonds with the multiple fetuses in her womb long before their birth:

> It's a funny thing about ultrasounds: They let you fall in love much earlier than you normally would. . . . I told Tom, "I love them all already. I want them all." (in Browder 1997: 122)

Two of my interviewees, Bruce and Tom, relate stories of connectedness to a fetus:

> At first it was just . . . in my own head . . . that I'm going to be a dad. And then I started to connect with this not-yet-person, who I didn't even meet, and then it was aided [by technology] . . . the sonogram, etc. (Bruce)

> My sister miscarried, and I was destroyed. I had started that bond. And then when she got pregnant again, I was kind of

prepared to feel that way, so I could say that I started to feel that bond the moment she got pregnant the second time. (Tom)

In sociomental bonding with a fetus, or a dead person, or for that matter a fictional character, the social reality of the "other" takes temporary precedence over its physical status (or lack of same). Even in forming weak, ephemeral sociomental connections, a social reality can exist at least concomitant to or "alongside" the physical reality; a social reality that matters in its own way.

We also form in our minds impressions of animals, cartoon characters, objects, and natural phenomena. Some people form connections that feel absolutely authentic in response to these phenomena. Although this book focuses on connections to people and personlike characters and beings, it is instructive to consider (if only briefly) the way in which people can orient themselves toward nonhuman phenomena so that they feel connected. If we can appreciate the way in which a bond can emerge between a pet owner and his or her cherished animal, or a child and his or her toys or favorite cartoon characters—fairly conventional occurrences—then we can better appreciate the potential strength of the bonds that form with human and personlike absent others.

When, for example, my son Ryan was four years old, Simba, the lion cub in Disney's *The Lion King* (with whom he had spent many hours viewing videos and playing interactive CD-ROM games), was a very real part of his life. His connection to Simba (and many other such characters) would have been readily apparent to anyone who could observe the complex, multilayered "world" of game playing in which he would immerse himself (games that would typically include both himself and Simba as participants). Simba, like so many children's characters—including those representing the animal world—is endowed with a human speaking voice and traits. Children, who may be less imaginatively constrained in forming sociomental bonds than many adults, tend to respond unselfconsciously to such anthropomorphizing. Young children seem to easily form social bonds of real consequence to them with fictional characters and with such inanimate objects as dolls and toys (Ball 1967). It is edifying (not to mention adorable) to watch young children verbally interact with their fictional video, toy, and CD-ROM "friends." When another of Ryan's favorite characters, "Brother Bear" from the Berenstain Bears series of books, videos, and computer games, would "ask" him at the end of a computer game to return to play with him again soon, Ryan's response to him was always an immediate, unwavering declaration of the strength of his connection: "OK, Brother Bear, I will!"

It is likely that a similar process of anthropomorphizing characterizes the bonds that both children and adults make with animals, fictional characters, spiritual figures and special objects. Those who conceive of, develop, write about, and distribute such things, as well as those who form connections to them, impute human traits to them, even though they are not human. We endow our gods with ostensible physicality, names, and even status characteristics such as gender and race. We name or relate "to" special dolls, stuffed animals, toys, photographs, and mementos (such as a wedding ring). We even treat computers as humanlike or *sufficiently human* (talking to them, naming them, blaming them for errors, etc.) to permit the construction of perceived mental connections to them.[10] Apprehending them *as* human, even though we know intellectually that they are not, our orientation toward such beings and objects becomes more pronounced. This creates and upholds the social reality of our connection to them.

Some people even feel bonded to such natural phenomena as plants, trees, oceans, rivers, and "land" itself. It may be tempting to want to draw the line regarding the "limit" of social bonding here (if one has not already drawn it during one of the preceding few paragraphs!) and to classify such feelings as something less than or different from true bonding experiences. However, people—and cultures—with minds flexible enough to find a sense of bonding in such places might agree with Christopher Stone (1974), who claims that like women, African Americans, prisoners, and the insane, all of whom had no legal rights or legal standing at one time, environmental matter such as trees and rivers might theoretically be extended legal rights and standing one day. We could grant rights to the environment, he proposes, because it communicates its wants and needs to us in verifiable ways (i.e., "the lawn tells me that it wants water by a certain dryness of the blades and soil—immediately obvious to the touch— the appearance of bald spots, yellowing, and a lack of springness" [Stone 1974: 24]). People also sometimes talk to plants, trees, and the earth. So, as we feel that a flower or an ocean "communicates," and we feel ourselves respond anthropomorphically, we could conceivably orient ourselves toward it in a subjectively meaningful way, perceive it as a personlike thing, and form a social bond with it. It is an arguable position.

Physical and legal corporeality, then, neither determines nor limits social connectedness (though surely it influences its quality and nature). We can form mental impressions with virtually any thing or being— particular or typified—toward which we have become mentally oriented and which has social reality for us (although this book deals primarily with human and humanlike manifestations as I consider them most fully *social*). Then we determine whether there might be some commonality between ourselves and these faraway others. As we do so, we form sociomental connections.

FINDING AND FORGING COMMONALITY

As we become oriented toward other people, we seek out information that will help us get to know them. We attempt to discern their social attributes and status characteristics: gender, race, ethnicity, socioeconomic class, age, occupation, level of education, marital status, and so on (Davis 1973: 95). Whether consciously or not, we set out to determine the extent of our "social overlap" with them (Cerulo and Ruane 1998); how similar or different we are in the ways that matter most to us.

We are constantly exchanging information as we share certain ways of presenting ourselves, including our postures, emotions, clothing, jewelry, hairstyles, tattoos, ways of speaking and behaving, and notes on all of our "favorite things." We display aspects of ourselves and try to detect aspects of others, sometimes relying on stereotypes when we do not yet have individualized information.[11] My interviewee Joe describes this process:

> When I see somebody with a Cowboy shirt or hat on, it tells me something about them. Not a lot, but certain characteristics that I might assess that they have. Same thing with the Lakers. Certain types of people like certain types of teams. Because teams have identities—flashy, whatever—whereas another team like the Detroit Pistons, it's kind of like they're blue-collar guys, they're work horses, you know, a hard-working team, "We're not here for the flash, we're just here to get the job done." So the teams kind of take on an identity, and you kind of place those characteristics on fans, cause a lot of times, that's what people like about the teams.

When we treat someone else as a "type," we are taking a kind of mental shortcut, helping us to decide (however automatically, or even incorrectly) which mental models to activate in various situations and how to organize our cognitions to make sense of our surroundings. This prevents us from having to approach every individual and every situation as wholly unique and from being so "flooded" with information that we cannot make decisions about what to do and how to think (although, to be sure, stereotyping also can result in the inability or refusal to see others as individuals when that is what is appropriate). It permits us to "sight-read the world" (Thayer 1990: 339).

When we believe that we share some social attribute(s) or status characteristic(s) with someone else, we may come to feel connected on the basis of presuming that the other is the "same type" as we are. My interview subject Joanne told me that she feels connected to other members of her sorority when she sees someone wearing the Greek letters that represent it; similarly, Joe told me that he feels a connection with other L.A. Laker fans when he sees them wearing the team's insignia or clothing. Such commonalities engender connectedness because they seem to indicate that some degree of *like-mindedness* or *oneness* exists among those who share the commonality. Through a lifetime of socialization, we learn what it means to be a follower of a political party, religion, TV show, singer, sport, profession, discipline, and so on. When we feel that we belong to such a group and it becomes part of our identity, we tend to feel strong, positive feelings toward the others in it as well as intensified attributions of similarity (Hancock and Dunham 2001: 327; see also Lea and Spears 1992). We presume that we are somehow like, and may even think like, those who seem to be the same "type." As Tonya says of a woman whose academic credentials, background, and occupation are similar to hers:

> I really think that an (academic) discipline teaches you a certain way to think, so we (she and I) must think somewhat similarly . . . I felt most connected to her.

We can discover and feel like-mindedness on virtually any basis any time a common identity with others is created: with people who enjoy the same television shows as we do, who were born in the same town, who went to our school, who enjoy the same sporting team, or who share *any* commonality that has meaning for us.

Of course, in assuming similarity, we can make mistakes. We can be wrong; the object of one's connection and oneself may *not* be particularly alike, but we can still come to feel connected in feeling that there is a common identity and in sharing information about aspects of ourselves that reinforces this sense of shared identity (see Turner, Grube, and Meyers 2001: 233). Ugo told me that his former school was such an important part of his life that he still feels a oneness with all others who attended it. He perceives commonality with them—even though he will certainly never meet most of them, and it is certainly possible that they may have very little in common with him. Still, he feels strongly connected:

> It feels like an invisible bond that nothing can destroy. [Why is it so indestructible? What makes it so powerful?] Because of the

culture [the all-male high school] that we both belong to. Even
though we may not know each other, the culture, that environment, is so strong, it's like it's built such a strong foundation—
like if I was to meet him, it would be like he's from school, he's
cool. [Even if they didn't attend when you did and you could
never have met them?] Exactly. Even those who graduated thirty,
forty years before us . . . it's very cool, it's an extremely positive
feeling, to know that there are people out there who you're connected to, and you don't even know it.

For Bruce, music is one of the commonalities that produces in him a
strong sense of like-mindedness and connectedness to others:

I may feel a connection with someone who likes and uses and
thinks is as cool as I do—that's a very poor sentence—I feel a
connection with people who play the same type of guitar as I do.
I don't feel the same connection to those who, say, drive the same
Buick as I do. But I chose this guitar carefully, and there aren't
that many of them out there, and . . . I feel a connection. I think
that's why people wear patches, you know, "I am a member of the
blah blah blah," and you wear it on your sleeve . . . and you feel
membership to a certain thing, and you feel connected to that.
And I could see somebody who uses the same drums as I do . . . I
think it's validating. Somebody else likes the same things I do.
And it's a shared experience.

Bruce feels connected to other guitar players and drummers because he
presumes that he shares certain experiences or states of mind with those
others. Although he also drives a Buick, he apparently does not feel
strongly enough about that commonality for a sense of like-mindedness
with other Buick owners to emerge.

Other interviewees share the commonalities most relevant to them in
forming sociomental connections:

I feel a connection with others who share my interests—like bal-
looning, gardening, dog training. (Nicole)

In my [professional] association, having the group in common,
there's a bond there. (Jose)

In reading a book, and with others who like that book . . . I identify [with those people]. (Bruce)

There's a person with my last name who works in our town, and I
feel like they're in my family, even though I don't really know
them. (Joanne)

The person sharing Joanne's last name is envisioned more as a typified than
a particular other. She senses some connectedness simply on the basis of
the name (and perhaps a familylike feeling that it may conjure up).

Connectedness to a fictional character tends to develop when we presume like-mindedness between ourselves and that character. Because we
tend to see fictional characters as representative of real people, we often
identify with those whose feelings or insights we feel we share (Fiske
1986). Sometimes we even develop an "implication" with characters that
is more complicated and meaningful than mere identification; we feel
that, in a fundamental way, we truly "know" them (see Brown 1989: 185).
Caughey notes that given the intimate way in which we apprehend fictional characters, it would be peculiar if we did *not* respond in this way
(1984: 49; see also Fine 1983: 232).

Reading seemed to engender some of the strongest sociomental
bonds in the people with whom I spoke; in fact, people who felt connected or bonded to characters in favorite books seemed to grasp the concept of sociomental connecting instantly and intuitively during my
interviews with them. They would knowingly nod when I asked whether
they had ever felt connected or bonded to a character in a book, and they
would then explain to me, often in great depth, what this was like for them.

It's almost as if "oh my god!" this person is so much like me, or
whatever. And you just want to finish the book, then and there,
and not put it down. (Jessica)

It's almost like finding a friend. I care about what's going to happen [to the character], because I know how I would react or how
that would make me feel. If something hurts that character,
you're hurting right along with them. [You think] "oh, that
would be awful if that happened to me!" So, it's just sort of a
"simpatico." There has to be something with the character that
I identify with in order to get a connected feeling. There's
something about the character that's like, all right, I've had that
happen to me, or all right, I'm like that. (Rhonda)

One of my favorite books is about my [ancestral African] tribe . . . and there were certain things that they did that I noticed that my parents did to me growing up. Like what they did to their kids, how they related to their kids, how they spoke to them, the respect that the adults and the children have for one another, and that feeling was the same as—it was like I was reading about myself. Like someone had been watching my whole family life the whole time and wrote it down in this book, and I never knew it, and one day I picked it up, and there it was. And it felt funny, it felt really good, too, it made me want to read the book more, it made me really think about the characters and what they were doing, and relate it to myself. I would actually say, "OK, this character is me, this one is my mom, this little guy is my little brother." (Ugo)

In television viewing, people also develop connections with characters:

It's like when I'm watching the soap opera I know how she's going to react, and it's the same way I would react; in certain situations, that's what I would do. (Anita)

It's like I really cared what happened to the character of Harley, you know really in the moment of watching the show, if she were upset I'd feel really bad for her . . . in the moment I'd get very caught up in wanting it to work out, or not wanting her to get caught, or whatever. Really caring, kind of like having my fingers crossed that it's going to work out, really doing that, like, "I hope she makes it through that car crash!" (Nicole)

Guiding Light characters (as well as many from *As the World Turns*) feel like family—you care about them—you get involved. (from the online soap opera group)

I really have watched *Guiding Light* for most of my life . . . I cried when they killed (the character) Maureen Bauer, and I was really touched. My mom thinks I am crazy for watching it for so long and taping it every day. But I don't care, the characters have become like family in a weird type of way . . . I do have to say that if they cancel GL I will probably not watch another one. It's like losing your best friend. (from the online soap opera group)

And from the movies:

> There are some characters I just make a connection to. I get all involved in their story and they just remind me of me. And it's almost like I get advice from them! Like in *Don't Tell Mom, the Babysitter's Dead,* this girl fakes a resume and gets a job. And the next day, I did the same thing, and I got the job! (Grace)

As characters remind us of ourselves or we feel we with have things in common with them, a sense of connectedness can begin to emerge.

People also form sociomental connections with celebrities on the basis of some presumed commonality. My interview subjects formed sociomental connections with the following celebrities:

Television and movie actress Neve Campbell:

> She's like me—her character is. And Claire Danes on [the television show] *My So-Called Life.* They're similar to me and my life. (Elizabeth)

Country singers Martina McBride, Shania Twain, and Lorrie Morgan:

> [Because] I'm a country singer too. (Claire)

Newsperson Paula Zahn:

> She just seems real. She tells me enough about her personal life that I can relate to her. She's a mom, and what she has to go through to get to work in the morning, and home at night. (Caitlin)

Singer Gloria Estefan:

> Because she came here from Cuba when young, worked her way up, and doesn't give up her American culture for her Cuban one. . . . I guess because there's not that many Latina actresses or singers; they don't even talk about that they're Latinas—they just totally assimilate. . . . She's just like really open about it. [Do you know a lot about her?] Yeah, from interviews and magazines. . . . I hope there will be many similarities between me and her. I mean, I want to be successful, and she is very, very close to her family . . . and I want to

do the same thing. Be successful, and at the same time have a family, be very close to my family. (Rosa)

Identification with celebrities, and the sense of like-mindedness that can result, easily lends itself to the formation of a connection.

And connectedness engendered in everyday Internet use is, if anything, potentially even stronger. People who join and become involved in online groups often assume a common identity with one another which implies similarity and affinity. In the exchange of online messages, a shared identity often is reinforced (Turner, Grube, and Meyers 2001: 233; see also Walther, Slovacek, and Tidwell 2001: 112). Online connecting has exploded in popularity, in fact, for just this reason—for countless highly specialized news groups, bulletin boards, electronic communities, chat areas, Multi-User Domains (MUDs), and Web sites attract like-minded people, many of whom desire and enjoy such connectedness and choose to return regularly.[12]

It's exciting to connect with people, people in which you have a passionate commonality . . . I feel like these people are in a sense my friends. (from the online soap opera group)

It's the feeling of being connected to others who you have something in common with. (from the online soap opera group)

Chat rooms allow people with similar interests to meet one another. I think that's very powerful. (Ken)

Perhaps because forming cyberspace connections can be so "exciting" and seemingly "validating," connecting in this way has become one of the primary uses of the Internet.[13] As M. Kadi observes, albeit rather facetiously (1995: 59), "When J. Individual is on the Internet, he or she does not engage in topics that do not interest J. Individual. So who is J. meeting? Why, people who are just like J."

Online or offline, we do not always detect like-mindedness in others. Other times, in assessing our level of social overlap with others, we perceive significant differences, yet still form a connection. In what I call *complementary differentiation*, one forms a connection despite (or perhaps even because of) these differences (as when "opposites attract"). These connections may be more latent and difficult to detect than those characterized by perceived similarity, but they may be just as strong, as in Maria's connection to a favorite author who comes from social circumstances different than her own:

> I find it interesting that we're so different yet we can have similar experiences and a connection.

Or, in Bruce's realization that it would make good sense to forge a closer connection to the people with whom he will have to work every day:

> I mean, I have forged friendships with folks I don't even really like. Because I know I have to be with them. So I try to find something that we can connect and talk about.

In general, one is motivated to share some aspect of another person's life when it has some relevance to one's own, whether or not social characteristics or motivations seem explicitly similar. Still, "underneath" a connection marked by difference is often hidden some fundamental commonality, some shared concern regarding a common issue (albeit differently expressed), which "anchors" the connection.

When we do perceive differences between ourselves and others—and some differences will inevitably occur when we forge connections—it bodes well for the overall quality of the connection if these differences complement (rather than diminish or destroy) our own traits. Of course, this does not always happen. Some people form connections and bonds with people who hurt, abuse, and diminish them. These connections may seem to offer nothing of value to the connector. But implied in the decision to remain connected—if, indeed, a person has any choice at all (which children and other legally, physically, or emotionally debilitated individuals may not)—is that the seemingly "weaker" half of the connected pair still perceives *something* in the other that he or she believes is either helpful or necessary to attain some goal (e.g., financial need, proximity to one's children, human contact, survival itself, etc.). The less empowered person may feel that the goal in question would be impossible to reach without the connection. Thus the differences between them can be perceived as complementary, at least by the individuals involved, and this perception can represent the basic point of commonality between the people involved that a connection usually requires.

When three or more individuals become jointly oriented toward some person, place, thing, or idea, a community of the mind can form. This core commonality or "hub" can be said to define the group, "draw members in," and represent its identity. It can be almost any person, place, thing, or idea imaginable: it can be an identification with one's nation, with a leader or charismatic personality, with a television show or favorite writer, or with a shared value, belief, or ideology. "It is sociologically very significant," Simmel states, "that isolated elements are *unified* by their *common relation* to a phenomenon which lies outside of them" (1950 [1908]: 145, emphasis added). Core group commonalities make communities of the mind possible and give them their unique and most prominent character (ibid., 145–53). This is true of communities both large and small.

As an example of the construction of a small community of the mind, consider the three individuals who can say that they are one of the children (the siblings) in my particular family of origin. This is a very specific, very strong commonality—let's call it "Chayko siblinghood." Each of the three of us is attached to the core commonality (being siblings in this family) and attached and bonded to one another as well. Although we have many other things in common—we share a fondness for the New York Mets, Bruce Springsteen, and our mother's meat loaf—it is only through our commonality as siblings that we have been able to discover and develop these "subordinate" commonalities.

My brother, my sister and myself are linked in a "hub-and-spoke" network—a series of triadic connections that can be envisioned as a bicycle tire. The "hub" or core of this structure is the linking commonality (Chayko siblinghood), and at the "spokes" are those individuals who are mentally oriented toward the hub (the three of us). Each triad in this case consists of two individuals and the linking commonality (siblinghood) that lies outside of us (at the "hub" of the "wheel") yet serves to connect us. It is the joint orientation to a commonality represented as a "hub" that permits separated individuals to become linked in a communal mental structure that then becomes characterized by the *nature* of the commonality (see Simmel 1950 [1908] on the triad, especially p. 145).

In small communities of the mind constructed much in this way and consisting of few such triads—work groups, committees, small Internet discussion groups, geographically dispersed families, circles of friends who live far from one another—the likelihood is that sociomental bonds with particular others within the community will emerge. Members may also have some form of contact. I once was on a conference organizing committee with seven other people whom I had never physically met (and have not met to date, as I was unable to attend the conference). We "networked" on the Internet and via telephone, and we completed our task successfully and congenially. Had the committee been larger, the odds would have been greater that at some point I would meet one of the members face-to-face or go on to form a stronger bond.

Somewhat larger communities of the mind coalesce around "hubs" that are less specific in nature than those that characterize small communities. The people in a community may share a general concern, such as enhancing educational opportunities for low-income students (as opposed to the more specific task of organizing a conference for professionals in that field), having an interest in the field of "sociology" (versus the much narrower and more specific interest in the emerging field of "cognitive sociology,") or being a fan of a mainstream movie star (as opposed to a "cult" media figure). As the criteria for inclusion in a group become less specialized, more and more people are eligible to be part of that group.

Communities of the mind can become very large and diffused. Still, Craig Calhoun argues, they can still very much "reflect social relations" (1991: 108). Large-scale groupings develop in response to commonalities and "hubs" that are so general and widely known—with such a low "common denominator"—that masses of people can find something to connect with in them. Nationalism is a prime example of this. What it means to be a member of a nation often is so broadly defined that many otherwise diverse people can still "qualify" for membership and feel a sense of community together. Other examples include occupational disciplines, racial, gender, ethnic, or sexual orientation categories, fans of cultural products and media figures, and political parties. Members of a religion also are bound together by shared beliefs and common worship of spiritual figures. Because of a common connection to, say, Allah, members can feel a commonality with and a connectedness to an enormous number of others. Though they may live halfway across the world or even in a past period of time, a very powerful, very real sense of community can still be generated. Common connections to leaders and principles also tie people together—quite powerfully and emotionally—in military groups (Freud 1967 [1922]: 25–36). Though they will have many individual differences, people in large communities are still able to share core commonalities and will perceive varying degrees of likemindedness or complementary differentiation among the group's members.

Communities of the mind also are built by careful design. Families, work groups, and neighborhoods can be "planned." Audiences are sought for products, services, and ideologies. Political constituencies are needed to elect and support candidates. Corporations and other businesses have a commercial interest and investment in seeing "clusters of interest" coalesce around their products and services.[14] To achieve such goals, physically separated people must be encouraged to jointly focus on some common phenomenon in the hope that they will develop a sense of one another and a common identity, become a community of the mind, and achieve the desired aim for the "designers."

To be sure, a cluster of people such as a political (or cultural) constituency may emerge spontaneously, from the ground up, in a groundswell of support for a person or an idea, but such groupings also are frequently designed in the modern age by those with a financial or political stake in their development. The accurate identification and successful creation of large "publics," consumer "markets" and fan "bases" for products, ideas, and services is a skill in large demand.[15] Advertising, marketing, and demographic specialists can be quite ingenious in successfully creating such constituencies, with an eye toward their becoming genuine communities whose members may be inspired to develop sociomental connections to one another and thus remain ever more firmly connected to the community.

Those who successfully create clusters of interest that sell things, elect candidates, or further other types of goals seem to have an excellent intuitive understanding of the concept of sociomental space and of processes of connecting in communities of the mind. For example, TV home shopping networks seem to shrewdly "use" viewers' joint desires to shop *and* to be part of an exclusive club to inspire them to feel connected to the program *and* to one another:

> The network emphasizes that it's a Home Shopping *Club* and that customers are club members. This imparts an intimacy, as do the hosts who announce their own engagements, weddings, and family births on the air. . . . The sales operators are trained to greet the callers as friends, and the network's computers are just as solicitous. The automated answering machine is personalized. . . . When operators set up a new account, they make sure to ask for the new member's birthday and anniversary. Another computer sends greeting cards to all members, enclosing coupons for their next purchase. (Carlin 1993: 40)

Of course, this seemingly warm community atmosphere has been created to further sales goals. Similarly, the Easton Press publishing company sends a mass-marketed letter to people on its mailing list, encouraging them to purchase a series of books using this as an appeal:

> Now, the world's greatest authors of science fiction will autograph their new works for you . . . much as if you were a personal friend. . . . When friends come over and admire the books, I tell them, "These are First Editions the great Science Fiction authors sign for me." . . . They'll also sign for you.

Though it may look quite personal, the ad obviously has been devised first and foremost for commercial purposes.

Even when individuals are brought together in deliberate, commercialized ways, though, they may still discover and develop a sense of common identity and genuine connections to one another. As they are jointly oriented toward common phenomena, they may come to feel unified. Regardless of the nature of the motivation and method by which they were "brought together" in sociomental space, they may come to self-identify as members of the group, find it meaningful, and form sociomental connections to one another on that basis.

While conducting my online surveys, I came upon just such a community. People participating in the Generation X online discussion group that I studied (people roughly in their twenties at the time of this research, the 1990s) seemed to struggle, rather overtly, with the question of *whether or not they were a true community.* They were well aware that they had been externally identified as similar in some way and had been "clustered together" as a consumer market. They knew that many businesses were doing all they could to identify the salient aspects of being in one's twenties to better reach them and sell them things. Yet many of them revealed that, in spite of their resistance to being grouped and identified in this way, some of the commonalities that had been identified *did* serve to link them in a community after all.

These "Xers" seemed to implicitly realize that the question turned on the issue of the *internal, self*-identification of collective identity and common experiences versus the *external* identification of similarity by others (see Uems et al. 1997). They began to explicitly grapple with the question of whether they were legitimately like-minded enough and had shared enough experiences to consider *themselves* a community. To do this, they compared notes on their attitudes toward life and the cultural experiences and symbols that were important to them:

> If you were old enough to own the *Saturday Night Fever* soundtrack on vinyl, but not old enough to see the movie without an adult, you are Gen X. If you were born before Cheech and Chong movies suddenly became passe, you are Gen X.

> When they start talking about lava lamps, bell bottoms, beads in the windows, then they're a boomer. If you talk about Big Wheels, *Schoolhouse Rock,* and the Bee Gees, then you're an Xer. It's also a worldview. How many of you feel like when you're old, you'll have enough from Social Security to make ends meet?

I'll bet the next generation division will be whether there were metal detectors in your high school (to detect guns) and computers in your elementary school. What say?

Remember Pink Floyd's "Another Brick in the Wall," *The Bionic Woman, Wonder Woman, Land of the Lost, Speed Racer, The A-Team,* and who can ever forget Kimba the lion? I always thought nobody remembered all the great stuff from the 1970s. Thanks for a trip down memory lane.

I resent and dislike the stereotype of the Gen X human being, but because I resent it, it is only proof that I am a part of it. Think about it.

I think that being part of a generation has nothing to do with stereotypes, except for possibly the mass marketing industry. Being part of a generation is about shared cultural experiences. Like having in common something as inane as the culture of the '70s during our formative years.

If you're wondering [whether you're Generation X], you probably are.

And one member seemed to bring together these strands of discussion:

I'm not into joining this bandwagon or that one, but I do have a lot of common experiences with people from my age group. I can go anywhere and share notes on childhood experiences like seeing *Star Wars* or Saturday morning cartoons, or listening to that horrible '70s Top 40 radio, and my subsequent discovery of punk rock and new wave. I don't really feel that I am associated with today's teens though except that I am part of the sub-group that they model themselves after and have already experienced a lot of the misery that they should be preparing themselves for! (Like, you know, the usual whine about crummy jobs and no future, etc.)

It is likely that for many who contribute to this online discussion group, membership in "Generation X" gives them the sense of community that may have been one of the attractions of participating in the online group in the first place. However, the members' voices also reflect their realization that external forces had much to do with the creation of this community.

This generation identifies closely with the mass entertainment media they use and have grown up with (Uems et al. 1997). For one thing, television, having been a large part of their lives, has given them a powerful set of commonalities. Later in life, these media-created commonalities become mental reference points. Though the members of this generation may or may not continue to debate the meaning of their experience, the ways in which they had been brought experientially together may continue to provide a subtle sense of connectedness for them.

As we become mentally oriented toward others and forge commonalities with them, then, sociomental connections are formed. With some people, however, our connection is more profound than with others. We may feel that we are "tuning into" them particularly well. Even though we do not meet them face-to-face, we want to call our connections with them true social *bonds*. With these people, we *resonate*.

RESONANCE

In getting to know (or know *of*) someone, we sometimes sense a kind of "resonance" with the other. We feel that we are somehow on the same "wavelength" with this person, even if we are only vaguely aware of it (Schramm 1954; Schutz 1951).[16] More explicitly, we may feel a profound sense of understanding the other or of being understood. I call this experience of "tuning in" to another in the process of forming a sociomental connection *resonance*.

Resonance is a concept rooted in the Pythagorean principle that "like is known by like."[17] As used in the science of acoustics, it refers to the "sympathetic" vibration of a sound wave as it strikes a body that vibrates in response at the same frequency (hence, the metaphor of the "wavelength"). For resonance to occur, acoustically, the structures involved must be somewhat similar to one another, implying some form of "like knowing like." The concept of resonance has been appropriated for use in the fields of physics, chemistry, biology, medicine, psychology, and communication to aid in the description and analysis of various sorts of systems. To demonstrate the application of resonance in social connecting, I draw from two of these fields: communication, and the model of communication developed by Wilbur Schramm (1954), in which he describes the way in which the senders and receivers of messages must "tune in" or resonate with one another if a message is to be received with any kind of accuracy;

and chemistry, in particular Linus Pauling's theory of chemical bonding (1948), in which he conceptualizes electrons as waveforms that contain frequencies that resonate in the presence of similarly structured electrons, resulting in a stabilized "interaction" in which atoms become "bonded" (see Miller 1990: 350–54; Schutz 1951).

As with the chemical bonds that form between atoms, there must be some similarity in "social atoms" for there to be a possibility of a bond. Even the fact that all social connectors are humans is, at the very least, a fundamental kind of similarity. But more critical to the emergence of resonance is the similar social structuring of minds (see Chapter 2); the ability to perceive, categorize, and think about the world in similar ways that touch off strong feelings of like-mindedness. People need and want to be understood. If, in connecting, they reach beyond general commonalities to establish specific intersubjective understandings—or even believe that they have done so—a sense of resonance can emerge.

The thoughts or actions of two or more people—the "senders" and "receivers" of messages, in Schramm's model—can become highly synchronized as understandings are established. The people involved can then be brought experientially "together." When certain stimuli "synchronize the internal intuitions of two or more individuals"—even when the people are not in one another's immediate presence—they create "a sense of cognitive cohesion" (Cerulo and Ruane 1995: 13). The synchronizing of the activities and mentalities of individuals can be achieved as spatially separated people experience the same piece of art or music,[18] view the same television program or listen to the same radio show,[19] videotape events and watch the tapes afterward,[20] use telephone sex and party lines,[21] rally around flags, sing anthems, celebrate holidays, and otherwise experience episodes of nationalism,[22] visit Web sites, message boards, and chat areas online or engage in virtual reality,[23] and follow schedules and calendars.[24] Stimuli such as these bring us experientially together and "can provoke a meeting of the minds" (ibid.).

A *quasi*-synchronization can also occur, among individuals who are not alive at the same time or who otherwise cannot experience things at the exact same moment and who can *only* be brought together in sociomental space. Unlikely as it may sound, our internal rhythms can become quasi-synchronized with someone physically separated from us in space or through time as we focus on things or share experiences in very much the same way. Alfred Schutz delineates how a musical composer and the music's listener, living centuries apart, can relate to one another, "tune in" to one another, and, in a sense, "communicate." As the musical thoughts of the former are transmitted to the latter, through the mediation of mechanically produced sounds and/or the symbols of musical notation, "the latter participates with quasi simultaneity in the former's stream of consciousness by performing with him step by step the ongoing articulation of his musical thought" (Schutz 1951: 90). In the moments of doing so, "togetherness" between the two separated people is generated.

Quasi-synchronization also occurs when writer and reader or artist and viewer "come together" in the appreciation of a cultural work. Their streams of consciousness and internal rhythms can become coordinated, and people in a sense brought "together," as the technology permits "access" into the minds of those who may have created cultural works but from whom we are temporally separated. Artist Jonathon Kenworthy describes the experience of observing 17,000-year-old Cro-Magnon paintings etched in the walls of the Lascaux cave in France:

> [The artist] is taking us through the world that he saw, through the creatures he hunted, into the innermost part of his mind. . . . What the caveman [artist] was doing in Lascaux is exactly what I'm doing now. . . . If a caveman walked into my studio today and started talking to me, I would not understand a word he had to say. He would be speaking cave language, whatever that is, and it would mean nothing to me. But if I look at his paintings, I have a complete area of feeling and view that I can share with him. This curious development of drawing the pictures of our minds is the most eloquent way of touching another person's mind that has ever evolved. It's a language without words, a language that links us through the whole history of mankind. If you like, *it's a fellowship from one human mind to another.* (in Restak 1988: 6; emphasis added)

Ralph Waldo Emerson illustrates how, in learning about people and events of the past, an individual can come to reexperience history, so that

> [w]hat Plato has thought, he may think; what a saint has felt, he may feel; what at any time has befallen any man, we can understand. . . . Every revolution was first a thought in one man's mind, and when the same thought occurs to another man, it is the key to that era. . . . We sympathize in the great moments of history, in the great discoveries, the great resistances, the great prosperities of men; because there law was enacted, the sea was searched, the land was found, or the blow was struck, *for us,* as we

ourselves in that place would have done or applauded. (1906 [1841]: 7–9)

As we sense how we ourselves would feel and act if we were present in historical moments, we can come to understand and resonate with those who came before us. Emerson concludes that we gain our own individual identities, in part, by reliving what others have lived through before and by connecting with the states of mind of those who have come before us. We are, then, in the most profound sense, both indebted and connected to them.

Two of the people I interviewed describe experiences of resonating with favorite authors:

> I will read a particular passage and think to myself, "I know what he or she was feeling when they wrote that. I know what precipitated that . . . maybe we've shared some experiences. I've done that. I know what that feels like." (Tom)

> You read something and it hits home, you're in accordance with what the author is saying, and at the same time the author is not there to physically interact with you and say, oh, I agree, I feel that way. . . . The person's not actually there, but you're like, "Oh, I see what you're saying." (Ricky)

Responding to e-mail messages that have been posted on a message board or discussion group some time in the past is a more modern manifestation of quasi-synchronization. Again, both the minds of the writer and the reader are "brought together" as the message is read and responded to. Of course, when people chat in "real time" it is even easier to synchronize rhythms and feel resonant with another person. People can feel a resonance with all types of distant or absent others, but especially, I found, with ancestors and family members (with whom it is particularly easy to sense similarity), fictional characters (to whom we often relate as analog depictions of real people), media figures and celebrities (whom we often feel we know intimately), and people we contact online (for connecting with others directly and often synchronously can provide an especially strong sense of cognitive cohesion).

Resonance can also emerge in group settings. In some instances of connecting within communities of the mind, the bonds formed take on an intense quality that Durkheim called "effervescence" (1965 [1912]: 246–51). A powerful collective force or "rush of energy" that people sometimes feel within them in circumstances of togetherness, effervescence is created as people sense that many others are similarly resonating with respect to commonalities that are important to them. My interview subject Bruce shares his feeling that

> it's great when you find somebody that loves the book that you love. The feeling is kind of "Oh, wow!" Or "Oh, me, too!". . . I think it's cool. I think it's neat. And I like those kind of connections. And I have even tried to work to sort of cultivate them. Like, fan clubs are really cool for people who like so and so. It means something to them. [Can you describe these connections for me?] Oh, they're definitely bonds. [You have no trouble calling them that, even in their fleetingness?] Nope.

This collective kind of resonance can range from passionately strong and ever present to comparatively transient, for "the incidence, intensity, and scope of collective effervescence varies according to the relationships, activities, and interactions characteristic of social groups" (Shilling 1997: 210).[25]

As people are brought experientially together in communities of the mind through the synchronization and quasi-synchronization of members' mentalities, opportunities for this emotionally charged kind of cognitive cohesion or effervescence occasionally present themselves. Any time television or radio programs are viewed "live" as they are aired or an event is participated in or "followed" live via the Internet, individuals can gain an especially strong and definite sense of the others who are technologically participating in the experience at the very same moment. When people are technologically "brought" to the same place, as in an inauguration, a coronation, the wedding or funeral of a person of national stature, or a major cultural event such as the Super Bowl, they experience those events simultaneously with large numbers of others, generating collective thought and attention (Purcell 1997: 104; Cerulo 1995), a focal point for collective energies (Durkheim 1965 [1912]: 246–51; Dayan and Katz 1992), and the sharing of a powerful temporal order (Zerubavel 1981: 64–69).

Our emotional responses to media events do tend to exist within a predictable range. In media use, most people care at exactly the same moments whether a victim is rescued or whether a villain is conquered, and when viewing comedic or tragic fare, most people laugh or cry at the same time. We will not have in common the exact same feelings, but our feelings are likely to have a similar quality or intensity and to be evoked within a given range.[26] Participating in collective rituals, then, can be reassuring, even "mystically empowering" (Pacheco 1990: 20). Surely, part of the desire for millions of people to view such events as the opening ceremony of the Olympics, a State of the Union address, or the dropping of the "ball" on New Years Eve in Times Square lies in the impulse to join together and to feel that they are in community with others who are feeling similar (and similarly heightened) emotions.

Collective experiences of resonance and effervescence can produce especially strong feelings of community and connectedness, as Bruce describes:

> You're at baseball game with 35,000 people you don't know, and a cool thing happens—say you were there to see someone get their 3,000th hit—and then you meet somebody who was at that same game, like ten years later—and you say, "Oh, you were there, too!" That is so cool. And that is a connection. Because you were in the same place, and you both saw something. That is a connection. And you never met them. But you can feel it, and you can really respond to it.

Comedian Jerry Seinfeld gives his impression on the power of television to create such feelings:

> When you know that everyone's watching something, like Clarence Thomas and Anita Hill—that was a great community experience. ("His TV Mirror Image" 1992: 16)

Radio talk show host Rush Limbaugh discusses the radio equivalent on his program:

> It's people all over the country . . . listening to my show and feeling the exact same sensations. (*WABC* radio broadcast, November 23, 1993)

New York Daily News columnist David Hinckley describes the pleasure of coming upon a favorite song on the radio:

> Playing a cassette of Bob Dylan or Bessie Smith, to me, has never produced the same surge of satisfaction as hearing the same song pop up on the radio. Maybe it's just the idea that someone else thought of this great song too, but that's not all of it, since very often I hadn't even been thinking of the song. If someone had

asked me what I wanted to hear at that moment, I might not have thought of what the radio played—which makes it better when the radio does. I suspect that's why a lot of people listen to talk radio, too—because they like being there at the precise moment when something pops up that they didn't expect. (1995: 48)

My interviewee Ling would concur:

I don't like to listen to my favorite songs all the time on tapes, I like to turn on the radio and if it comes on, it's more special. At that moment.

And actress Jess Walton even feels a sense of collective activity in doing crossword puzzles:

I can't wait each week. I do the one in the daily paper, too. There's an immediacy to it; the fact that everyone in the city is struggling with the exact same puzzle. (in DiLauro 1995: 17)

In times of national or international crisis, it is common for people to turn to the media for information, comfort, and a sense of community, as we did during the terrorist attacks of September 11, 2001.

Regarding the American preoccupation with CNN and other television networks' reports of the first hours and days of the Gulf War, columnist Anna Quindlen observed that

[i]t was not because of the press of news that we seemed incapable of turning the TV off. The television had become a kind of modern communal meeting place from which to absorb history aborning. It was America's back fence, the one place in this time of dislocation where we were all connected, all having the same sensation at the same time. . . . It gave you the feeling of America sitting in a circle. (1991: 19)

As we did in the days and months following the September 11th terrorist attacks, we turned to the television ostensibly for news of the crisis, but what we got, and perhaps had unwittingly sought, was a sense of togetherness and collective resonance (see also McCarthy 1991). *Electronic communities*—communities of the mind generated in electronic mass media use—have great capabilities to induce shared experience, collective identity, a sense of community, and resonance in members (Chayko 1991,

1993a, 1993b). Our desire for all this can be so great in times of crisis that we can feel an almost overwhelming compulsion to watch the news or log on to the Internet. Our need to feel connected can be so strong that to turn the TV or computer off can leave us feeling frighteningly detached.

As we resonate with one another, we form connections and communities that have a real (yet, of course, mental) shape and structure. *Mental networks* and paths are formed that can be identified and studied. Though they are not visible in literal space, their location in sociomental space can be examined, and they can tell us much about the nature of the sociomental connection that has been created.

MENTAL NETWORKS

When a sociomental connection has been formed, a kind of "mental path" is established between two individuals. I borrow liberally from sociological network theory in developing this concept. In network theory, ties of direct contact between people in given settings (i.e., kinship groups, workplaces, friendship circles) are charted and studied, usually to determine the flow of resources, material goods, social support, and information "along" these network "paths." The ways in which these ties and patterns of ties constrain the behavior of the people involved are then analyzed.[27] I conceptualize these paths, however, as mental phenomena, and am more concerned in this work with the ways in which information, subtle forms of influence, and emotional intensity (as opposed to material goods) "flow" along them, and with the ways in which such paths become linked together to form mental networks and complex mental structures (see Garton, Haythornthwaite, and Wellman 1997).

Even when the people involved in a sociomental connection do not know, have never seen, and cannot accurately visualize one another, a kind of mental pathway exists between them, along which information may be passed or people may otherwise influence one another. It is as though a passageway to many potential forms of social exchange and social relationship has been opened. The people involved may not be aware of this passageway or "use" it in any but the most weakly realized fashion, but due to the sociomental connection that exists, they have an increased opportunity to use it at some point in the future. Thus many more outcomes to an interpersonal association (including face-to-face relationships, friendships, and even love affairs) are possible when a mental pathway has first been opened between two people in the form of a sociomental connection.

The speed and force with which some face-to-face connections are made and immediately come to feel like strong, real social bonds is a testament to the mental pathway (or sociomental connection) that *must have existed* between the two people involved prior to their meeting in literal space. Singer/actress Della Reese, for example, has described how easy it was for her to work with actor Redd Foxx for the very first time, stating that, "Redd and I come from the same point of understanding, so the rapport between us was *already there*" (on the *Arsenio Hall Show*, Fox-TV, November 30, 1991). Such "instant rapport," a situation in which interpersonal rhythms seem to be immediately established and talk flows freely and easily, can be understood as the result of a mental pathway—the "point of understanding" of which Reese speaks—having previously been established between two people. Because a prior sociomental connection had opened up a path between them, a sense of "instant" connectedness was possible between Reese and Foxx.

Many of us have had such an experience: an "instant" rapport or chemistry (even "love at first sight"), characterized by a strong sense of interpersonal similarity or commonality, a "oneness" that seems to emerge full-sprung. We may, for example, discover someone who shares our affection for a favorite team, who hails from our hometown, or who enjoys the same television show. When this happens, most people feel unexpectedly, often pleasantly, confronted with the evidence of a bond that has seemingly existed, albeit physically dormant, "all along." We find that we can talk and feel connected rather easily and quickly; we can skip over the type of formalities that generally characterize initial meetings and get more quickly to the heart of a relationship. We feel, in some significant way, that we already "know" that person, because the mental pathway between us is "open," with a strong emotional "charge" flowing along it.

Maria, for example, told me that she had not met a brother of hers who lived in Puerto Rico for the first fifteen years of her life. But in addition to the occasional phone call or letter, she was told many things about him. As a result, when they did meet, they become "quickly attached. I think I became close to him because we are similar." Jeremy, too, describes an "instant" connectedness to faraway members of his extended family:

> I never interacted with my mom's side of the family because of the distance involved. . . . So the storytelling and the pictures are all I have. . . . Then this past Christmas, my mom's cousin and my cousin came up from Uruguay to visit . . . and I felt very comfortable with them, it wasn't like they were strangers to me, it felt like they were family, and I had never seen them in my life.

Though the "instant" activation in literal space of sociomental bonds is only manifest when such people happen to (or decide to) contact one another physically, it indicates that a kind of mental pathway can exist between people *before* or *instead of* face-to-face meetings. Most sociomental connections will not and cannot be physically activated—we would do little else if we were to try to physically meet everyone with whom we had something in common—*yet the pleasure found in such occasional activation is evidence of the potential strength of sociomental bonds, and indicates the power of a "simple" commonality to open the door to a mental pathway connecting two people.*

In communities of the mind, a web of such pathways, which gives the group a kind of mental structure, develops.[28] Recall that each individual in a community of the mind, jointly connecting with a core commonality, becomes *triadically linked to each other individual, whether particular or typified, who has made such a connection* (see, again, Simmel 1950 [1908] on the triad, especially p. 145). These links are, in effect, mental paths in mental networks that link members not only to the "hub" of the community but to one another. Even if barely recognized explicitly, these "sensed" mental paths stretch out in many directions simultaneously (hence, the metaphor of the "web"), bringing members information and knowledge of one another and giving them cause to feel that they are very much a part of a group.

With members linked to the core commonality *and* to one another, a community has the potential to develop a complex internal structure. The larger the community, the more likely it will consist of several (or many) smaller mental networks and webs of connections, through which ever more specialized and ever more specific ideas and bits of information will flow. Most large communities of the mind consist of a number of smaller, more specific hub-and-spoke-shaped networks that represent the "factions" (or diversity) of the community, subsumed within a grand, overarching network that still connects all members and represents the similarity or oneness they all share.

Depending on its size and complexity, a community of the mind can consist of a few or many mental networks. Each community develops its own unique pattern of networks that intersect and are "laced" together. Some people in the community will feel part of more than one network or faction, while others may feel "part" of only one aspect of the community. Christianity, for example, is an enormous community of the mind that can be represented and thought of very differently by different people, who tend to fall into different "camps." The overarching, core commonality is that members define themselves as "Christians," but there often is great disagreement within the community about exactly how that should be interpreted— the great divide between Catholicism and Protestantism being the definitive example of this. So various interpretations of Protestantism and Catholicism have emerged, and many different self-proclaiming Christian religions and sects have developed, each of which constitutes a faction of the larger community and is usually represented by different symbols, religious figures, and rituals. As individual members of the community resonate with these different interpretations of Christianity, they are most likely to form the strongest connections with those in the same "camp."

Larger communities of the mind generally have many factions and camps that correspond to the ways in which various people identify with the community. Few communities, especially in modernity, can remain homogeneous enough in thought and behavior to maintain a collective identity that is perceived identically by all members (though such "rigid-minded" communities as the Amish, a cult, or a terrorist network strive to attain this in an attempt to keep themselves strong, durable, and "pure"). Most are rather diverse and thus are fluidly and imperfectly bounded.

With their wide, rambling structures of mental connections and networks, large communities of the minds can be thought of as *mental worlds* of people who cooperatively create and share something that matters to them. I appropriate Howard Becker's conception of the "art world" here, in which

> groups of people . . . cooperate to produce what they, at least, call art. . . . This might include people who conceive the idea of the work (e.g., composers or playwrights); people who execute it (musicians or actors); people who provide the necessary equipment and materials (e.g., musical instrument makers); and people who make up the audience for the work (playgoers, critics, and so on). Although we conventionally select some one or a few of these as "the artist to whom responsibility for the work is attributed," it is sociologically more sensible and useful to see the work as the joint creation of these people . . . [an] entire cooperating network that radiates out from the works in question. (Becker 1976: 42)

Large mental worlds or communities of the mind can coalesce around any of a number of phenomena (which may or may not be a "work of art"). A wide range of individuals can form an "entire cooperating network" that "radiates out" from the core commonality. This network, though, is invisible and is primarily characterized by mental pathways and webs of connection.

With this approach we can even conceptualize communities of the mind that have a commercial or political (or other organizational) purpose as *jointly* created by those who have deliberately set out to "draw" individuals together *and* by those who have become connected to the community and to one another within it. For along the mental pathways that connect them may flow all kinds of ideas and emotions that can provide commonalities and a sense of connectedness for these individuals. People with power, money, aims, and agendas can create (or attempt to create) communities of the mind and mental worlds, but the interest, knowledge, sophistication, and *agency* of individuals in these worlds can still create and influence outcomes.

When one is chosen for demographic reasons to be part of a political focus group, for example, one can play a part in the changing of a candidate's political platform (which can surely have a ripple effect on a large number of people if elected). The feedback of fans and followers can cause the producers of cultural products to make changes to those products that are then available to a large number of people.[29] The Internet is providing followers of various phenomena with an unprecedented opportunity to provide others in their mental worlds with direct feedback. In explicit fashion, they are using the mental networks that have been created. And audience members and consumers play a critical role in even highly commercialized communities of the mind, as one of the soap opera viewers of *Guiding Light* I surveyed realized:

> GL is making its way up the ratings ladder, so we (the fans and writers) must be doing something right!!!

As this viewer seemed to understand, cultural products are indeed jointly (though not necessarily democratically) created by people playing different roles in the community.

As with all social forms, especially modern ones, some people are always more "included" and involved in communities of the mind than others, communities are never perfectly bounded or impermeable, and people move in and out of their boundaries constantly (Scherer 1972: 61). Communities melt into and "interpenetrate" one another (see Chayko 1993b). Mental pathways and boundaries, "sensed" rather than seen, often are murky and unclear, and communities of the mind remain untidily formed structures. Still, the overall pattern of all of the interlocking sociomental connections in a community can be thought of as constituting the particular mental structure of that community, giving it its shape.

People form sociomental connections in countless ways, in countless sites, wherever points of commonality emerge. They connect dyadically and communally, with particular and typified others, in arrangements that coalesce internally (from the "ground up"), or in response to some external agent. Mental orientation, commonality, resonance, mental networks, and whole mental worlds are discovered and developed. But to endure and to really have an influence, they must somehow be sustained. In Chapter 4, I take a look at the processes by which sociomental connections, bonds, and communities of the mind are kept mentally "alive."

4

Till Death Do We Disconnect?
Keeping Connections Alive

We are never constantly "with" any one person at all times—in literal space *or* in sociomental space. We keep connections "alive" when we recall them, whether in between situations of face-to-face contact or instead of ever having had such contact. Activating our memories, thoughts, and fantasies—retrieving them from our long-term memory "stores"—helps us ensure that those with whom we have become connected remain with us, and that their social reality is maintained.[1] They also help us "resynchronize" ourselves with others to help our sociomental connections remain and feel as vibrant as possible.

It is quite common for people to form social connections in face-to-face settings and then only rarely to see one another physically. When instances of getting together face-to-face "fall off," people must maintain their connections with one another (if they desire continued connectedness) from a distance (see Fiebert and Wright 1989). Some intimate and long-lasting bonds involve little or no face-to-face interaction.[2] All but four of my fifty primary interviewees reported that they had formed at least one strong social bond with a person they saw face-to-face just once or twice a year or less, and over half (twenty-seven) mentioned that they had developed strong bonds with a person they saw only once every five years or less. Of one such friendship, Tom says,

> It's in remission, but it still exists. It's being neglected, but that's not to say that we couldn't dust it off.

79

It is through symbols, rituals, and talking and thinking about others to the extent that we can feel we are "carrying" them with us that we mentally "dust" off and maintain our connections. Engaging in these processes of bond maintenance ensures that we will at least periodically evoke the mental images that represent sociomental connections. They help us sustain all of our connections—even those characterized by plenty of face-to-face interaction—and thus they are vital in helping us sustain a social order.

SYMBOLS

People use symbols to help make mental connections more tangible, and the memories of them more easily accessed and brought into the conscious mind. Durkheim (1965 [1912]: 251–52) writes of how members of groups tend to become fixed on totems as tangible representations of groups, keeping the images of the totem in their minds and attaching real sentiments to them, because the social reality of a group (even a dyad) is too complex to be mentally retained in its entirety. When a group is dispersed—or the people involved in a social connection are not in direct contact—totems continue to bring those with whom one is involved to mind and even in a sense to "reassemble" the group mentally.

There are literally limitless potential totems—people, things, ideas, images—around which people coalesce, which they similarly see and fix upon, and through which they develop the impressions of one another so central to social connecting. Photographs were among my subjects' favorite such symbols, often taken or displayed specifically to remind people of absent others.

> I see the picture and I immediately think of [my friend] and what she's doing, and her goofy dogs. . .it's like staying connected with her. All of us are so busy, so it's kind of nice, it's like a reminder when I'm under stress that my friend is still around and accessible. . . . In fact, anytime I see a woman walking two dogs, I think of her. (Nicole)

> I don't know if I've ever even stepped back and asked myself, "why do I want that photo of me and my groomsman on the wall," but I would gather that who you have up on your wall. . . are the people that you don't see everyday. You may not need pictures if people are right here, living next door. . . . If you

looked at my wall, at the pictures, most of them would be of people that I am close to, but are not around. For example, I have a great friend nearby named Rick. I don't have any photos of Rick on the wall. (Bruce)

I have a photo of him [my brother] I keep in my kitchen. And a little toy "Oscar" he gave me. But I've never thrown it away, I've always kept it . . . for the same reason I've kept every letter I've ever received, every picture I have, because I'm scared if I get rid of that I'll get rid of the memory as well . . . I think technology helps you keep memories alive, in a world especially like mine, where I just move so often, and so many people are a blur. Even my friends in junior high, who I have no contact with, no clue, nothing with, no idea, I still like to have pictures of them, because even though they don't play a major role in my life now, they did then, and they were very important, and I don't want to forget them. (Rebecca)

I don't feel like I need the photos, but when I do see the photos, it brings back more memories. (Anita)

Symbols lead us, as Suzanne Langer tells us, "to conceive their objects" (1957: 6)—the objects, in this case, being the people with whom we form connections. As photographs generate memories, they bring "the other" back into one's mind and help the connector sense, visualize, and thus renew the connection.

Rebecca and several others whom I interviewed used music as a symbolic reminder of other people:

Songs completely remind me of my life, and I think that's why I'm so sentimental about songs. [Is a there a particular song that reminds you of your brother?] Sure—the Beatles' "I Should Have Known Better." [Do you ever choose a song specifically to remind you of a person?] Yes. (Rebecca)

Billy Joel's "Piano Man." She [my friend] loves that song. (Rhonda)

When I hear salsa music, it reminds me of [my aunt]. (Rosa)

A way of "enhancing and coordinating group feelings" (Gates 1992: 58), music helps evoke social connections and communities of the mind particularly well. Disc jockey Paul Cavalconte tapped into this idea as he said during his radio show one morning, "Hearing an old song is like meeting an old friend" (WNEW-AM broadcast, February 6, 1991).

But symbols can, in fact, be virtually anything:

> Being in school reminds me of [my mother]. (Jose)

> When I see something green. Like clothes. Because she [my sister] really loves green. Or when it's hot out, because she's got asthma. (Joanne)

> Whenever I'm trying to solve a problem . . . [my friend] comes to the top of my head. She's the problem lady. (Elise)

> Hearing something about Cuba reminds me of my family. (Rosa)

Symbols constantly touch off mental images and impressions and bring them into the conscious mind, helping us retrieve temporarily dormant memories and connections.

The more specifically a symbol relates to an absent person, the stronger the memory it can arouse. Sometimes Cindy goes to her long-distance boyfriend's favorite park, or eats at his favorite deli, just to feel connected to him:

> And then the sandwich I get there is kind of like comfort food. I miss him . . . but I also feel that connection.

Regarding her long-distance friend, Jessica tells me:

> If I see something he likes, or hear something that he'll think is funny, I'll be like, "Oh, Rodney would like that."

For Bruce, a gold earring became a special, consciously selected symbol of the strong sociomental bond he continued to feel for a friend who had died in a car accident several years prior to our interview.

> Jason always wore a gold hoop earring in this ear. And I would wear one now and again. And I decided that as a sort of tribute to him, I would wear my gold hoop all the time. And I didn't take it out for like five years . . . and then it sort of rotted . . . and then I didn't need it anymore. I was "walking the dead." I thought about

him a lot. And when I saw it [the earring], I thought about Jason, which of course was at least daily. I thought about him all the time, and it was because of that thing. And it helped immensely. It helped immensely. Because I kept him with me. And I needed to, because I wasn't ready to let go of him yet. Because he was such a good friend and he was gone and I needed something to connect me with him. And for me, that was it.

As Brian says:

[The symbol] can really be anything, seeing anything. It can really come out of anywhere, *because the connection is always in my head*, so that little action, just like that, triggers it. You relate to something, and your head starts going. (emphasis added)

Sociomental connections can be thought of as perpetually "in our heads" (or our hearts), needing only to be "triggered" to be brought to consciousness at any given moment.

Symbols also help large numbers of people recall their commonalities and help them mark off the boundaries that define them as a unit. The set of all people who understand the power of a given symbol—a pink triangle, an American flag, the theme song to *The Brady Bunch*—can be considered "in" a community of people who are the "same kind," which is the kind that can interpret the meaning of the symbol and has shared some similar experiences. Others who do not share these experiences and memories and for whom the symbol is "just another thing" are at least temporarily excluded from the group.

Symbols can serve as focal points that large numbers of people can "rally around" and use to identify one another as members of the community.[3] In cyberspace communities, people use a wide array of special textual symbols that are continuously invented and disseminated through online networks. These aid in communication and in the construction of personal bonds and also give communities their own special identity. The creativity involved in this use of typewritten symbols often is remarkable, ranging from shorthand (the soap opera online group I studied uses such abbreviations as IMHO, in my honest opinion, LOL, laughing out loud, ROTFL, rolling on the floor laughing, and IOAS, it's only a soap) to keyboard art. MUD users have created the following types of pictographs or "emoticons" (Reid 1995: 172):

:-) or :) a smiling face, viewed side on—tilt your head to the left
;-) or ;) a winking, smiling face

:-(or :(an unhappy face, or "unsmiley"
:-(*) someone about to throw up
8-) someone wearing glasses
:-P someone sticking out their tongue
:-O someone screaming in fright
:-& someone whose lips are sealed
*<I:-) Santa Claus
!#!^*&:-) a schizophrenic

Such symbols "provide a form of shorthand for the depiction of the physical and emotional condition" that permits users to "read each other in far more than a textual fashion . . . [and] experience human dramas as strongly as they might in actuality" (ibid., 176). Ever more specialized and tightly knit communities are maintained, then, as people create, understand, and use symbols similarly.

People who follow mass media and participate in fantasy role-playing games also develop systems of symbols and languages together (Fine 1983: 12; Baym 1995). Rush Limbaugh, for example, whose nationally syndicated radio show has focused on current events from a conservative Republican point of view, has developed an entire vocabulary of catch phrases and mannerisms, all of which he and his callers adopt. He has introduced certain issues with special "updates," and employed special fanfares and songs. Callers who wish to indicate their agreement with Rush greet him with the word "ditto" and are called "ditto-heads." Similarly, some television shows introduce words and phrases into the lexicon that become highly identified with the show and can identify fans of the show to one another (e.g., *Seinfeld's* "yada yada yada," *Saturday Night Live's* "Isn't that special?"). Such words and phrases act as verbal shortcuts, giving the community of the mind a special identity and helping members maintain the boundaries, determining who is in and who is out of the group. And as people talk about their connections and communities in everyday life, the connections are strengthened and maintained.

TALK

People "live in a community by virtue of the things they have in common," John Dewey observes, "and communication is the way in which they come to possess things in common" (1915: 4). People communicate *with* and *about* their distant connections in a variety of ways, using an ever-unfolding array of technologies. Years ago, when people saw most people they were close to daily, their talk only rarely needed to serve the function of connecting distant others. Today our spoken communications often help us sustain sociomental connections as we tell one another about the incidental and important people and events in our lives.

Individuals "feel they are united whenever they refer to one of the groups of which they both are members" (Davis 1973: 61). By orienting themselves to some commonality and then reorienting themselves time and time again by talking about it, "togetherness" is solidified. Families often share stories and experiences that bring physically separated members mentally "together."

> I've got family in Puerto Rico. I've never met my oldest brother. And even though I've never met him, I've spoken to him on the phone a couple of times and seen pictures of him, and yeah, there is a connection with him. I've heard stories about him. And I love him. (Jose)

> All my life having been told I am like him [my grandfather] in personality, physical appearance, sound . . . I think it's more comforting than anything else. I've never met this man and everything is based on things that I've heard. . . . The bond is there; it's very strong. (Bill)

> My great-grandmother—there's a giant picture of her in my mom's house. Everyone's always telling me we look alike and that I've got some of her traits . . . I've heard a lot of stories about her. And yeah, I feel connected to her. (Grace)

Clearly these deeply felt bonds rest on the commonality of shared identity, communicated in the stories that are passed down throughout families.

Much of this talk and storytelling now takes place online. Mabel told me about her experiences encountering members of her family—usually her brothers and sisters—in cyberspace. While surfing the 'Net, she would sometimes notice through "instant messaging" that a family member was online. Chatting with them online in real time brings an entirely new dimension to her relationships with them, she tells me:

> The other day I chatted with my sister online. She just lives a few towns over, but it seems we never see each other. Well, we talked online for over an hour. And—this is the funny part—we've never

gotten along so well! In a strange way it was better than being in person because we didn't get into the same old stuff about mom and dad, and "Oh, you broke that lamp in 1978 and I got blamed for it"—it's much more of a chance encounter, and I think it's overall much more pleasant.

Mabel even found that family members with whom she ordinarily did not get along were somehow more enjoyable to spend time with online:

> Family members of mine with whom I don't get along very well in person—there's always some element of antagonism—I get along very well with online. We're talking more because of online communication. You get to say whatever you want without being interrupted—the very things you perhaps couldn't do when you were as kid. As adults, our opinions, views, and lifestyles are drastically different at this point. And when we get together for the obligatory family holidays—I always call it the horror show, and that is essentially what it turns out be—we communicate much less. . . . We don't want to start fights, and it doesn't happen online.

By communicating with absent family members in a variety of ways, Mabel finds that her relationships with them are expanded in scope, more manageable, and more easily maintained.

Talking to and about one another, then, can extend or strengthen some connections. Cindy has met the man who has since become her professional mentor exactly once, but she keeps in contact with him through e-mail, the telephone, and letters, and she feels that their connection is as personal as any sustained in face-to-face interaction:

> How can it be personal? . . . . It feels like it is. If people said, "Oh, gee, do you know so and so?" I would say "yes." I wouldn't say, "Oh, well, I met him once." I'd say, "Oh, yeah, I know him." I mean, I know his hopes and dreams. Usually, you wouldn't know that with somebody you just met, unless you were communicating all these ways. It would take you many months or maybe years to figure out what someone's hopes and dreams were. . . and I think it's because we were simpatico on some level.

Because they are "simpatico"—like-minded—Cindy is motivated to maintain her connection through technological mediation.

Technologies of communication, used in infinite combinations with one another, are nearly always available to assist connectors who wish to communicate in particular ways. As Cindy and her boyfriend maintain a long-distance relationship, various technologies have become indispensable, she told me, in helping them remain connected. When she has something to tell him, she asks herself:

> Do I repeat it all on the phone, in the e-mail, in the letter? That's too much. So I parcel it out. I think "Oh, I want to tell Roger I saw five deer on the way home tonight." So I'll put that in the letter. That's a letter-y kind of thing. I won't put it in the e-mail, I may not mention it on the phone. On the phone, I'm going to talk to him about making plane reservations. On the e-mail, I'm going to talk to him about crap that's happening at work that I don't want to waste a phone bill on. So I think I do evaluate information and decide which channel it's going to go through the best or quickest, or get me the kind of response I want back . . . I'd say using different media deepens our relationship, because they allow us to communicate the same information so many different ways. . . . My boyfriend thought, "Now that we have e-mail our phone bills won't be so high." Well, the reality is that they're higher. It's just supplementary. It hasn't replaced anything. If I read his e-mail, it might make me want to call him.

"Mediated talk"—using a variety of channels—helped my interviewees sustain connections.

> [The Internet] extends some of my relationships. I'll talk to someone on the phone *and* e-mail them. I look forward to it. I remind people, "E-mail me." (Tonya)

> I think the telephone is way more important where my boyfriend's concerned, but e-mail would be way more important where my sister's concerned, because she's in South Africa and that's how we communicate. (Jessica)

> Sometimes I fax [letters to my family back in Korea], and if I can't I write, or if I can't do that I phone. (Kim)

> I sustain my interactions with a combination of e-mails, phone calls, and face-to-face interactions. (Jeremy)

Of course, people have preferred ways of communicating with others and favored technologies with which to do so:

> I use the phone to keep in touch with all my friends. People in my neighborhood, like the guy across the street, are the only ones I see *only* face to face. Everyone else I call. And to me, e-mail just seems one-dimensional. (Bill)

> I don't like telephoning. I'd rather write letters. The telephone is definitely personal, but when I get off the phone I often think of something I could have said or should have said, you know, after the fact. But if you write a letter, you can go through a draft or two. (Randy)

> [I like] e-mail. . . . You can reach so many people. And it's less expensive. I don't always need to keep seeing people . . . the e-mail just connects you somehow. . . . You can check your e-mail any time, you can reply any time . . . I love it. (Luis)

> For more intimate things, I'd probably use the letter [to communicate]. [Why?] It just feels much more personal to me. E-mail is kind of how the movies are . . . that surreality. Writing is more concrete. (Ugo)

> Often, I prefer the phone to e-mail. If I have something that [is] important to say, I'd just as soon pick up the phone. (Rhonda)

Many of the people with whom I spoke told me that regardless of the technology used, they would explicitly ritualize their contact with certain others to ensure the continuation of those bonds.

> I speak to my dad [overseas] several times a year, see him once a year, and always call on major holidays. (Tonya)

> If he [my brother] called last, then I know it's my responsibility to call next. And we always try to call on the weekend. (Maria)

> There's always a certain routine. How're you doing, how's the house, how are the kids—her grandchildren, my nephews and nieces—how are my brothers, how do you feel, did you eat. She always asks me some of the same things too. (Jose)

We pretty much discuss the same things over and over again. (Luis)

Quite simply, talking helps us feel close to people we do not see very often. It also helps to talk *about* the absent person.

I feel so close to my aunt, but I rarely talk to her. I ask Mom how she is, how she's doing. (Claire)

Yes, I talk about my family overseas a lot. (Nora)

I talk with my mom about her [a family member I have not seen since I was five years old], I talk with my fiancé about her, and my brothers. . . . It makes it [the connection] more tangible, maybe. (Jeremy)

All those times I don't speak to him or hear from him or whatever, in speaking about him and thinking about him, he's always there. He's always close. It's kind of like when someone passes away and they say they're dead and gone, but they're still very close to home, like a spirit, their spirit is still with you. It's the same kind of thing. (Ugo)

The "spirit" or essence of a connection, then, remains in the absence of face-to-face interaction, in large part because we work so hard to "keep it alive."

In thinking and talking about others with regularity, we "revisit" the objects of our connection in sociomental space. We can feel "closer" to them there. Such connections are more likely to endure, and as we develop rituals of engagement, we resynchronize our rhythms with those with whom we are connected and can periodically and predictably reconnect with them.

RITUALS AND SERIALIZATION

Rituals help us become fully involved in an experience of sociomental bonding in an ongoing fashion. They can help us maintain such bonds over a fairly long period of time. When we are thus involved, we "sustain some kind of cognitive and affective engrossment . . . some mobilization of one's psychobiological resources," as Goffman (1963: 36) views it. When an individual becomes highly involved in a physical or mental situation, cognitive processing is deeper and the effects on the individual are greater (Roser and Thompson 1995). Cognitive involvement has been linked to deeper message processing (Petty and Cacioppo 1986), greater cognitive complexity (Rothschild and Houston 1980), and lasting information retention (Burnkrant and Sawyer 1983). Thus cognitive involvement in the act of connecting leads to a greater chance of the bond becoming strong and sustained and of having a lasting impact on the individual.

People become particularly engrossed in experiences that are frequent and regular and that are structured to be continuing and open-ended.[4] No shortage of serialized experiences is to be found—they are found in physical and sociomental space—at home and at work, in mass media use, on the Internet, in belonging to associations and special interest groups of all kinds, and so on. Both in technologically mediated and face-to-face situations, when an activity lends itself to serial participation or involvement, there is a good chance that a participant will become regularly engrossed in it.

Serialized experiences are structured to resemble "real life" in their "unfinishedness" or "ongoingness" (though their content certainly may not be very realistic, as in science fiction novels or horror films). Because they are ongoing, participants can become slowly and gradually "drawn in" to the social reality that is created. People can temporarily forget (or consider irrelevant) that they are becoming engrossed in a social world "alternate" to that which we ordinarily consider "everyday life." When plots or situations or discussion topics are not neatly wrapped up, and dramatic characters are realistically crafted and presented and given a chance to grow and learn and "live" with the consequences of their actions, people who enjoy them often want to keep "coming back for more." Janice, for example, came to realize that she cared about fictional characters a great deal,

> especially if you follow a series. And you do feel connected to those characters, because you've been watching them for a year or two or three.

Jessica would agree:

> I've been watching it (the television show *Beverly Hills, 90210*) since it came out, when I was a freshman in high school, and just watching it for so long, and knowing what each and every character has been through, it makes me feel like I've grown with them, or they grew with me, through the years I've been watching it. It makes you feel a part of it.

Randy discusses the pleasures of serialization in fiction at some length:

> Sometimes I'll read favorite books over and over again . . . you
> sort of know what's coming, but you forget the exact words.
> [What kind of books do you read over and over again?] Tom
> Clancy, Grisham, W.E.B. Griffin, who writes military sagas,
> novels that have five or six books to them, that have central char-
> acters that evolve throughout the series. I've read some of them
> probably five or six times . . . I definitely get involved with the
> characters, and then something you don't think should happen
> happens, and you get really pissed off.

Serialization provokes by its very design (and occasionally by riveting or satisfying content as well) this type of emotional involvement, this "caring what happens." It would probably be more surprising if people who became immersed in serialized social realities *did not* become cognitively involved in the experience than if they *did*.

Interactive, call-in talk radio shows provide another example of the kind of serialized programming that can inspire strong involvement. In talk radio, individuals can communicate with one another and with a host about a variety of topics which often are both involving and challenging on a regular or daily basis. There is usually no end date for the program in sight; programs that have been in existence a long time are assumed to have a long life to come. Callers are remarkably loyal to radio talk shows, calling in again and again and becoming regulars with whom the hosts share jokes and anecdotes just as one might with a friend. They often "seem to want an ally, someone to be on their side," Carin Rubenstein notes (1981: 90). "In their boldness . . . [callers] become the proxy voice of . . . listeners who are afraid to call in; the advice, support, and friendship they receive flows out to everyone in the audience" (ibid.). Of course, some listeners will not want to or bother to call in but the nature of these programs is so personal that listeners can become drawn in and feel strongly involved nonetheless, and they may feel that those who do call in are indeed their "proxy voices." A listener told New York radio talk show host Bob Grant during Grant's final radio show on WABC-AM (which had been abruptly canceled), "Words cannot express the emptiness I feel. It's like an assassination" (WABC broadcast, April 18, 1996).

The worlds of daytime soap opera and professional sports are perhaps even better examples of serialization in pop culture: series of events that extend continuously and indefinitely (seemingly infinitely) into the future. Involvement in these worlds is possible on a nearly constant basis. Though sports have "seasons," the media provide a steady update of relevant issues and personnel transactions that fans can tune into and debate year-round. Games and matches are broadcast and presented much like a story, containing plots, subplots, heroes, villains, and beginnings, middles, and (always temporary) ends. There is always another game for a sports fan to look forward to, even when one must "wait till next year"—and, of course, there usually is the prospect of many more seasons to look forward to. Fans also often follow more than one sport, the seasons of which conveniently overlap, so that one need never be without a contest of some sort to follow.

Sports fans can become intensely involved with and strongly bonded to their favorite teams and players. Consider the very personal nature of the sociomental bonding indicated in these excerpts from fan letters sent to Yankees' baseball great Mickey Mantle after fans learned of his alcoholism:

> I followed your career since I can remember, read everything I could find about you, and watched you on TV and movies . . . I did try to emulate you as an athlete and that probably is a part of why I went into physical education/coaching. . . . When I first heard of your drinking problem I had many emotions, even at thirty-eight years of age you are still a "hero" to me.

> Although we've never met, I feel that I know you very well. I've even read all your books . . . I'm sorry that I haven't written to you long before now.

> Please get well soon. I need you.

> All my best to you, my lifelong friend. (Please forgive my familiarity but I have known you all of my forty-three years.) (Mickey Mantle Foundation, 1995)

Obviously, following the career and the postcareer life of Mantle for forty-three years helped this person feel that he "knew" the baseball great in a personal and meaningful way.

Similarly, soap operas fans can become deeply involved with and bonded to their favorite shows, actors, and characters. With new episodes presented continuously (five days a week, fifty-two weeks a year) in serialized form, soap operas inspire fervent, ongoing sociomental connections and communities. The soap opera press reflects and feeds this interest with a steady, multimedia stream of information, promotion, and debate. Soap opera magazines frequently receive letters and e-mails such as these:

Rex [a character on *The Young and the Restless*] was the sweetest man on the show. I loved him like he was part of my own family. When he died I felt the pain and the loss that Katherine felt. (letter sent to *Soap Opera Weekly* magazine, January 3, 1995, p. 41)

The story that continually stirs my emotions on *Guiding Light* is that of Matt and Vanessa. It is outstanding. I really care about them. I longed to have them back together after the past year of sadness they endured. (letter sent to *Soap Opera Digest* magazine, October 28, 1997, p. 141)

I was struck by the feelings that I had on the last air date of *Santa Barbara*. It was as if some close friends were moving away, never to be seen again. (letter sent to *Soap Opera Update* magazine, March 23, 1993, p. 16)

Regarding the content of soap operas:

It is not so much that "life is like that"—it doesn't need content analysis to establish that more dramatic things happen in soaps than "in life"—but that the generic lack of closure, in combination with the realist premise, offers a homology between soap-life and real-life. Like us, soap opera characters have to live with the consequences. (Brundson 1984: 86)

Of course, sports fans and participants must "live with the consequences" of their contests' outcomes as well. As with sports, soap operas provide "a stable network of friends and neighbors . . . continuity. People don't just watch soap operas, they live with them" (Rosen 1986: 44). And, as in soap opera viewing, following favorites over a period of time is one of the main reasons people enjoy sports (Wenner and Gantz 1989). Sociomental bonds engendered in serialization, especially in following sports and soap operas, thus seem especially strong and enduring.

This sense of deep involvement can occur any time people enjoy a form of technological connecting in a *ritual* way. To one degree or another, many of us develop rituals and structure our lives around media.

We incorporate media-generated routines into everyday life, arranging our lives so that, for example, one can feel connected to a favorite newspaper columnist first thing in the morning, to a radio talk show host on the way to work, to co-workers and friends face-to-face at the office, to a character in a book read at lunchtime, to a roommate or some friends later, to actors and characters in television shows watched (live or on tape) in the evening, to online buddies after that, and to a favorite writer in a magazine read before bed. Each genre has rituals that people can count on as well: soap operas and prime-time television shows (the recycling of familiar plots and character types, the relatively homogenized neighborhoods and families they depict); sporting events (laden with rituals, rules, and "sameness," both within and across teams and sports—such as long-standing rivalries); radio talk shows (in which each show has its own host, theme music, types of topics and callers, and special features); and computer use (with specialized vocabularies and content). Regarding the sameness of TV programming,[5]

> Television is deeply committed to offering viewers the same thing over and over again. In many cases, of course, it's the same programs—an awesome amount of the cable television day is filled with sitcoms that were first broadcast during the Johnson administration. . . . On television, we enjoy the exact repetitiveness . . . just as children want the same book read *the same way* each night before bedtime . . . which means that if television is a drug, as the outraged often claim, then it is a drug of a very specific sort. Not a hallucinogen, taken to open the door into new perception, but a drug almost guaranteed to rouse the same feelings day after day after day. (McKibben 1992: 35)

Whether or not one agrees with the metaphor of the "drug," the rituals and serialization involved in TV can certainly produce a "sameness" of experience that yields a sense of familiarity that keeps many viewers "coming back for more." For while talk shows, magazine, newspaper and newsletter columns, and the Internet are all forums for debate on a variety of issues, few problems are solved outright; the debates, and the bonds that can form, continue and can easily deepen. A series of exchanges— a lack of closure—is built into these forms and into the bonds that can develop in response to them.

Involvement in ritualized acts of sociomental connecting is most apparent when individuals feel that they are taking part in meaningful experiences and are actively processing the information to which they have been exposed. But involvement is also possible when individuals are not consciously aware of the meaning of the experience for them and are superficially or more passively processing information (Grunig 1982). People can become highly involved with mass media even when they are using it simply to relax or are not attending closely to it.[6] In electronic media use, many people become highly involved in programs without even realizing it, often becoming quietly engrossed in the worlds that are created and coming to care deeply about the people and situations depicted.[7] One soap opera fan indicates the depth of her involvement and familiarity with actress Martha Byrne in an online "chat":

> Martha, I'm a huge fan! I feel that we grew up together! (*TV Guide* online, April 22, 1997)

Another fan says that actress Mary Stuart

> was like my second mom. She was there, in mom's kitchen, every afternoon when I cam home from school for lunch. Then later, when I started traveling for work and found myself in strange cities in which I knew no one, all I'd have to do is turn on a TV at 12:30 P.M. and that wonderful friend whom I grew to love was there to offer me comfort. (from an America Online soap opera message board)

Of course, there is a fine line between involvement and obsession, which we shall examine more closely in Chapter 6.

As technologically derived rituals provide order for the individual, they also provide a sense of comfort and stability. We can come to believe that such connections and communities of the mind will last for a reasonably long time. We come to depend on them to be there and, in a more latent sense, to provide order and structure to our lives. Offering reassurance in their familiarity, rituals are evoked and replicated and we feel safer and more comfortable (Brundson 1984: 86). When we form Internet connections that we anticipate will be long lasting, we allow ourselves to become quite friendly and to feel a pronounced affinity with those to whom we are connecting (Walther, Slovacek, and Tidwell 2001). When a series of experiences is predictably generated, people can begin to feel comfortable investing emotional energy in them. The serialized form "allays *real* anxieties, satisfies *real* needs and desires, even while it might distort them" (Modleski 1982: 108, emphasis in original; see also Kubey and Csikszentmihalyi 1990: 174).

Routinized social bonding helps individuals maintain "ontological security"—the deeply rooted, unconscious confidence that human beings desire regarding the constancy of their social environment (Giddens 1990: 92, 1979: 219). We cannot emotionally bear the possibility that the world may change overnight; we need to know that the world is as it should be in order to feel safe. As social action is routinized and coordinated among individuals, our world remains ordered and secure.[8] When sociomental bonds provide this for us, it is little wonder that we are so inclined to keep them "alive," often for very long periods of time, and to keep those to whom we are connected mentally "with" us.

"CARRYING" THE OTHER WITHIN

Sometimes we maintain our sociomental connections simply by feeling that we are "carrying" others mentally with us and thinking about them in that way. As we think about the images that represent our connections to us, we "carry" mental replications of significant others in our minds and memories.[9] Though these thoughts may be fleeting or dormant, they may also be extremely vivid and dynamic. We may "play out" actual or fantasized scenarios in which we are sharing an actual experience with absent others. We may envision past or possible future encounters with them: mentally rehearsing asking a boss for a raise or a friend for a favor, recalling memories of absent (or dead) family members, or fantasizing about starting a romantic relationship. In doing so, we reconstruct and reinforce the connection and embed it in our minds (see Neimark 1995). "You imagine things that will happen in the future and think about those of the past," my interviewee Ling explained. In doing this, she said, you "experience things again."

My interview subjects reported that they think about their sociomental connections with absent others with great frequency—an average of three times a week per sociomental connection that they named. As my interview subject, Rhonda, put it, "I can be just as close with someone I don't speak with as compared to someone I do speak with." Thinking about others so often that we come to feel that they are a "part" of us or "with" us helps us sustain our sociomental connections.

> Although [my friends and I] may not talk as much as I would like to, they're a big part of me, and I still remember them and think about them. (Joe)

> When I think about her [my aunt] it's like it keeps me connected to her . . . I feel like she's close to me. (Anita)

I like to be reminded of the ties I've had with people, or the feelings I've had with them, and that I can feel them again because of that reminder is cool to me. I like that. (Bruce)

Since I want the relationship, if there's a hindrance [to meeting in literal space] I think about it a lot, and I try to compensate for it. . . . It's comforting for me to know that I care about them and they care about me . . . I don't focus on the separation. (Jeremy)

When we are close to someone, we may feel that in an important and a real way, he or she is with us.

To "carry the other within" was a metaphor I encountered frequently.

I carry thoughts of [my partner] with me during the day. And I store up what's funny, what's interesting, what's shitty, and I tell him when I get home. So in a way, I sort of carry him with me all day. (Mabel)

I feel like I have all my friends with me, and I think about them. (Joe)

They're very much a part of me. (Tonya)

I shall be carrying thoughts of all of you with me. (from the on-line literature group)

My interviewee, Nicole, provides a neat visual image with which to picture a community of the mind:

There are little things that remind me of them all day, so they're still with me . . . *I feel like I've got this support group that I carry around in my head.* (emphasis added)

And magazine editor Betsy Carter says of her family:

They are my team, and no matter where I am, I carry them all with me. (Carter 1996: 14)

Physical separation from our friends and family may seem less upsetting, less *remarkable* to us when we feel that we are keeping our loved ones mentally near us or even "in" us.

When the sense of carrying the other within is especially strong, some people may not even feel the need to make contact very often:

> Some friends, I don't have to call a lot, or keep in touch with all the time. . . . Even the next time I see them, you don't have to talk about everything in your life. It's almost like the person hasn't left. It's like just another day. (Ling)

> I think he feels that comfortable that our relationship will never change . . . he'll just see me the next time he sees me. (Rebecca)

> It's like she's with me, so I don't need to call her. (Anita)

> I always have all these people in my life, so I never feel lonely. And I always feel they're available . . . and it's not like I really miss my family all that much because I feel very connected to them. Like with Joan . . . I don't really miss Joan, because I feel like she's always there anyway. I mean, I'd love to go for a walk with her and stuff, but I feel her presence anyway. . . . Someone told me about a study that showed that when people got married and they first were sleeping in bed together at night, usually they were squished together, and that over the years, they tended to go to different parts of the bed. And it was thought that that meant the couple was growing apart. But now, what I'm hearing is, what that actually means is that the couple feels confident that one another is going to be there, and they can have their own space, they don't have to cling onto the other person. They know the person's going to be there . . . and they don't need to actually have a physical, tactile reminder of it. (Nicole)

In thinking about others and developing confidence that we will remain connected to them (as Nicole depicts so colorfully), we reinforce and maintain sociomental connections and bonds. Of course, certain types of bonds lack a great deal when there is no face-to-face interaction (e.g., parent and child, lovers, etc.).

When we carry a person with us mentally, we may dream about her or him with some frequency.

> I've only seen my grandmother six times in my life, but I feel like it's much more often, because I think about her and dream about her. . . . We're very close. (Bill)

I still feel really close to my grandmother, who's passed away. . . .
It hurts sometimes, and I try not to think about her, but when I
do that, I dream about her. (Rosa)

Sometimes I dream about [my grandfather] or think about him *as
though he's still alive.* (Randy; emphasis added)

As we have seen, it is when we no longer think about or are influenced by
another person that they cease to have social reality for us.

To completely break a sociomental connection and fail to *ever* think
about the other is very difficult. It is almost unavoidable that at times we
will think about people who once had some significance for us, at least occasionally; certain symbols remind us of others, even when we would prefer that they didn't. Many of my interview subjects told me that they still
frequently thought about certain people with whom they had formerly
had a relationship and therefore could not be certain that their connection
to them was severed permanently. When I asked Rebecca whether she
thought much about the person to whom she was previously married, she
replied, "No, but it's a constant effort." Ken told me that he had *not* broken off many relationships in his life because it was a futile exercise. No
matter what he does, he told me, "an element of the connection remains"—*in his mind,* I would add. Luis originally described one of his
connections as broken, but then he reconsidered:

There *is* something that remains . . . but it's definitely just in my
head.

Rhonda would agree:

I think the connection will always exist, as long as I wonder how
they're doing. Because we were such close friends. But the connection is stretched, I guess, as far as it could be.

If we find we must work very hard to sever a connection—to keep from
"activating" it mentally—it is likely that some element of the connection
and the commonality that originally linked us still exists. It is hard to
break a connection in which a significant commonality lingers and remains relevant. If, on the other hand, a connection is not so hard to sever,
most likely the commonality (or its importance to the connector) has diminished sufficiently. Elise notes:

We were really close friends for like ten years . . . but I saw him
last June, and there wasn't anything in common anymore. . . . Our
lives have really diverged. . . . It [the connection] was broken.

Elise could have defined the "in-between" state as either a "connected" or an "unconnected" one. In choosing to think of her friend and herself as no longer connected—because their common ground was no longer evident—Elise was able to interpret this relationship as being completely "over" and in the past, and she therefore could better maintain the "break." For her it is, for all intents and purposes, no longer alive; she says she has allowed those thoughts associated with it to fade, and she is not reminded of it anymore. (Of course, as we have seen, connections can be "dusted off.") As Rebecca noted with regard to her ex-husband, it is quite difficult to completely sever a significant, enduring bond; the restructuring of any long-held mental model generally takes a great deal of effort. People with a long, unrequited love or the long-lasting memory of a loved one can attest to the difficulty of breaking those bonds; because we "keep" people alive in our minds and close to our hearts, physical absence simply cannot be counted on to do the trick. Our thoughts are not as easy to extinguish as is the physical presence of someone.

A variety of mechanisms, then, keep distant people "mentally alive" as significant others for us in our minds. We use symbols that evoke particular memories, we talk about and even dream about people, we ritualize our mental encounters with them, and we even "carry" them, in a sense, with us. Clearly, sociomental bonds *matter* to people. To determine something of their qualities—and to learn more about the role they play in people's day-to-day lives—I examine four of their most prominent properties in Chapter 5.

5

How Real Does It Get?
Properties of Sociomental Bonds

In 1893, Emile Durkheim asked, "What are the bonds which unite men with one another?" (1984 [1893]: 41) and it remains a difficult question to answer satisfactorily. What exactly *are* sociomental connections? What do they "do" for us? Are they strong, reciprocal, and intimate in nature? Are they "really" real?

It is indeed a challenge to probe the essence of sociomental connectedness (or of connectedness in general), but a metaphor, again, may help us begin. We can think of a social connection as a strand of thread that reaches from person to connected person, "tying" them together wherever they might be—even during periods of little or no physical contact. Then we can begin to consider some of the qualities of these threads: are they thick or thin? Strong as rope or weak as gauze? Durable as twine or ephemeral as tissue paper? Warm and intense, as a "live" wire, or cold and lifeless, as a dead branch on a tree?

My interview and survey participants had much to say about the properties of sociomental bonds and communities—what they think of such connections and how it feels to form them. Though there are surely a wide range of qualities that can characterize sociomental connections— they must exist in nearly as many manifestations as there are people who form them—four properties were most prominently mentioned by the participants in my research. Sociomental bonds, I was told, have the potential to be strong, bidirectional or reciprocal, authentic, and intimate.

In this chapter I take a look at these qualities of sociomental connections, their meaning for connectors, and the place they occupy in people's lives. I explore the potential strength of the connections (which I consider "bonds" when they are particularly strong), the somewhat surprising degree of bidirectionality or reciprocity that can be achieved in the act of sociomental connecting, the perceived authenticity of connections, and the level of intimacy that may develop. These aspects of connectedness are, it turns out, axes along which *all* types of relationships either persist and flourish, or fail to do so.[1] For since virtually all social connections and communities are characterized by periods of absence among their members, all social connections can be considered largely sociomental. We can learn much, then, about the ways that we think and live and relate to one another in general by examining these properties of sociomental connecting.

STRENGTH

It is difficult to "measure" something as subjective as the "strength" of a social connection. Certainly the boundary between "connections" and "bonds" is drawn both subjectively (for one person's connection may be another person's bond) and intersubjectively (for people define relationships collectively). In their weakest states, sociomental connections exist without much cognitive or emotional depth, as in a connection we might make with a person with whom we have discovered only the merest trace of a common interest. In their stronger states, sociomental bonds can have greater cognitive or emotional depth, as in an intense experience shared by two devoted e-mail "pals." In between would lie a vast universe of sociomental connections and bonds with different levels of strength, each of which would likely be experienced differently by each of us.

In weak forms of social connectedness, people form connections of only marginal significance to them. In my interviews, people sometimes described connections in flat, unenthusiastic terms. Because she was not a TV enthusiast, Tapashi did not feel that she formed strong connections while watching TV:

[TV] makes you relax . . . you just watch it, and that's it.

Bill finds e-mail so one-dimensional that he refuses to use it or to try to form connections that way. Of the people he might encounter via e-mail, he firmly states:

They don't know me, and I don't know them.

Kim has decided to not maintain most of her long-distance connections with acquaintances from her homeland overseas:

> I'm too busy to write or call . . . what's the point? And I don't use my computer to write to them because my eyes hurt when I use it.

Furthermore, when our communication with others is simply task based and has no great emotional component, it is more likely that the connections formed will be relatively impersonal (Walther 1996). In many instances, then, we do not take others very far into our minds and hearts, and the connections we may form are, at best, rather weak.

In slightly stronger forms of connectedness, people report some degree of socially oriented engagement with the others to whom they are connected. They may describe such connections as "interesting" or "fun" but not "meaningful" or "strong." Many online connections exist at this moderate level of connectedness. When the cyberspace connectors I surveyed were asked about the appeal of online connecting, some told me that they went online for reasons such as these:

> Because I enjoy reading all the postings. (from the online literature group)

> To learn more about the subject than I do. (from the online science group)

> It's just plain fun! (from the online soap opera group)

> Because I find the people very knowledgable and helpful. (from the online soap opera group)

Such people either do not have or are not in touch with a strong sense of shared identity or purpose with the others in those communities. To use our model of sociomental space, they can be seen as sharing a sector of that space with other community members, but not as being located especially close to them. On the "periphery" of their communities, they are simply not as emotionally attached to the "hub" of the community—and to its other members—as more strongly connected members might be.

But sometimes sociomental connections and bonds develop that are much stronger. We may cultivate and nurture certain sociomental connections. The development of rituals, especially in conditions of serialization (see Chapter 4), can contribute to the deepening of the connection.[2] The bonds that result can be strong and enduring and both emotionally and cognitively intense. "Emotional intensity" refers to one's degree of affective involvement in the bonding situation, while "cognitive intensity" refers to the degree of knowledge or information a person has regarding the bond. Since cognition and emotion are often fused, with one generally accompanying the other, we can assume that in most cases of strong, intense sociomental bonding there is both a cognitive and emotional component.[3] Fans of actress Dana Delany explain why they have formed strong bonds with her:

> She is able to portray her thoughts and feelings on her face alone—she provides the medium for us to hear the message of each episode and understand its meaning. She connects emotionally with the viewer.

> She brings excellence to a complex role that draws the viewer in and demands interaction.

> She can convey more emotion with a look than another actress can with a soliloquy. Or perhaps she just allows the viewer to experience their own emotions.

> She helps me feel. (Viewers for Quality Television newsletter 1990)

People "may naturally feel a sense of friendship with personae they watch over time and feel that they have come to know" (Perse and Rubin 1989: 63), and when these personae "help others feel" and "allow them to experience their own emotions," it is hardly surprising that the connections and bonds they inspire might become quite strong indeed.

Strong, deeply felt sociomental bonds and communities of the mind also form in two other conditions. First, when the linking commonality is something people find especially relevant to their everyday lives (e.g., family, work, religion, special interests and hobbies, favorite books, sports teams or TV shows), the connections formed tend to be strong and meaningful. Bill, a broadcaster, notes:

> I feel connected to Frankie Crocker and all the people I listened to on the radio growing up . . . you feel you're in a sense of community with them. And now we're all in the same business. [Would you like to meet him or any of the others?] Meeting them wouldn't matter. It could even detract. It could break the bond.

And Joe, who is a huge fan of pro basketball's Los Angeles Lakers, feels connected to other Laker fans because:

> We're all interested in the same thing . . . and it has nothing to do with race or class. . . . It's us vs. them . . . and we've all got something in common, and we're all there to enjoy it.

The attraction for Bill and Joe is not in anything that fellow community members can do for them face-to-face, but in the way it feels to be mentally connected to them. The same is true of Randy, who says that having gone through the Marine Corps—a highly meaningful part of his life—has given him a set of important connections:

> I'm a strong believer in that people who have suffered together definitely feel a bond, and the military, in the beginning, is definitely suffering. So anyone who's gone through it, you sort of feel like you know them a little bit. If they've been in the same branch of the military, you feel like you know them a bit more. I could really relate to someone who's been through the Marine Corps.

Randy told me that he "feels that he knows" fellow Marines, even those he only reads about or hears about from others and knows he will never meet face-to-face.

Strong bonds also are engendered when the people involved feel threatened and/or marginalized, thus yielding a heightened desire or need to feel a sense of community with one another. When groups of people are not part of the societal mainstream (e.g., gays, members of racial and ethnic minorities, smokers, vegetarians, members of cults or antigovernmental militias) or are facing a specific fear or threat (e.g., illness, disability, loneliness), the community provides not only the pleasure of associating with others but also a means to defend, support, and protect one's group (and, it then follows, oneself). Jessica, who is of a Caribbean background but lives in the United States, explains the allure of sociomental bonding in the ethnic organization to which she belongs:

> It's just the fact that everyone [in the organization] is West Indian, everyone is from the Caribbean, you feel some sort of connection, some sort of home-ness, because you're all from the same area, the same Caribbean background. . . . Even though we're from all different countries in the Caribbean . . . we're similar . . . it's comforting.

A member of the online science group explains:

> I've always had an interest in science . . . [but] the people I know
> "face-to-face" (friends, family, co-workers) are largely indifferent
> to, if not actively bored by, this stuff. So I'm here to interact with
> others with similar interests.

And a fan of the often-beleaguered New York Mets I surveyed online
complains of feeling constantly marginalized because of his identification
with the Mets:

> Win or lose, we always end up defending ourselves as Mets fans.
> Losing: "You like the *METS*?! *WHY*?? They *SUCK*!!!" Winning:
> "You like the Mets? Sure. *EVERYBODY* likes the Mets, it's the
> cool thing to do right now." We're *ALWAYS* on the defensive!!

This individual's use of the pronoun "we" is an indicator of the communal connectedness he feels to other fans on the basis of this perceived
marginalization.

People also feel a strong need to connect with others sociomentally
when they are threatened in some way, which is why so many people go online to form support groups in response to illness, disease, stress, isolation,
or when other difficulties arise. They reach out to others for understanding,
fellowship, and empowerment. This fellowship with others who have been
through similar situations and are almost always available to "talk," "listen,"
and share information is sought and found online at all hours of the day and
night. Participation in "support communities," especially health-related
ones, is an extremely common use of the Internet; the effects of such communities on members are significant and often overwhelmingly positive, especially when face-to-face support is lacking (see Turner, Grube, and
Meyers 2001). Consider this passage written by Jay Allison, who began
posting updates of the condition of his infant daughter (who had spent
weeks on heart and lung apparatuses) on the "Parenting" sector of a large
Internet community called the "WELL" (excerpted by Howard Rheingold):

> Before this time, my computer screen had never been a place to
> go for solace. Far from it. But there it was. Those nights sitting
> up late with my daughter, I'd go to my computer, dial up the
> WELL, and ramble. . . . At 3 A.M. my "real" friends were asleep,
> so I turned to this foreign, invisible community for support. The
> WELL was always awake. Any difficulty is harder to bear in

isolation . . . I found fellowship and comfort in this unlikely medium. (in Rheingold 1995: 61)

As he shared the moments of this crisis with Allison, Rheingold discovered that he and many others in the online community had come to care about the Allison family quite deeply. "I've never met them face-to-face," he says of the family, "although I feel I know something powerful and intimate about the Allisons and have strong emotional ties to them" (ibid.). Such is often the experience in (and the appeal of) Internet communities (see Turner, Grube, and Meyers 2001).

Offline as well, threatened and marginalized groups have a definite incentive to form strong bonds, and they do so in great numbers. One consequence of the oppression with which many minorities have had to contend is that community-building movements among these groups have proliferated. For example, the multiple linguistic, tribal, and ethnic divisions that exist among African Americans are often redefined as a single, common ancestry, and the collectivity labeled, simply, the "black community" (see Higginbotham 1992). Creating a sense of a common, jointly experienced past is a response to threatened identities and an uncertain fate and allows a group to consider itself (and then even to go on to become) a strong, cohesive unit. This can be comforting and empowering, can inspire the formation of sociomental connections, and can create the sense that even in their diversity, African Americans are indeed

a nation. The best of us have said it, and everybody feels it. I know it will probably bother your white readers, but it is nonetheless true that black people think of themselves as an entity. (in Higginbotham 1992: 267)

In similar fashion, some gays in the mid-nineteenth century, in response to their status as threatened outcasts, formed communities which coalesced in and through their underground writings, extensive symbol systems and occasional face-to-face meetings (these groups were called the gay "beats" and flourished most visibly in San Francisco). Collectively, they began to defy existing definitions of homosexuality, forming a highly significant community of the mind that has influenced subsequent generations of gays—a community in which homosexuality could be valued as both legitimate and self-affirming:

In their rejection of the nuclear family, their willingness to experiment sexually, and most importantly, their definition of these choices as social protest, the beats offered a model that allowed homosexuals to view their own lives from a different angle. Through the beats' example, gays could perceive themselves as nonconformists rather than deviates, as rebels against stultifying norms rather than immature, unstable personalities. (in D'Emilio 1983: 187)

The sociomental connections that developed within the gay beats likely were quite strong and could easily pave the way, at some point, for face-to-face connections. People who form communities as a consequence of being marginalized and/or threatened may have a desire for connectedness that is especially acute and that may not be so easily met in the mainstream of social life. The sociomental connections that are sought and formed, then, can become especially strong, thus reinforcing the strength, boundary, and significance of the group. And they also can be bidirectional or reciprocal in nature.

BIDIRECTIONALITY AND RECIPROCITY

Recall that a kind of mental pathway exists between people who are sociomentally connected (see Chapter 3). Information and subtle forms of influence can be said to "flow" along these pathways. Because this can occur in two directions, like a "two-way street"—both toward and away from a connector—I consider those sociomental connections made with actual, living people (as opposed to those made with fictional characters or with the deceased) *bidirectional* and *potentially reciprocal*. As information and influence flow from one person to another along a mental path, the possibility always exists that some such influence may "flow" back to the first person in return (thus establishing *bidirectionality*) and perhaps even go on to be reciprocally exchanged or felt (the potential for *reciprocity*). In other words, there are fewer hindrances to the establishment of a variety of forms of relationships when a path has been formed than if such a pathway were not in place (see Bourdieu 1985 on "probable classes," p. 725).

Bidirectional connectedness is *directly* established when people write to, e-mail, talk on the phone to, or otherwise communicate with a person to whom they feel connected. There are many less obvious and *indirect* ways, however, that people create bidirectional connections. Consider the following letter printed in a letter to the editor forum of *New Woman* magazine, in which the letter writer describes her sociomental connection to the writer of an article in the magazine, Elizabeth Berg:

[The article] affected me deeply. At the end of the article, when Elizabeth Berg said she wished she could be telling me this information as a best friend, over coffee, she was actually getting her wish. . . . After reading her story I took the information, as she had hoped, far into myself. . . . Thank you, Ms. Berg, for bringing it home so effectively. If you are ever in Wyoming, please call, and I will take you to coffee. (in Edwards 1995: 16)

Berg had obviously influenced the reader, but because the reader wrote a letter that was published, the *potential* that Berg might come to read it, learn of her feelings toward her, and be influenced in kind was established. At that point, the possibility even existed (albeit remote) that Berg would take the letter writer up on her offer.

Although the latter outcome would most likely not happen, this example is illustrative of the enhanced potential for people to influence one another once a mental pathway has been opened. This particular mental pathway opened when the reader of a magazine article felt such a strong sociomental connection that she decided to express her feelings in letter form. Once such a mental pathway is established, many outcomes are possible—perhaps one of the *least* likely being a strong, reciprocal friendship between writer and reader, but the *most* likely being the creation of a true "meeting of their minds." When this happens, subtle forms of influence and comfort—of not being alone, of being understood, of somehow sharing one's thoughts—can flow *in both directions*.

Of course, simply having her article published and knowing that others would read it could affect Berg, even if no one wrote a letter to the editor (or contacted her regarding the article) in response. She might still be cheered (or concerned) by the reaction she would hope or presume that she had elicited; she might feel an enhanced (or a diminished) motivation to write for publication again. Some public figures are quite aware of the bidirectional nature of the bonds created between themselves and their fans. Jerry Seinfeld has noted that he feels a definite two-way connection with the audience of his television show *Seinfeld*, simply because he knows that people are out there somewhere, watching and enjoying his show (as its high television ratings, even in syndication, have made evident):

It's like an electric connection with millions of people that is both intimate and distant at the same time . . . episode by episode, we'd send these silly little ideas out, and the ratings, like a message in a bottle, would slowly come back: "We hear you. Keep sending." And that's the *relationship* I miss most: sending shows out as if through a long vacuum tube, and you getting back to us like millions of pen pals each week. (Seinfeld 2001: 19; emphasis added)

The "long vacuum tube" that Seinfeld speaks about is a direct parallel to the idea of the mental pathway. For, as he told Barbara Walters, he perceives his relationship with his fans as absolutely bidirectional:

> It's like I'm having an affair with these people. It's very intimate and not like anything else. (on the *Barbara Walters Special*, ABC-TV, November 24, 1992)

Actress Nancy Lee Grahn uses the word "relationship" to describe the bidirectional nature of her connection to her show's (*General Hospital*) viewers:

> The most essential relationship I have as an actress is with the audience. I am always communicating with you. When I act something that works, I feel your satisfaction. When I act something that doesn't . . . I can hear you saying "What the hell was that? That would never happen!" And I feel your pain. We're in this together. (*Soap Opera Digest*, July 3, 2001, p. 22)

In this passage, the way in which even supposedly distant media figures and fans influence one another (or metaphorically "hear" one another) and "send" information along mental pathways is clearly demonstrated.

Similarly, actress Suzanne Somers has said to those fans who expressed condolences over the death of her mother:

> I've always said I feel like I know all of you. Thank you for being my friends. (on the QVC Shopping Network, March 15, 1998)

And rock singer Bruce Springsteen says that:

> I know this is idealistic, but part of the idea our band had from the beginning was that you did not have to lose your connection to the people you write for. I don't believe that fame or success means that you lose that connection, and I don't believe that making more money means you lose it. Because that's not where the essence of you lies. That's not what separates people. What separates people are things that are in their heart. (in Marsh 1987: 75)

Springsteen, who has made many gestures of friendship to his fans over the many years of his career, refuses to consider himself "separate" from his fans, even those he will never meet. Sharing what he calls the "essence" of what is "in his heart" with his fans and receiving feedback in kind, he pursues the goal of remaining connected "with the people I'd grown up with, and the sense of the community where I came from" (ibid.). Even the most well-known celebrities, then, reaffirm the reciprocity and bidirectionality of their connectedness with fans and followers.

In addition, as public figures answer fan mail, sign autographs, make personal appearances, and even make subtle adjustments to their lives as a consequence of their followers' existence, bidirectional connections are evidenced (see Harrington and Bielby 1995: 48–65). To effectively reach others, those in public life must "restructure, manipulate, or even discard the messages they would send according to the conditions, composition, and feedback of their target audiences," Cerulo (1995: 91) observes. Two broadcasters in my interview sample told me how caring about their fans affects them and their programs:

> My listeners connect with me, and I connect with them. When I haven't heard from Ed [a listener] in a few weeks, I start wondering, "I hope he's okay!" (Kara)

> I love to speak with listeners [on the radio] when possible, because I feel a certain connection. (Bill)

As media figures come to feel connected to members of their audiences, they "give expression to their recipients' own concerns, tensions, aspirations, and hopes . . . [and] they deny all distance between themselves and the audience" (Kecskemeti in Cerulo 1995: 91). The closeness and the reciprocal nature of the connection formed between entertainer and fan, writer and reader, or creator and consumer are thus further enhanced.

Of course, the possibility also exists that very close, possibly even face-to-face, relationships may be formed as a consequence of the establishment of a mental pathway. This is an important characteristic of sociomental connectedness. Although sociomental connections will not *always* result in a two-way relationship, they increase the *likelihood* that some form of relatedness may occur. They provide the initial point of commonality that a connection or relationship requires.[4] When we share a sociomental connection with someone, there is an increased potential for physical connectedness to them (see Wellman 1988: 37). Grace touches upon this when she states that:

> I'm [a] member of a sorority, and if I went to a job interview tomorrow and found out that she was a member of the same

sorority, we'd have something to talk about, and you just know we'd be connected! [Do you think that would help you get the job?] Oh, come on, of course!

As Brian describes one of his communities of the mind:

It's like your own little world . . . and if you met one [of the others in it], who knows, maybe he'd be your best friend.

Mental pathways and networks *can* and sometimes *do* lead to physical ones. When they do, material—not merely cognitive and emotional—resources can be delivered face-to-face and can "flow along their paths."[5] Networks of physical support, then, can emerge much more easily when people have previously been mentally bonded. Stated another way, the more people share relevant commonalities, the more likely they are to form sociomental connections that may actually become "activated" in literal space.

The tacit perception of bidirectionality is a significant property of sociomental connections. Although connectors generally know that people who are far away or famous will likely not return their exact feelings or level of interest (a factor in face-to-face relationships as well), they still may sense in the "other" some form of subtle response flowing in their direction along the mental path that connects them. The more keenly they sense this, the stronger the resonance and sense of connectedness may become. Thus sensing bidirectionality (and the possibility of reciprocity) makes sociomental connectedness a bit more tangible and enticing. It also provides a subtle incentive to the creation of connectedness and enhances the authenticity of the experience.

AUTHENTICITY

Connections made with absent others can be experienced as quite real and genuine for those who make them. This, in fact, is one of the most common themes echoed by both my face-to-face and online research subjects. People often are not sure why (just as they may have been surprised by their strong reactions to the deaths of, say, Princess Diana or Martin Luther King Jr.), but they can truly come to care about people with whom they feel sociomentally connected, and they can feel that the bonds formed are absolutely authentic.

This is because things that do not exist in literal space but only in the spaces of our minds can be perceived by the brain as quite real.

Mental constructs are perceived by us as having their own reality, which cannot only seem *just as real* as things "out there" in literal space but oftentimes indistinguishable from it. As psychologists and neuroscientists have determined, the same centers in our brain are activated by imagination and by literal, visual perception (Neimark 1995: 85). Due to suggestibility, misattribution, bias, and the general persistence of mental images, we can easily confuse and conflate that which gets stored in the brain. We can unconsciously transfer a memory "from one mental category to another—from imagination to reality, from this time and place to that one, from hearsay to personal experience" (Begley 2001: 53; Hannigan and Reinitz 2001). This is how people can be unsure whether something in their past actually happened or whether they have imagined it. It is how Macbeth can grasp a handful of empty air when he believes he sees a dagger:

> Art thou not, fatal vision, sensible
> To feeling as to sight? or art thou but
> A dagger of the mind, a false creation,
> Proceeding from the heat-oppressed brain? (Shakespeare, 1981: 2, 1)

Macbeth's dagger, though "a false creation," is not "false" to his brain, which has recorded the vision of it just as faithfully as it has recorded the hand with which he reached for it.

The mental images and replications of others that we "carry" with us can be understood as creative blends of fact and fiction, for "images are alchemized by experience and emotion into memories," psychologist Elizabeth Loftus explains (in Neimark 1995: 85.) Any mental image—whether of someone we have met face-to-face or someone we know of sociomentally—can be a part-fact/part-fiction hybrid. Memory is imperfect and malleable. People can be prompted to "remember" things that never existed or happened: to remember "nonexistent broken glass and tape recorders; to think of a clean-shaven man as having a mustache, of straight hair as curly, of hammers as screwdrivers, to place a barn in bucolic settings that contained no buildings at all, to believe in characters that never existed and events that never happened."[6] Literal experiences and imagined things are recorded in the same place in our brains (the hippocampus). The same cognitive processes are used to encode, process, and retrieve them. We do not generally interrupt the flow of everyday experience to sort images and feelings into their appropriate categories (e.g. "images deriving from the physical world" and "images deriving from the mental world"), taking care to respond to them in distinct and different ways. As we go about our day-to-day business, we tend to "code" face-to-face and sociomental experiences similarly, often with equal "realness." A member of the online religion group I studied reveals:

> I didn't come here looking for friendship, and am thus surprised at how some of the regular posters have become real people to me. Some of them just have a very personal way of expressing themselves that I've come to recognize and, sometimes, to like very much. This has nothing to do with spelling or mental brilliance or even depth of faith, for that matter. I think what draws me to some people here is their authenticity and their willingness to be imperfect. But even the ones I don't especially like have touched my heart to the extent that I sometimes worry about them and wish I could reach through the computer and help them, somehow. In fact, now that I stop to think about it, it is amazing how "real" some of these distant, unseen, frequently anonymous message board posters have become. But, of course, they *are* real!

Because we so rarely discuss experiences of sociomental bonding openly, the reality of connecting online can take us, as it did with this connector, completely by surprise. Social connections formed and maintained solely in the brain can be experienced very much as those characterized by spatial copresence (Neimark 1995: 85).

In a classic study, Robert Merton investigated the 1943 war bond drive and singer Kate Smith's ability to sell $39 million in bonds in a one-day radio broadcast appeal. Merton traced Smith's effectiveness to the way that she was personally received by listeners, and he concluded that her listeners experienced "an emotional response; their inner self was in tune with Smith" (1946: 62). This resonance and synchronicity often yielded a sense of connectedness in buyers that felt extremely authentic. He quoted the mother of a young woman who purchased a bond:

> My daughter was wildly excited after she had made the phone call, and when some of her friends came in afterwards, she ran around the room from one to the other crying, "*I bought a bond from Kate Smith!*" (Merton 1946: 66; emphasis in original)

Though this example seems rather charming in its 1940s' naivete, the concept is far from outdated. We still experience sociomental connecting as resonant and authentic. Even situations that are clearly fictional can feel very real. Cindy, one of my interviewees, says she most enjoys reading novels that "just feel like real life to me." Of her favorite character, Cindy shares, "I want to see what's going on in her life right now!" Horton and Wohl (1956) explain this phenomenon, stating famously that, "The conditions of response to the [distant] performer are analogous to those in a primary group. . . . The most remote and illustrious men are met *as if* they were in the circle of one's peers."[7] Because we do not continuously stop and sort fiction from fact, one type of social reality from another, and face-to-face from sociomental, it is easy to care about absent *and* present others with equal and analogous intensity and authenticity.

Though Cindy and most others who form sociomental bonds using a technological mediator can differentiate fantasy from reality, they also can easily forget that a mediator is assisting in the creation of a connection (as is often the case in connecting via technology). Our ability to "ignore" technological mediators speaks to just how prevalent they are in our lives in facilitating social connections, how comfortable we generally are with them, and how commonly we do form sociomental bonds. We take them for granted. Triadic structures generated through technological mediation often feel like dyads, which increases one's sense of them as genuine, and as cognitively and emotionally similar to—"as if" they are—face-to-face connections.[8] We experience sociomental connections as part of real social worlds—organized outlooks built up by people of a common identity and solidarity, communicating and connecting with one another (see Shibutani 1955: 566; Fine 1983).[9]

We form hundreds of sociomental connections through the process of technological mediation and, as we have seen, we reaffirm or maintain them in thinking about or remembering them frequently (Caughey 1984: 22). We cannot possibly be aware of this process every time it occurs. In addition, our bodies are not always able to classify experience as "mediated" and therefore something "different than" (or "less than") an experience derived from face-to-face contact. If, for example, we are watching TV or a movie and a character moves quickly in our direction, our visual perception system will make us aware of this and prepare us for an actual retreat or a confrontation. Our bodies will probably even move a bit as we spontaneously respond to the "person coming toward us" (Reeves, Nass, and O'Toole 1995: 8). We feel real feelings and weep real tears when we experience moving passages in books, television shows, and movies. The *Guiding Light* online group demonstrates this:

I cry a ton happy and sad! I bawled when Lujack, Maureen, Eve, and Nadine died. On a happier note, I cried during Reva and Josh's wedding, and the twins' birth.

I've cried so many times I can't count. All the deaths mentioned above. . . . I'm pretty much good for tears of sorrow or tears of joy every week!

I cry too much about this show. I just cried yesterday when the babies were hurt. I was thinking about my girls. The worst episodes lately for my poor eyes were when Henry died. I lost both of my grandfathers last year, and it really hit home.

This is really weird but I always used to cry during the X-mas shows and afterwards when the cast was all gathered around singing and waving. My husband thought I was nuts! I didn't cry this year, probably because the show wasn't that great, and there were a lot of cast members missing in group shots. I also cry whenever they dedicate a show to someone or remember someone.

When there is cause to be happy, angry, or excited when connecting to a media figure or character, we feel genuinely happy, angered, or excited, often perceiving technologically generated experiences as "natural," not "framed," events.[10]

    This is a common response to the highly technological nature of our lives. It does not mean that we cannot tell the difference between reality and fantasy. Rather, it implies that as media- and technology-savvy viewers and readers, we blur and "play" with the concepts and "frames" of reality and fantasy more freely than our predecessors did.[11] We flirt with the concepts of reality and fantasy and play with them a little, generally without losing touch with "everyday" reality. We use mass media so frequently and regularly that we have become experts at performing the mental shift from "everyday" social life to these "alternate," media-generated social worlds. In fact, "real" friends often discuss the antics of their "media" friends (Meyrowitz 1985: 120; see also Brown 1989 for examples of this).

    Fictional characters such as those we watch on TV or read about in books are viewed as *simultaneously* real and constructed.[12] We care about them much as though they were real, while knowing full well that they are not. Mentally approaching characters "as if" they were real heightens the pleasure of the experience and of making sociomental connections (Harrington and Bielby 1995: 105). We assign a special kind of reality to a fictional character and immerse ourselves temporarily in that reality while usually knowing "deep down" that this character will never show up on our doorstep, is entirely separate from the actor portraying him or her, and is simply the figment of its creators' (and the audience's) collective inventiveness.[13] Most of us do not mix up actors and the characters they play (except in a playful sense) or expect a movie idol to fall in love with and marry us. (Contrast this sophistication to the panic that gripped audiences when motion pictures were first introduced, or that which the "War of the Worlds" radio broadcast initially inspired.) Modern minds are far more flexible, more able to hold and resolve seeming contradictions, than those existing at any time at the past. "The playing adult steps sideward into another reality," Erik Erikson says (1985: 222), a reality in which figments of the mind and of literal space comingle to amuse and engage us.

Sociomental connectedness can actually supply a healthy source of fantasy involvements and situations. Fantasy often is ridiculed as a waste of time, and those who fantasize—women in particular—are ridiculed for spending their time and energy frivolously.[14] But fantasy, like sociomental connecting itself, is an ordinary human mental activity and is neither especially good nor bad, except in the extreme.[15] Of course, we sometimes need to make a quick decision as to whether something falls distinctly into the realm of fantasy *or* reality. The realms do not always easily and unproblematically "merge." At times we feel a strong need to gauge what is "really" happening and what is not. In an age of virtual reality and artificial intelligence, of computers that replicate many functions of the human brain and machines that are becoming ever more humanlike, this can be an enormous challenge. As I have written elsewhere:

> In modern, everyday life, it is difficult (and becoming impossible) to definitively classify experience as "real" or "not real"; it is more helpful to determine the degree or "accent" of reality in an event. The frames we once used, conceptually, to set the real apart from the unreal are not as useful as they once were; they are not as sturdy; they betray us. As they become ever more fragile, we require new concepts and understandings. (Chayko 1993b: 179)

Since our brains record so-called "real" and "unreal" (and "fantasy") events so similarly, and modern technologies conspire to blur these realms as well, it may be time to conceptualize reality itself more flexibly, as I will discuss in Chapter 6.

In modern life, each person must negotiate his or her own means of crossing the boundaries between one's inner and outer worlds, between internal and external realities, between the real and the fictional. According to D. W. Winnicott (1971), an "intermediate" area of experience keeps inner and outer worlds separate but interrelated.[16] As a baby carries a blanket or a favorite toy (a *transitional object*) to help her understand and negotiate the boundary between "self" and "not one's self" with ever-increasing security, so must adults use *transitional phenomena* to navigate this ill-defined "intermediate" area of experience and to build a bridge between the inner world of the mind and the external world "out there". It is in social arenas such as the arts or religion, Winnicott believes—that is, in creative expression—that we learn to interpret and deal with those internal and external realities that might otherwise seem incompatible with one another.

Sociomental connectedness, I propose, can serve this purpose excellently. Possessing an "intermediate" degree of reality—with both real and fantasy elements—sociomental connections can help us build a bridge between the world "out there" and the world in our heads, for such connections are the province of both. Playful in many ways yet serious in terms of importance to us, sociomental connections, like the security blanket, may help us find our way through a murky cognitive landscape in which multiple realities coexist. This may, in fact, be one of their prime attractions.

Children are granted a "freedom to experience objects as simultaneously real and not real" that adults are not as freely granted (Harrington and Bielby 1995: 135). It remains difficult for adults to acknowledge sociomental connections as authentic and meaningful, let alone to understand the key role they play in helping us navigate the world. Still, there may be a great payoff in our learning to see them as possessing *degrees* of reality, for "no human being is free from the strain of relating inner and outer realities" (Winnicott 1971: 13). Once we can see them as truly authentic, we can appreciate why some people find them to be truly intimate as well.

INTIMACY

Social bonds, especially when developed in situations of strong, bidirectional, authentic involvement, can be quite intimate. Individuals in close, intimate relationships usually are deeply, emotionally involved with one another, though emotion may not always be displayed (some emotionally "quiescent" people only share or release their emotions upon the dissolution of a relationship, a release that can be exceptionally powerful and can reveal the intimacy of the connection—see Berscheid 1983: 112–13). Though the magnitude of one's feelings for another may not be outwardly expressed (or even inwardly noted), if one has formed a strong social bond with another person, it is likely an emotional one. It is as though a social connection has been given a "shot" or "charge" of emotion.

This emotional charge can provide the sense of "warmth" that seems to characterize intimate bonds. When individuals become intimate, their time together appears to them, phenomenologically, as "warm time" in the flow of a day or week (Davis 1973: 39). It takes on a special quality that is different, somehow, than time spent with acquaintances or less intimate friends. It is the closest, strongest, most involving and generally most intense form of social bond, yet it does not necessarily require face-to-face contact or even sustained mediated connectedness. Intimacy can be either enduring in nature—characterized by frequent, reciprocal, long-lasting contact—or situational, characterized by sporadic, transitory, more ephemeral situations of connectedness.[17] In either case, the bonds that form can be personal, comforting, quite emotional, and deeply significant for the individual.

When people become intimate, we can say that they are "very close" to one another in sociomental space. The mental "path" that connects them can be envisioned as "shorter" than that which would connect them to a mere acquaintance. If we were to chart or map the connections, as network theorists sometimes do to visually depict the connections among people in a face-to-face network, the "lines" that would connect sociomental intimates would be shorter, "thicker," and more firmly drawn than they would between people whose connections are weaker.

The warmth of intimate bonds provides individuals with spatial orientation (Davis 1973: 43). When lonely, an individual essentially "wanders" through her or his environment and feels disoriented and lost. Intimacy anchors us mentally. The "test" of intimacy, then, is not proximity in literal space (such as living in the same house as another person, or being "closely" related by blood or marriage) but proximity in sociomental space. In online connecting, we frequently see creative depictions of the closeness and the mental proximity that accompany the intimacy people share.

> There are some people that I "met" here that I have developed meaningful relationships with. We chat about things that are bothering us, and we often pray for one another. (from the online religion group)

> I do feel connected . . . I feel there are some Christians out there who think the way I do, and I feel close to them when they post. (from the online religion group)

> I think it's fun when we get to know each other, and it's interesting to find out what we think about things other than *Guiding*

Light. I feel like I have a whole new family of friends online. (from the online soap opera group)

People often seek and find intimacy online. Initially a skeptic with regard to the ability of the Internet to generate real feelings of community, John Perry Barlow describes people's online responses to him after they had read a posting of the eulogy he gave when he buried the woman he described as the love of his life, Cynthia Horner. He also shares *his* response to *their* response:

> Over the next several months I received almost a megabyte of electronic mail from all over the planet, mostly from folks whose faces I have never seen and probably never will. They told me of their own tragedies and what they had done to survive them. As humans have since words were first uttered, we shared the second most common human experience, death, with an openheartedness that would have caused grave uneasiness in physical America, where the whole topic is so cloaked in denial as to be considered obscene. These strangers, who had no arms to put around my shoulders, no eyes to weep with mine, nevertheless saw me through. As neighbors do (1995: 56).

Stark in its depiction of intimacy, Barlow's experience shows us how people who cannot extend their arms to one another can extend their hearts nonetheless. A member of the *Guiding Light* online soap opera group I studied discovers the same thing when she shares this intimacy with the group:

> My father-in-law passed away last Friday and . . . I have to admit something to you all that I didn't dare tell my husband or family—I managed to sneak away and watch GL. . . . Through the tears and heartache I still had to watch.

This confession elicits the following responses from the group members:

> I'm so sorry for your loss. But please don't beat yourself up about sneaking a peak at GL. . . . Sometimes you just need to grab onto something that's familiar and will take your mind off your sorrow. God bless you sweetie.

> I am so sorry about your father-in-law—my prayers are with you. Hey, nothing wrong with a little GL break through the daily struggles of life—that's what it's for.

We are here for you.

I'm very sorry for your loss. I do understand your wanting to still watch the show . . . there is something comforting in doing what you usually do, and GL is like an old friend you can count on to be there.

The last inspires a response from the person who had posted the original message:

Oh, you have just made my day! I was feeling so guilty about escaping to keep up with my favorite soap, but you're right, GL is an old friend and I do find comfort in watching. It's nice to know that someone understands.

Intimacy can even grow so strong over time that online connectors begin to get to know one another more or less as "whole people" and to form multiplex bonds.

Depending on the circumstances, topics, and people involved, bonds that form in cyberspace can either be narrowly specialized or broadly multiplex (Wellman and Gulia 1999: 181). In the online forums I studied, the most intimate, multiplex, sociomental bonds were in evidence in the soap opera and literature groups. Members of these groups not only expressed their emotional states freely, they seemed almost driven to learn as much as possible about one another. That may be due to the nature of the connecting elements (both involve serialization which, as I have noted, tends to engender heavy involvement) but also may be due, in part, to the predominantly female constitution of the groups (for the online sports group, which also dealt with a "serialized" sports season, did not demonstrate such a pattern of intimate exchanges). Probably as a consequence of their early experiences, emotional warmth and intimacy are more generally characteristic of women's experiences of social bonding relative to men's;[18] while men's relationships tend to be oriented toward doing and discussing physical activities, women's tend to be oriented toward talking about personal feelings and concerns.[19] At any rate, in the soap opera and literature groups, primarily composed of women, intimate social bonds were freely and frequently constructed and were often a source of discussion themselves.

Sociomental bonding permits individuals to visually "hide" from others, and thus it may encourage the development of some intimacies. In being completely anonymous, one may become much less inhibited; one may look and act however one wishes, without ever being seen. On the one hand, certain types of intimacies can only be exchanged face-to-face. On the other hand, even in literal space, people often prefer to be in a private setting, or to hide in some way, in order to "give rein to" their most intense affections and most intimate exchanges (Weitman 1970: 350). The anonymity afforded by telephone and computer technology often results in lower inhibitions by users, who may behave more freely and "open themselves up" to intimacy more than in face-to-face encounters.[20] As the mental component of such an encounter predominates over the physical, some may even find that a greater level of intimacy is reached:

> The great thing is you get to know one another before you see each other, so there's no preconceived notions of how the other person is by what they look like. (from the online soap opera group)

> When you date people, the first thing you have is the physical component. I learned all about Sandy's inside person before I met her physically. (in Olafson 1993: 2)

> [Online connecting] takes away the physical insecurities people have. And I think that's a good thing and a bad thing. (Mabel)

From the online science group comes this thoughtful perspective:

> It could even be argued that we are communicating on a deeper level than we would be able to if we were face-to-face. A lot of things get lost and misconstrued in oral arguments. With this, everything is in writing. One often edits and rephrases for clarity. Putting things down in writing is far different than just blurting something aloud. Many posts only come after much reflection and a sorting out of thoughts. So although we miss the tones and facial expressions of the people with whom we are communicating, it could be argued that we are still communicating on a more profound level.

Even online a profound sense of knowing someone's "insides" can develop. Yet some argue that the intimacy created in technological use is illusory, devoid of the investment one must make in a face-to-face relationship (see Stoll 1995; Beniger 1987).

Whether or not one considers a truly intimate connection to have been made in the mind seems to depend primarily on two things: the context in which the bond is formed and the mental flexibility of the individual considering the nature of the bond. It is somehow easier to "forgive" a lack of face-to-face copresence—and to permit an intimate bond to develop—when its context is the work world or a leisure interest, as opposed to the family, a marriage, a "best-friend"-ship, and so on. In the more traditionally "personal" spheres of social life at least some face-to-face copresence is traditionally seen as imperative.

> With a soulmate, love-type relationship, for me, face-to-face is necessary. There's some folks who are married and live in different states . . . I'd put a bullet in my head. For this type of relationship I think (face-to-face) contact is necessary, and I've had those kind of relationships suffer because of lack of contact. With friends that are not that kind of "soulmate," love kind of thing, you can maintain it at a pretty good level when you're not around, and that's helped by e-mail, or the mail, or the phone, or sending tapes—all that stuff really helps. Absolutely. (Bruce)

Nineteen of my fifty primary interviewees told me of at least one face-to-face social bond that had been broken—due, they felt, to physical separation. They told me that without sufficient face-to-face interaction, these bonds (which had been among their most intimate) could not be sustained. Jose expressed the general feeling among these individuals when he said that "technology"—as it is used to mediate connectedness in cases of physical separation—"shouldn't be 50 percent of a relationship. Maybe 20, 25 percent." The idea that intimate relations are the exclusive province of face-to-face interaction is a deeply held perspective.

Still, we must consider the possibility (at least theoretically, but increasingly practically) that particularly motivated and flexible-minded people *can* and *do* seem to conduct deeply intimate relationships without ever having face-to-face meetings. Online relationships may be the best example of this. In computerized worlds such as MUDs people actually translate the computer environment into a "set" that they design in great detail to express, enact, and uphold their bondedness with one another (Reid 1995: 175). In it, people can become strongly attached to those they come to consider friends—even lovers:

> The most common action taken by such partners ("virtual lovers") is to set up virtual house together. They quite literally create a home together, using the MUD program to arrange textual information in a way that simulates a physical structure which they can then share and invite others to share. These relationships may

even be consummated through virtual sex, enacted as cowritten interactive erotica. More technically gifted players may also create objects, which other players can interact with, that textually mimic the behavior of pets and children. (ibid.)

Certainly, some consider such acts "merely a game" and definitely "not real." The people most intensely involved in them, however, might disagree (Reid 1995; see also Fine 1983). Online connectors frequently report that some of their closest friendships exist "in" cyberspace, among people they seldom or will never meet face-to-face (see Wellman and Gulia 1999: 180). Research also suggests that groups of people that "meet" over the Internet tend to become more intimate over time.[21] As one individual put it:

> I don't care how much people say they are, muds (sic) are not games, they are *real*!!! My mud friends are my best friends. . . . They are my family, they are not just some dumb game. (in Reid 1995: 175)

Far from being "just a game," objects and relations in the created world are "treated as if they had the properties of the everyday counterparts—houses are lived in, roses are smelled, and hugs can hold together friendships" (Reid 1995: 182).

Such behaviors reflect both technological sophistication and quite a bit of mental flexibility, in that the individuals involved must figure out how to cooperate to create aspects of their lives together using tools and rituals that they also create. Players perform acts representing sexual relations (both consensual and nonconsensual), and some players even contend that they "marry":

> The virtual bride and groom are married by another player who virtually reads, and actually types, the wedding ceremony. Tokens are often exchanged, virtual representations of flowers and rings attached to a player's virtual manifestation through the manipulation of the textual description of the character. The wedding is usually attended by a number of fellow players, whose participation in the event bolsters its imaginative reality in the shared minds of the MUD community. The forthcoming nuptials are often publicized in the communications media. (Reid 1995: 175)

This is a vivid example of people creating a world, a reality, in what Elizabeth Reid calls their "shared minds."

Players also have met online in the "shared world" of the chat room or MUD, have become intimate there, and then have met face-to-face.

> I met Mark, who I'm now married to, on a MUD. . . . We spent a lot of time chatting and we got closer and closer. It was really good—I could tell him anything and he was really supportive. We ended up building this castle together and everyone on the MUD treated us like a couple. I could tell that he was interested in me, and at first I was reluctant to get involved but he was so nice and he said that he really loved me and in the end we had this MUD marriage. It was so beautiful—I burst into tears half way through it! After a few months I had the chance to visit the East coast (sic) and we met while I was there. He was different from what I expected, mostly in the way he looked, but we got along really well . . . we got married last year. (in Reid 1995: 176)

Interview subject Bruce's feelings regarding the importance of face-to-face contact for what he called "love-type soulmates" notwithstanding, some people certainly can form bonds of friendship, love, and even "marriage," which feel very intimate to them, are framed as real, and have very real consequences for them, without ever meeting face-to-face. These people have learned to define, interpret, and experience social bonding far more flexibly and fluidly than those who simply cannot imagine bonding in such a way (let alone do so).

To be sure, the potential for deception in an online relationship can be quite high. One can never be sure that there has not been deception involved in the sending of a message, or that one has received the actual message that was intended. There is ample opportunity to disguise one's identity, motives, and meaning online (see Turkle 1997). But this all occurs in literal space as well (see Goffman 1974, 1959; Bateson 1972 [1955]).

Deception is actually exceedingly common in face-to-face encounters. Psychologist Bella DiPaulo has found that most people deliberately tell a misleading lie once or twice a day, that they lie in approximately one-fifth of social exchanges lasting ten minutes or more, and that over the course of a week, they deceive about 30 percent of those with whom they interact face-to-face. Dating couples, she found, lie to one another in about one-third of their interactions (possibly more than they deceive other people in their lives), and most "big" lies—deep betrayals of trust—occur between people in intimate relationships. A certain degree of deception seems inevitable in *all* forms of interaction; deception may even serve as a kind of social lubricant that actually makes it easier for people to get along and thus help to sustain connectedness (in Kornet 1997: 53–55).

As people get to know one another, then, they gain increasing amounts of information on which to base their perceptions. Of course, in the end, these perceptions can still be wrong. But despite these complications, we persist in forming social connections with distant or absent others. Though the potential for deception may indeed be greater in cyberspace, this still may not impede the development of intimacy, just as it may not in literal space. As Rheingold remarks:

> You can be fooled about people in cyberspace, behind the cloak of words. But that can be said about telephones or face-to-face communication as well; computer-mediated communications provide new ways to fool people, and the most obvious identity swindles will die out only when enough people learn to use the medium critically. In some ways, the medium will, by its nature, be forever biased toward certain kinds of obfuscation. It will also be a place where people often end up revealing themselves far more intimately than they would be inclined to do without the intermediation of screens and pseudonyms. (1995: 64)

For intimacy is no stranger to distance or to darkness.

Sociomental connections, bonds, and communities, then, can be characterized by a great deal of strength, bidirectionality and reciprocity, authenticity, and intimacy. Not all connections will exhibit all of these properties, of course, and many more will be uncovered and identified. Sociomental connections exhibit a great diversity of qualities, and they can influence us in many ways as well. I discuss some of these influences—the social "fallout" of sociomental connectedness—in Chapter 6.

6

The Social "Fallout"
of Connecting at a Distance

Modern individuals "stand" at the busy, well-traveled "intersections" of myriad social connections. Our lives are characterized by rapid social change that can take a mental and an emotional toll on us.[1] It sometimes feels as though our ability to find our way in the world around us can hardly keep pace with these changes. Social boundaries are constantly shifting, requiring us to constantly learn and relearn appropriate and acceptable norms and rules of behavior. Feelings of anxiety, anomie, stress, depersonalization, alienation, and fear can proliferate under the "mask" of increased freedom (Merelman 1984: 107). We seek a sense of stability in a world that sometimes threatens to spin out of control.

The combination of transience and privatization that has come to characterize suburban life has eroded the bonds of neighborhood, family, and kinship that once helped people cope with the demands of their lives. Women—for whom housekeeping and child care is still a primary responsibility—may feel these effects particularly deeply. Research indicates that women rearing children at home may be more prone to depression than working mothers, and that working mothers suffer depression more often than working men. And the stresses of modern life have resulted in an overall increase in anxiety for both women and men (Wright 1995).

Technological advancements now occur at breakneck speed. Countless opportunities (and obligations) of social interaction seem to swirl around us, competing for our time and energy. At the same time, and perhaps as a response to these conditions, we now make an unprecedented number and variety of sociomental connections, bonds, and communities.

127

The impact of sociomental connecting—on individuals and on society—is great, but as with all complex social phenomena, its influence is neither obvious nor simple to determine. As it brings us together, it may also be contributing to social problems that we can only begin to understand— the anomie, the alienation, the anxiety of our time.

So what is the "fallout" of living in a world so thoroughly defined and deeply influenced by sociomental connectedness? Though there are hazards to consider, there are benefits as well, and sometimes, there are effects that cannot so easily be designated "good" or "bad." At the same time as physical presence becomes less of an imperative for conducting business, it remains a critical component of strong families, while its role in education is debated, for new applications of computer technologies have made inroads into all of the institutions of modern life. Online banking and shopping flourish, yet their face-to-face counterparts remain vital. Many chapters of the story of the impact of twenty-first-century technology on our society and our social connections are yet to be written.

In this final chapter, I deal with some pressing concerns related to social connectedness in the Internet age. Do the dangers outweigh the advantages? Are we experiencing, as many fear, a loss of community? Are technology and sociomental connectedness playing a transformative role in shifting conceptions of community, of the self, of humanity itself? How can we best understand this "togetherness" in which people are literally apart?

Here I speak to these issues, considering what we can take from this analysis of sociomental connectedness that will help us better understand our world and ourselves. I examine the delusions and dangers that can accompany connecting at a distance, look at the nature of the connectedness and community that can be created, and discuss some implications for the modern self and society. Finally, I propose that we use these perspectives on connecting to better understand the modern social condition and our place in the Internet age.

DELUSIONS AND DANGERS

Clearly, sociomental connecting has its downside. Any comforts and intimacies found while connecting in this way would surely be cold comforts indeed without sufficient face-to-face bonding to provide balance and completeness to a "portfolio" of social relationships. Face-to-face connectedness is, and must remain, the interactional bedrock of society. A child needs hands-on affection and attention. A lover needs to hold and be held by another. We need physical stimulation and need to respond in kind in order to be fully human. Symbolic representations of hugs and kisses placed at the end of a letter or e-mail are radically different from the real thing—and most of us certainly consider loving symbols vastly inferior to their face-to-face referents.

To be sure, some people do withdraw to an unhealthy degree from face-to-face connectedness. Seduced by the ease with which sociomental intimacies can seem to develop, or perhaps fearing, rejecting, or tiring of the complexities and responsibilities of interaction in the literal realm, they form sociomental connections in excessive proportion to those they form in literal space. They may even become obsessed or delusional, believing that these connections are, indeed, wholly reciprocal in nature. They may not know how to deal with different kinds of connections appropriately or how to manage their internal and external realities (let alone the "intermediate area" that bridges them), and, thus, may feel overwhelmed by these many tasks and roles.

When an excessive amount (or what a culture considers an excessive amount) of a person's social connections is formed in purely mental ways, we classify the situation (and the person in question) as "odd," perhaps delusional, or even psychotic. Collectively, we may be even more inclined to make such classifications when "too many" of a person's connections seem to be with dead, fictional, or nonhuman others. To be sure, such a connector may indeed be delusional and may be disregarding entirely the importance of face-to-face forms of bonding. But who is to say definitively what constitutes "too much" sociomental bonding? Where is the line to be drawn between rigid and flexible—or normal and psychotic— levels of sociomental bonding?

Just as individuals do, a culture (or subculture) constructs a collective definition of "what is real." We all live simultaneously in many mental worlds ("multiple realities" or "spheres of reality"): the reality of everyday life, the "erotic reality" of sexual activity, dream and fantasy worlds, religious experiences, drug-induced hallucinations, child's play, and fictional and media-generated social realities, to name just a few.[2] Interestingly, these realities are often experienced simultaneously; as Davis puts it, "It is one of the most remarkable features of human existence that we live not in one reality but in two (at least) and that we continually alternate between them, often against our will" (1983: 10).

In our tendency to reify our social world (Zerubavel 1981: 43) we often classify the "reality of everyday life" as the one and only *real* reality. We have become accustomed to thinking about it as the only "natural" one. All other realities then become consigned to the category of "artificial" or the realm of the "crazy," either rife with delusion or just somehow "less than." "Everyday life" is assigned the ultimate position of primacy. Yet the proliferation of "other" realities poses a constant threat to this rigidly conceived system. As Schutz illustrates:

> If one conceives of [everyday reality] as the "daylight" side of human life, then the marginal situations constitute a "night side" that keeps lurking ominously on the periphery of everyday consciousness. Just because the "night side" has its own reality . . . it is a constant threat to the taken-for-granted, matter-of-fact, "sane" reality of life in society. The thought keeps suggesting itself (the "insane" thought par excellence) that, perhaps, the bright reality of everyday life is but an illusion, to be swallowed up at any moment by the howling nightmares of the other, the night-side reality. (1973 [1945]: 98)

Realities other than the "daylight" of "everyday reality" tend to become categorized as artificial ("night-side") experiences. It is as though to collectively recognize them as truly real or authentically equivalent to the reality of everyday life (which in and of itself is not a clear, unified concept) poses too great a threat to the social order.[3]

As we go about our lives, though, realities other than "everyday reality" routinely rear their threatening heads. We are members of many communities of the mind and make many sociomental connections, each of which, as we have seen, bears an "accent" of reality. But rather than acknowledge this openly, we tend to deny it, fearing social stigma (the "fear of being labeled crazy," as Harrington and Bielby put it [1995: 135]) *and* the breakdown of our carefully ordered system of categorizing realities. When the feelings generated in experiencing one of these communities are comforting or in some way temporarily "more real" to us than the reality of everyday life, our entire understanding of "what is real" is thrown into question, a situation that many of us are unprepared to consider head on.

For most of us, the separation and hierarchy of realities is an incredibly powerful social fact, constraining much of our way of thinking and dealing with life. Many people believe (or feel the need to *claim*) that a bond formed with an absent other is somehow inauthentic, evidence of delusional thinking. But this is quite a rigid way of approaching these issues. Though the general thought style of modern Western society is, overall, a rigid one, underneath it a subtle but definite negotiation with the boundary or "frame" of "what is real" continually takes place.

The fact that those connections and communities which are formed with respect to spiritual and religious realms are treated as absolutely real by many in the societal mainstream demonstrates a major inconsistency in this conservative thought style, and a very interesting paradox. While feelings of connectedness with celebrities or fictional characters often are criticized by the rigid minded as strange and unreal, social relationships with possibly fictional and certainly dead spiritual figures such as gods, angels, and saints are frequently framed not only as real but as having immense life-and-death significance (see Goffman 1974; Chayko 1993b). Forming religious and spiritual sociomental connections is deemed normal and even essential to living a good life by millions who might view other forms of sociomental connection with suspicion.

In no other way is the arbitrary, conventional basis of the classification of "what is real" so vividly revealed and the definition of the delusional called into question. The "line" between reality and unreality is revealed as a reification, a cultural creation. Only those with the power to classify reality "correctly" and to impose systems of classification on others can relegate others to categories such as "delusional," "psychotic," "child-like," or "insane" (and therefore relegate the people in such categories to places considered "appropriate," such as mental institutions—or kinder-gartens!). This is *not* to say that insanity does not exist and is not a potential outgrowth of excessive mental connecting—it is. I wish only to emphasize that an informed debate is necessary to intelligently and fairly draw such distinctions, so that sociomental connections do not persist in being defined as *inherently* and "obviously" unhealthy—a notion with which I strenuously disagree.

As a rigid style of thinking does dominate society, people with creative ways of forging connectedness are sometimes not taken seriously. And as we all have at least some elements of rigidity in our own minds, we may be understandably tempted to regard connections formed with non-human others, "ghosts," plants, inanimate objects, and other things and beings that test the "limits" of sociomental connecting as "obviously un-real" (or at least "weird"). But we must remember that the lines to be drawn here can and will be drawn differently by different cultures. Many Eastern cultures, for example, will be highly accepting of and encouraging of bonding with dead or dream-state others and with plants or natural ob-jects. Religious subcultures will be very forgiving of even the "excessive" formation of bonds with spiritual others. Western cultures will better tol-erate bonding with "imaginary friends" among children than adults. There is plenty of diversity among individuals and cultures when it comes to classifying reality.

Incidentally, the general Western prejudice against the figurative in favor of the literal is a social convention as well. It may derive from ancient times in which priests, kings, and emperors discouraged disobedience to their laws by claiming that their words were the "authorized," God-given truth—fixed, literal, and unchangeable. Ever since those early times, Western cultures tend to privilege the literal over the figurative, the thing over the idea, and the body over the mind, but as it is the job of sociology to point out, *in another culture or social sphere it could easily be otherwise.*[4]

Since deeply held thought styles and mental models are difficult (though by no means impossible) to challenge and change, traditional ways of thinking about social connectedness continue to become defined, by default, as correct and solely appropriate. But there is a danger in this as real as in excessive sociomental connecting. In dismissing sociomental connecting outright as "unreal" or fake, we ignore, shun, and trivialize a form of human communion in which we all engage. We become divorced from aspects of our everyday lives which are crucial to understanding ourselves and our place in the world. The result is that we become increasingly alienated from parts of ourselves, from one another, from seeing "society" as it really is. This alienation can lead to stress and depression and their very real physical effects—or, at the very least, a sense of unease or uncertainty as we live our everyday lives.

An appreciation of sociomental connectedness can help us resolve the tension of sublimating forms of human communion and can show us how we can value all of our interests and desires and aspects of ourselves. It also can inspire and inform much-needed dialogues regarding coping with and managing the incredible array of connections with which we are enmeshed. We can develop a more nuanced understanding of the process of connecting in all of its manifestations. And such knowledge has never been more important.

For there are, indeed, definite dangers inherent in connecting at a distance (which is not surprising, since there are dangers in all forms of connecting). The exploitation of the powerless is a possibility that becomes even more frightening in the absence of face-to-face information and accountability. For example, the Internet seems to have spawned a resurgence of pedophilia because avenues for the exploiters of children to reach vulnerable children and one another (for organizational and commercial purposes) are now more extensive and easily traversed (Nordland and Bartholet 2001). In a study conducted by the Crimes against Children Research Center at the University of New Hampshire, Durham, almost

20 percent of the 1,500 children surveyed reported unwanted sexual solicitations online from people they did not know (Thomas 2001: 1D).

Many modern organizations—from advertising and marketing specialists to totalitarian governments—use technology to exploit the process
of "connecting people together" to its fullest. This can have outcomes that
can range from mildly annoying (an intrusive telemarketer, unsolicited
e-mail) to highly fearsome (Goebbels' Nazi Germany propaganda, online
hackers who electronically ruin credit, spread viruses and alter identities,
those who prey upon others they encounter online). Still, even when risky
or dangerous, sociomental connections—just like face-to-face ones—can
give members an undeniably satisfying, even seductive sense of togetherness. The lure of an unscrupulous televangelist provides a particularly good
example of this. Even as he or she misleads a group of people with fiery
fear appeals solely for commercial purposes, the sense of belonging to a de-
vout community of followers can have real feel-good effects on members.[5]

That the computer age is creating a new echelon of elites based upon
technological sophistication also is worrisome. Those with access to and
knowledge of computer connectivity can take advantage of technologically
illiterate social members much as media owners can manipulate media
users, but with a twist: these new "owners" can, with sufficient technological know-how, be "one of us"—the previously disempowered and those of
low status (see Allman 1993: 63; Pursell 1995). Subtle forms of manipulation among "everyday" people can therefore proliferate and be even more
dangerous in their invisibility and newness. Concerns about the "digital
divide" between those people who own, manage, or work at a sophisticated level with high-tech products and those who do not have such skills
(whether due to their lack of knowledge, education, financial resources, or
feelings of self-efficacy) are well placed (see Hoffman, Novak, and
Schlosser 2000; Easton and LaRose 2000). It will become more and more
difficult for people without computer skills to become fully integrated into
and benefit from a digital society.

Threats to privacy are a real and related concern. Personal information and one's actual "movement" online are very easy to track. Private information is increasingly accessible publicly—to law enforcement
agencies, marketing companies, hackers, and so on. Those who are unaware of this or who lack the power to do anything about it can easily be
lured into dangerous situations. Laws may emerge to protect the unsus-
pecting from some of these dangers, but as David Gelernter notes (2000:
74), "laws are bad weapons in the fight to protect privacy." Privacy concerns in cyberspace are quite real.

Some, however, refuse to worry about the potential danger represented by modern invasions of privacy. Gelernter claims:

> So what else is new? Technology always threatens privacy. These threats usually come to nothing. They have been defeated before, and will be in the future, by a force that is far more powerful than technology—not Congress, the law or the press, not bureaucrats or federal judges, but morality. . . . Life will get better: not because of the technology revolution but because of a moral rebirth that is equally inevitable and far more important. (2000: 74)

Whether one agrees or disagrees, Gelernter reminds us that we can never be certain of the exact ways in which technologies will have their impact and of the ways in which people may respond.

Dangers such as these occur, in slightly changed forms, in all social settings. Delusion, psychosis, obsession, and addiction will probably always be with us. "Haves" and "have-nots" will emerge in social settings from Silicon Valley to Russia, as people live in different class-based worlds with very different opportunities and lifestyles. The problems, risks, and frustrations that accompany sociation in any form are found in the sociomental domain, but they take on new forms and there is new concern when people are physically separated from one another. It is worrisome that the people I interviewed—even the high-tech connectors—did not seem fully aware of such dangers.

> [Online is] the safest way to communicate socially. You risk very little. I think that's why a lot of people don't go out to bars and clubs . . . there's a lot of pressure [in them] to look right, to act right, to drink a lot. I don't drink, and I'm not out scammin' or cruisin', and rarely can you go into a bar to have a conversation with someone you don't know without an assumed sexual overtone to it. You can't just walk into one and talk about the New Hampshire primary [like you can online]. (Mabel)

> There's no risk involved in e-mail, I don't think. And it's convenient. . . . The e-mail is a very nonthreatening way to kind of "buzz" people about things. (Cindy)

Without exception, my subjects felt that there was little danger to be found in cyberspace. In the Crimes against Children study, only 23 per cent of the children surveyed expressed any real concern about the potential dangers inherent in encountering others online (Coughlin 2001: 3). Online connecting may seem to entail less social and psychological risk than face-to-face contact, at least initially—it may *seem* safer. And compared to face-to-face communities, many members of adult sociomental groupings do retain, and exercise, the ability to enter or exit many communities of the mind at will (unless, of course, in the case of brainwashing and/or coercion).

This is why information about, and open discussion of, sociomental connecting is so critical. To protect themselves from risky or harmful situations, people must realize that as they use technologies, they often are forming social bonds and communities with very real risks and dangers. Once in the habit of discussing such things, people can become all the more aware of these dangers and better "armed" to defend against them. Only educated individuals can make truly informed choices about the causes and consequences of their use of technology. There is evidence that the current generation of people in their teens and twenties is becoming more media savvy than those in any prior age group (Collingwood 1997; Uems et al. 1997). We must extend this "savvy" to cyberspace connecting and to the sustained discussion of all forms of technological connectedness—of delusions, satisfactions, and hazards.

We also must preserve and encourage the salience of face-to-face connectedness. To find and achieve a kind of balance between the literal and sociomental domains can only be healthy for individuals and for a society. But it is a real challenge in the modern world. Face-to-face interactions take measures of time, energy, and commitment which often are in short supply. "Community," at least as traditionally defined, seems to have been threatened, possibly lost.[6] We have come to expect and desire efficiency, calculability, predictability and control in virtually all areas of social life (see Ritzer 2000), including our social connections. New times and changed worlds require new paradigms of understanding—a rethinking of what we "know" to be sure, a recasting of "knowledge."

RETHINKING COMMUNITY

Many forms of civic membership and formal engagement are, to be sure, in decline. As Robert Putnam observes, people are "bowling alone" more frequently (though as Richard Reeves rebuts, they more often form groupings as they work together).[7] People are finding new outlets for membership in a variety of organizations (Ladd 1999) and experimenting with looser forms of ad hoc face-to-face connections (Wuthnow 1998). But others, certainly, are turning excessively inward. It is easy to point the finger of blame to technology, to argue that "easy to start, easy to stop" sociomental connections and "easy to enter, easy to exit" communities of the mind are responsible for the decrease in certain forms of civic engagement and community and family life.

It is generally a mistake to assign a single cause to a social phenomenon, however. The social world is far too complex; wide-ranging phenomena are always intersecting in subtle ways to produce unexpected results. Technology has just such a complex, and reciprocal, relationship with society. Any change in society tends to produce a change in technology, and vice versa, and as these changes build upon one another, they "shape the world in which we live, shifting its contours and rearranging its parts, just as oceans move sand dunes" (Westrum 1991: 4; see also Meyrowitz 1985: 5).

The introduction of new technologies into existing social patterns has always worried those who prefer the preservation of the status quo. The development of writing, for example, concerned those who cherished pure orality (such as Socrates, who believed that writing things down would destroy people's abilities to keep concepts in the mind).[8] Centuries later, the introduction of film and radio troubled social critics who feared the creation of a populace scarcely able to tell the difference between fantasy and reality. And as television and computers have become household fixtures, many fear their potentially harmful effects on people (particularly children), with the ultimate fear being the separation of people from one another in important, and perhaps permanent, ways. Some people it seems, will distrust any new technology as it emerges, always fearing that interpersonal relationships and society itself will undergo a deleterious transformation for which technology is directly responsible.[9]

This distrust of technology rests upon what Claude Fischer calls the "impact-imprint assumption"—the belief that a technology influences society directly and usually negatively as it transfers its properties to individuals, groups, or institutions (Fischer 1985). Manifestations of this belief include the following assumptions: that labor-saving devices have decreased labor in people's homes, that the automobile has caused people to change residences more frequently that before its widespread use, and that cars, railroads, and telephones have inspired people to abandon localized experiences in favor of long-distance ones (ibid.). But research actually indicates that none of these three outcomes is a necessary response to the introduction of the technology in question, or even occurs more often than not. Time spent on housework has not declined in the era of time-saving appliances (Vanek 1978), residential mobility has actually declined in the twentieth century, possibly because the automobile allows people to stay in the same residence even when they change jobs (Long 1976), and transportation and communication media actually stimulate more local contacts than distant ones (Willey and Rice 1993; Fischer 1985 details this complete argument). The impact-imprint logic, then, is misleading, for technologies often have unexpected and contradictory consequences, some of which may cancel one another out.[10]

The impact of technologies always expands in ways that their creators and producers did not originally intend and often could not have imagined. Writing, for example, originally developed merely as a way of keeping tax records. Gutenberg's printing press and movable type were created as a better and more permanent way to produce Bibles. Alexander Graham Bell's telephone was designed and intended as an aid to the hearing impaired. The unpredictable patterns of growth of these technologies led to major transformations in their use, in social life, and in processes of thinking. It oversimplifies things greatly, then, to focus on the extent to which sociomental connections may have displaced face-to-face forms. Technologies do not necessarily displace one another. People end up using technologies to complement one another and to fulfill different (and ever-changing) functions and gratifications.[11] Technologies can even "boost" one another and "boost" face-to-face interaction.[12]

Though there may be an initial "honeymoon" period in which a new technology is used to excess, the people I interviewed and surveyed indicated that, in time, newer technologies had generally become "folded into" their lives alongside older ones (albeit with effects that are hard to immediately discern). Bruce spoke, as he often seemed to, for many in saying,

> I don't think I have any less real-life friends because of my interaction on the Internet. . . . For me it's totally additive. It's just more interaction . . . it's a really neat opportunity.

In my research I did not detect a wholesale shift from one kind of technological mediation (e.g., reading, letter writing, face-to-face contact) to another (e.g., TV or Internet use). The people in both my "low-tech" and "high-tech" groups *all* reported using technologies in combination with one another as they form connections, *adding* technologies that are as high-tech as an individual feels comfortable with to the low-tech mainstays (writing, telephoning) that all subjects employed.

It is very much worth noting that some face-to-face encounters are rather impersonal and dissatisfying (Calhoun 1986: 335–38). When people feel that technology can ameliorate the impersonal aspect of some situation, they may forego face-to-face interaction for a mediated form (though, to be sure, they may forego face-to-face interaction because of laziness and seeking convenience as well).[13] Automatic banking machines, for example, save customers from the experience of waiting on a long bank line only to meet face-to-face with a teller who might not necessarily conduct the transaction as quickly and efficiently as a machine might; handling it—as is understandable—as a human being, not a robotic model of efficiency. Thus a simple banking transaction, limited in scope but potentially time consuming and bothersome to those who are used to speed and convenience,[14] might sometimes be more effectively handled by a machine. In situations such as these, technologies can "automate precisely those things that now depersonalize humans, those tasks that involve us only as automatons, in the colloquial, not the literal sense, and as potentially annoyed and annoying parties" (ibid., 337). Furthermore, when lengthy or unsatisfying tasks are technologically automated, people theoretically have additional time and energy to spend on more satisfying endeavors—and could conceivably spend *more time* building face-to-face communities, friendships, and families (though this is far from a guaranteed outcome, and another potential result is the deterioration, loss, or manipulation of human relationships).[15]

Interestingly, interpersonal sociability and connectedness are often positively correlated with media use. Media-disseminated ideas and information frequently serve as fuel for discussion—to persuade others, to gain prestige, and as fodder for "small talk," among other things—which can result in an increase in social exchanges, emotional support, interpersonal engagement, and sociability. Much use of media (especially radio, television and movie viewing, and computers) is in and of itself a social activity, which also can lead to face-to-face meetings and the development of relationships, as might be generated among members of fan clubs, for example.[16] Sometimes, technologies enhance face-to-face interaction.

Negative correlations between mass media use and sociability also have been found. These relatively fewer studies suggest, however, that it is usually in instances in which individuals use media to "escape" from real-world situations and interactions that they withdraw from face-to-face interaction as a consequence.[17] While collectively these findings may appear to contradict those that find media use positively associated with sociability, the contradiction can be at least partly reconciled by recognizing that motivations for and consequences of media use may differ because social actors are using them differently and thus are being differently affected. When people want to stay in touch with others, pass the time in the company of others, feel less lonely, and gain social support, they are at least as likely to utilize conversational aspects of computers and telephones as they are to communicate face-to-face (Flanagin and Metzger 2001). People are most likely to use those technologies which best help them satisfy their needs, gratifications and desires (see Flanagin and Metzger 2001; Turner, Grube, and Meyers 2001).

Most people desire and require face-to-face contact. Fears that modern technologies are displacing face-to-face communication, then, seem extreme and thus far unwarranted. Technologies have multiple and contradictory consequences; they are used by different people in different ways at different times.[18] The ways in which technologies transform social relations and social environments, then, will not *necessarily* be negative *or* positive, for "there is no *a priori* reason that different technologies, or even similar ones, need have congruent effects, nor that all their effects need to be consistent, nor that everyone or every society need react similarly" (Fischer 1985: 288). Rather than being "responsible for" particular things or social patterns, it may be more helpful to consider technologies as shaping and reshaping the contours of the social world in conjunction with one another *and* with face-to-face interaction.

When we form sociomental connections, we often sense that we are not alone, that others with whom we have much in common are "out there" somewhere, and that we are *in community* with them. My interviewee, E. J., describes what it is like for people to feel linked in this way:

> It's similar to going into a movie theater, huge crowd of people, and you're watching the same thing, not necessarily talking to one another or communicating with one another—but you are, just by your mere presence, and acknowledging each other's presence, and yet you're all focused on the movie. That technology links all of us together, even though we aren't communicating verbally. We're communicating in a pre-verbal sense.

As E. J. says so well, there is something in the acknowledgment of others' presences that connects people and even serves as a crude form of pre-verbal "communication."

If Auguste Comte is correct, and feelings of community are rooted in our nervous systems, then perhaps it is not surprising that the mass media, which Marshall McLuhan considered "extensions" of our nervous systems, should evoke a sense of community in such a deep-seated way.[19] When people become jointly engrossed in a communal experience, they experience a social world *together*.[20] As human beings, we need such experiences. In a deep, latent way we internalize a sense of one another's presences, of the mental networks that even link us to others who share our interests. We can come to feel, albeit on a tacit level, a free-floating sense of community, a comforting sense of belonging to a unit larger than ourselves.

In our technological world, a proliferation of mass media—books, magazines, newspapers, newsletters, online forums, and specialized television and radio shows—keeps most people well informed that they are not alone in their communal interests or tastes. Even the smallest newspapers or magazines, for example, draw fairly large numbers of readers (the very definition of mass media), and most readers know this. The mass media create large audiences for an endless supply of topics, ideas, programs, and personalities. Whether one follows a soap opera or a sport, a political ideology or an academic discipline, we know that there are many others who are similarly interested, maybe even involved, in much the same way as we are. We learn much about the audiences for these cultural products—the "others" in our communities—because media organizations want these products to become (and to be seen as) popular and successful. Information about popularity ratings is always available; fans are sometimes encouraged to take part in informal polls in various media to determine the "best" or "hottest" actor, show, or thing; audience responses and trends are publicly noted (see Fiske 1988; Gans 1988, 1974). We now know that many others share many of our interests, and that specific communities of the mind that coalesce around those interests can be discovered simply by switching on a radio, television, or computer, or by opening books, magazines, and newspapers.

By arranging one's life so that favorite media products are nearly always available—by habitually tuning into favorite programs or keeping favorite books on the nightstand—one need never feel that he or she is far away from the others that populate a social world and thus can avoid a certain type of social isolation. This can be accomplished deliberately if one has an awareness of these types of connections. My father, for example, recently discovered that audio recordings of books are available at the town library, and, in his semi-retirement from work, he treats himself to a continuous stream of them. Though he also reads voraciously, he now always has an audio book handy as well. "It's such good company," he says.

In these busy times, people will often be "cut off" from others or will feel somehow "out of sync" with them. Communities of the mind can help people become, and remain, "plugged into" a variety of experiences; a web of connections and a world of others instantly available. Participation in these communities can minimize the portion of their lives in which people feel "cut off" from others. Instead, they can feel surrounded by a "world" of others instantly available to them. As they are readily accessible, communities of the mind can provide a convenient and relatively stress-free way for modern individuals to make social connections, and for people who are necessarily cut off from others, such as the elderly, ill, disabled, or homebound, to feel much less isolated (Cerulo, Ruane, and Chayko 1992; Turner, Grube, and Meyers 2001). People who are introverted may prefer to form connections via technological mediation. Though, again, this would be troubling in the extreme, it also can be thought of as an ideal way to stave off certain unavoidably lonely moments.[21] Regarding her set of sociomental connections, Nicole says:

> I always have all these other people in my life, so I never feel lonely. And I always feel they're available. . . . It's not like I really miss my family all that much because I feel very connected to them. Like with [my friend] Joan . . . I don't really miss Joan, because I feel like she's always there anyway . . . I mean, I'd love to go for a walk with her and stuff like that, but I feel her presence. . . . It makes me feel safe. I feel connected.

Others share exactly how connecting online helps them feel less alone:

> Being on this Web site definitely always reminds me that constantly there are people . . . who really are crazy about [football] like me. (Rebecca)

> Just knowing you are all out there will help me feel better. (from the online literature group)

> I am not alone!!! Finding you folks is like coming home. (from the online soap opera group)

> When I found this discussion group, I was elated! It's just nice to know that I'm not alone, I should say *we* are not alone! (from the online soap opera group)

This sense of connectedness to others can become intensified when we not only sense that others are out there but become aware (as "elation" indicates) that we are resonating with them. As people become increasingly adept at "shifting" into alternate social worlds, especially those that may provide a strong sense of community, authenticity, involvement, and intimacy (such as those generated in serialization), the implicit terror that would be found in being "cut off" from the rest of the world at any given time can be greatly diminished. Indeed, the togetherness that we find and the reality that we "shift into" in these social worlds can be less precarious, less prone to disruption, and in certain ways more satisfying than the reality of everyday life (Goffman 1974: 439–95). This may be why when people feel a strong need to stay "in touch" with others, they often choose to use forms of mediated communication (such as the telephone, e-mail, and Internet messaging) rather than face-to-face communication—a finding that attests to the superior "distance-bridging ability" of such technologies (Flanagin and Metzger 2001: 172).

Sociomental connections in all of their forms can give connectors a real feeling of validation, a feeling that their interests (and selves) are solid and sound, and that there are others who feel as they do. When she forms sociomental connections in the reading of books, Mabel thinks:

> It's nice on a number of levels. It's nice to know there's a writer out there touching on some subject that's important to you. People don't like to feel alone with what they're thinking or what they're feeling or what they're doing. So if you have some author validate it, whether in fiction or nonfiction or an essay, you think, "Whoa." It's nice. You feel a little bit more secure. Because it's not "just me." You feel like there [are] other people that wonder about this, other people that worry about this.

In discussing online connecting, Bruce notes:

> I think it's validating. Someone else likes the same things I do.

Alicia tells me that one of the reasons she enjoys listening to talk radio is because she "likes to know that other people agree with me," and thus she feels her interests are validated. Engaging in a rewarding activity with someone who also finds it rewarding adds to our own sense of pleasure (Roloff and Solomon 1989: 292), and it may help us feel that there are people in the world who are like us and who understand us.

Tapashi tells me:

> [I like chat rooms because] you talk so freely without the face-to-face stuff. [People] understand what you mean when you say something; you don't have to go on and explain over and over what you're trying to say. When you just say it, they understand, really quick . . . [and] when someone understands what you're trying to say, really fast, it makes you feel like, OK, at least someone understands me.

For Rashima, getting "lost" in a good book can give her that feeling of being understood:

> [When I read books], it feels like others have gone through the same experiences that I have, and it just makes me feel better to know that someone relates to what I'm feeling.

Feeling "plugged in"—though often in a tacit sense—is certainly a prime benefit of sociomental connecting:

> If you don't [read the papers, listen to the radio, and watch TV], you feel like you're not plugged in, you feel like you're completely out of control, and it's almost like a spinning sort of situation. And what happens is, you feel out of touch . . . I despise that feeling. (Bill)

> If technology were for some reason to be just void, I think I'd be lost. I don't know what I'd do. (Jessica)

Sociomental connecting does introduce—for better or for worse—an element of control into the otherwise haphazard world of social interaction (which also is found in the use of caller ID or answering machines for screening out those with whom one does not wish to speak, without the other person even knowing that such "screening" has occurred). Controlling or "harnessing" sociomental connections is certainly one way in which people can manipulate interactions to satisfy their needs more precisely. Of course, this also can impede the development of other interactions that might be fruitful.

Community membership and connectedness, it should be remembered, is always a complex, and certainly not always a positive, thing:

> I am very angry at all of you . . . I specifically asked someone to give a quick synopsis of Wednesday's show and not one person responded to it. I thought we were all friends here. (from the online soap opera group)

> One thing that never fails to disgust me is the use of new technology to further hate causes. Hate groups are now using e-mail to threaten minorities in vast numbers. (from the online sports group)

[Online chat rooms] can get really frustrating. . . . There [are] people just like in physical social spaces who lack couth and restraint,
who come in to start an argument and be really antagonistic.
Those people come into a "real" room too. For example, if we were
in the room "Atheistic Existentialism"—and I don't even know if
there is such a room, I'm using an example—you could get a holy
roller come in and say, "You're all going to hell." Or in any political
room, you're going to get the right versus the left. (Mabel)

Connecting with others *always* brings the risk of troubling or unsatisfac-
tory outcomes (see Goffman 1983: 4).

Sociomental connecting should not be construed as a panacea that re-
duces negative aspects of interaction any more than it should necessarily
be considered a threat to positive interactions. Still, a nostalgia—
some would say a *hunger*—for traditional forms of community remains
(Rheingold 1993; Calhoun 1991: 114). When I recall seeing my brother,
sister, and parents every morning and evening around our kitchen table
when I was growing up, I do so with great fondness, especially since we
are now geographically separated from one another. But was I so fond
(and appreciative) of this—and of them—at the time? Of course not. The
forms of community that we are all experiencing—at this moment—will
become the nostalgia of the future. People often compare their lives to the
past (and the future), and find the present time wanting in some way
(Wright 1995).

To fully appreciate the effects of sociomental connectedness, we
might begin by stripping the concept of community of much of its normative tone. There is little to be gained by comparing sociomental structures
with face-to-face forms in some attempt to find them "better" or "worse"
in any significant way. All communal life has the potential to offer members a sense of belonging, of not being alone, of being understood, of
being harmed, of warmth and pain and, inevitably, of physical separation.
When social forms defined as "traditional" are seen as absolutely ideal,
those defined as modern must, by default, be considered problematic. It is
tempting to "mythologize the past as somehow better, more moral, more
human than the present."[22]

But life without modern technology was hardly utopian. Violence,
cruelty, and suffering have been hidden "behind closed doors" in even the
most closely knit, picturesque, upscale, and/or "tranquil" communities—in
both traditional *and* modern times.[23] Premodern life often was difficult
and short, characterized by barbarism, periodic starvation, slavery, incur-
able disease, and death (Wright 1995: 52). Poverty and homelessness were

rampant at the turn of the twentieth century and during the era of the Great Depression:

> [m]ilking cows was not just a direct—even tactile—contact with nature; it was also a fatiguing chore. Scything the grass or grain smelled good, but it made backs ache and was different from singing *Oklahoma* on Broadway. Net migration has been *to*, not *from*, urban areas, with their impersonal markets and bureaucracies. Indeed, one could say to those who long most for the tight, close ties of small communities in urban settings, unstained by modernity, "I sentence you to a week in the Middle Ages!" (Hernes 1991: 126; emphasis in original)

The premodern past looks rather coarse when "stripped of the gauzy romanticism of myth" (Kevles in Wright 1995: 52).

Our current era, of course, has its own unique difficulties. But many of the technological developments that characterize this age will, in time, become staples of social life, "folded in" with the rest of our lives, as the telephone has been. Future generations may look back on the development of the Internet and the connections it helped them form with a sense of nostalgia and fondness. Rather than idealize any form of communal life, then, let us conceptualize the sociomental domain as a social arena in which can be found cooperation or conflict, interdependence or independence, happiness or suffering—and, generally, some of each. Community may not be so much lost in the modern era as it is simply changed; liberated, in a sense, from spatial constraints.[24]

Emile Durkheim realized that "mechanical solidarity," in which ties of blood and similarity are sufficient to unite people, is not viable in modern industrial society. Rather, a "new" organic solidarity would be required to ensure social cohesion and integration. He hoped that this solidarity would emerge as a consequence of the interactions and interdependence found in certain "secondary" groups that would mediate between the individual and the political system in a society and produce a "cult of the individual" (1984 [1893]: xlii–xliv). Durkheim had in mind professional groups and associations which, he felt, could produce the same kind of solidarity as religious groups. He could not, though, have conceived of the kinds of technologically generated communities of the mind found in the modern era. Located as they are between the individual and the state, governed strictly by neither but influenced by both, and consisting of the collective ideas, interests, and sentiments of those who participate in them, communities of the mind are well situated to generate cohesion by affinity. They can help highly differentiated, urbanized, complex societies to structurally cohere and their members to become more fully integrated into them.

To paraphrase Mark Twain, reports of the death of community seem quite premature. We may be connecting in subtle, difficult-to-detect, and sometimes brand-new ways, but there is no need to see overall levels of social connectedness as necessarily in decline. As people discover that they have the ability to connect with others in a variety of previously unimaginable ways, they may find that they can satisfy *some* of their needs for togetherness and community with others mentally. They also should realize that they will not be able to satisfy every communal desire in this way. Lucas gives his view of the advantage of face-to-face interaction in business:

> Electronics won't replace in-person relationships in the business negotiation. Not even the phone or video conferencing can replace it. [Why?] Well, when you're negotiating to buy a company or something like that, or even negotiating price with a major customer, there's a lot of bluffing, there's a lot of reading emotion on the other person's face, and even video conferencing takes some of the personal interaction out. So we won't even attempt to do those kinds of things [electronically].

As a member of the online religious group states:

> As much fun as it is, we all still need to sit down with folks "in the flesh" and not become engrossed by this little world here.

As this person implies, the "trick" is to balance one's sociomental and face-to-face connections.

Community has always existed, and continues to exist, in a variety of forms: the hunter-gatherer tribe, feudal principality, Greek city-state, pre-industrial village, modern small town, and urban neighborhood, for example, all represent very different forms of community, each of which emerges in a certain social climate and time and is an expression of the culture of the people who constitute it.[25] None of these is inherently utopian; none has been entirely free of social stratification, prejudice, or tyranny. I suggest that we think of community as a dynamic phenomenon, a process subject to change, rather than a set of fixed, idealized arrangements. I also suggest that we think of the modern self in just as "flexible" a way, and that we cultivate mental flexibility in ourselves and in our children so that we may be better prepared to handle the complexities of modern life and modern modes of connecting.

RETHINKING THE SELF

Our cultural preoccupation with the self and with uncovering the qualities of one's identity is so seemingly prevalent that it is worth noting that such a concern is very much a modern Western social construction. Though the notion of an individualized self has been traced to the ages of Homer (Onians 1951) and St. Augustine (Taylor 1984), as of the late eighteenth century most people still tended to view themselves more as "exemplars of more general categories—members of a religion, class, or profession, or the like" than as individualized selves (Gergen 1991: 11; see also Lyons 1978). In cultures not predominantly literate, complex, or specialized, people tended to define themselves by that which they received from others, as opposed to the more modern mode in which the self is defined as that which is separate and different from others (Tuan 1982: 141–43). The modern, predominantly Western conception of the self came to the forefront throughout the nineteenth century, as urbanization, industrialization and transportation and communication technologies helped make freedom and opportunity (including the freedom and opportunity to shape a unique "self") accessible to many more people. Many non-Western cultures still construct nonindividualist conceptions of the self.[26]

We have come to think of the self as a fixed, singular entity, located in or accompanying a body, although the widespread belief in immortality indicates that many of us also see the self as something that can transcend the body, perhaps in the form of the soul. For Mead (1934), the mind is the locus of the self. As we learn to assume the attitudes of the groups of which we are part, or to which we are oriented as reference groups we begin to build a kind of "framework" upon which the self is constructed. In mentally regarding ourselves from the vantage point of particular or typified others, and either making accommodations to these others or resisting doing so, we develop a sense of self, or, perhaps more accurately, "multiplicities of self," representing different facets of ourselves.[27] Psychologists have even identified the phenomenon of *possible selves*, the multiple conceptions that people harbor of what they might become, would like to become, or are afraid to become (Markus and Nurius 1986).

Since others—many of whom we apprehend sociomentally—play such a large part in the development of the self, we can think of *any* self as a sociomental entity, an intrapsychic construct that develops in the process of becoming oriented to others sociomentally. The self has always been a dynamic entity with the potential for great change, but never more so than in modernity, when technology has quickened the pace of societal change *and* of self-development. The sociomentally constructed self is ever-expanding, increasingly differentiated, and distinctly individualized.

A mere century ago, people knew of comparatively fewer "others"; today, they are involved in making many more connections than ever before. These connections are more freely chosen and tend to be more widely scattered "around" the individual (in literal and in sociomental space) than in premodern times (in which one's social circles tended to be much more highly concentric). Now, membership in one social circle does not necessarily invoke membership in another (Simmel 1962 [1908]). This has real implications for the self.

The more communities of which we are a part (and of which we are aware and can use as reference groups), the greater the diversity of perspectives to which we will be exposed. Also heightened, then, are our opportunities to "take the role of others" (Mead 1934) and to use others as a "mirror" (Cooley 1964 [1922]) through which we can envision and construct identities. Our identities can become increasingly complex and multilayered. When communities of affiliation are freely chosen and not prescribed for us, we must take on the responsibility of creating and modifying this complex self, for the "community" cannot do it alone. The construction of self-identity thus becomes a lifelong journey in which people face "identity crises," gain and lose "self-esteem," and deal with "self-consciousness"—all in the pursuit of "self-actualization." The construction of the self becomes a project (not to mention a thriving set of medical, cosmetic, therapeutic, and "self-help" industries).

We must create a self without the "blueprint," or cultural codes, that traditional groupings used to provide for us (Merelman 1984). Membership in a Puritan community, for example, "told" you how to act, what to think, and who you were. With little competition among communities—for the family, the neighborhood, and religious and educational instruction were all likely integrated within the larger community—social boundaries were unambiguously fixed. It was easy to see what groups stood for, what they would require (in terms of time, energy, and loyalty), and where they began and ended—and the same was true for their members. The individual's duties and expectations were firmer in such a society. It would likely never occur to a person whose life was circumscribed by insular, concentric communities to spend a lifetime trying to discover "who am I?" The individual was probably, in many ways, not too terribly different from the others around him or her. With comparatively little opportunity to internalize perspectives from other groups, the members of such a community endlessly referenced one another, receiving feedback that was similar far more often than novel. They would all "take the role of" practically the *same other.*

Today, most of us have a far more diverse range of contacts and mental points of reference. According to Simmel, this expands our sphere of freedom (1962 [1908]: 130). We take on the roles of many others; our selves are highly differentiated, more heterogeneous. Individuals can, and generally do, become highly, perhaps inordinately, concerned with the development of identity. Lacking fixed, group-based guidelines, the boundary between the self and others is loosened, and thus we crave what we feel we need—a strong, cohesive sense of self (Merelman 1984: 30). For a self-confident, flexible, and open-minded person, this can be an interesting, even an exciting, search. For a person more vulnerable, however, it can lead to a kind of nightmare of ambiguity and anxiety, feelings of existential insecurity and rootlessness, a sense of disconnectedness to others and within oneself, and the possibility of exploitation as others perceive and capitalize upon apparent "weaknesses" (Merelman 1984: 31; Giddens 1990: 92–98).

As a multitude of mental lenses and reference groups are internalized by each modern individual, the horizons of the self are proportionally expanded (Shibutani 1955). The web of connections "surrounding" any given person will develop a pattern and shape so distinct (and so continuously changing and expanding) that it could not possibly be duplicated by another individual. No one shares the particular combination of communal affiliations as any other. The sociomental self, then, can be viewed as the point of intersection of many overlapping social circles, some of which represent communities characterized by face-to-face interaction and many more of which are communities of the mind, but all of which make possible a higher level of individuation than at any other time in human history (Simmel 1962 [1908]; see Zerubavel [1997:17–18] on the "web of sociomental affiliations").

As people develop many aspects, many "sides" to themselves (through identification with numerous reference groups), the process of identity construction becomes more complicated. People must take on a large number of roles simultaneously, displaying only "parts" of themselves in each situation and getting to know most of the others they encounter less "completely" than in earlier times. They may come to wonder whether others are presenting them with a "genuine" or "real" self, and thus may become guarded and mistrustful; they keep different "sides" of themselves hidden in different contexts (Goffman 1959). They also may feel less and less sure of "who they are" and more intent upon finding out.

This "loosely bounded" self is the result of the ability each of us now has to determine much of his or her own identity, the result of the reduced hold that any one group has on the individual. Rather than being determined in large part within a fixed set of groups that often greedily place demands on the individual (Coser 1974), selves are constructed as individuals join and identify with a wide variety of groups, often freely chosen. People may experience strain and conflict as they attempt to juggle and manage these roles, but their selves also have the potential to grow strong, well defined, and highly refined:

> It is true that external and internal conflicts arise through the multiplicity of group affiliations which threaten the individual with psychological tensions or even a schizophrenic break. But it is also true that multiple group affiliations can strengthen the individual and reenforce [sic] the integration of his personality. Conflicting and integrating tendencies are mutually reinforcing. . . . [They] may induce the individual to make internal and external adjustments but also to assert himself energetically. (Simmel 1962 [1908]: 141–42)

The modern self must become flexible enough to make the adjustments required to successfully navigate the many communities that influence it and "assertively energetic" enough to integrate these often contradictory "aspects" into an entity that coherently and viably represents that self.

We can envision the self as encompassing *multiple* states of being that are subject to change, as opposed to being singular and constant (Turkle 1997). People often adopt multiple personae on the Internet, especially in complex area such as MUDs, permitting them to explore, "try out," or even "communicate with" different aspects of themselves. Some invent entirely new identities, changing (or "playing with") their natural gender, race, or sexual orientation (see O'Brien 1999). Sherry Turkle's discussion of such personae is worth quoting at length:

> When people adopt an online persona, they cross a boundary into highly charged territory. Some feel an uncomfortable sense of fragmentation, some a sense of relief. Some sense the possibilities for self-discovery, even self-transformation. . . . A woman in her late thirties who just got an account with America Online used the fact that she could create five account "names" as a chance to "lay out all the moods I'm in—all the ways I want to be in different places on the system." Another individual named one of her accounts after her yet-to-be-born child. "I got the account right after the amnio, right after I knew it would be a girl. And all of a sudden, I wanted that little girl to have a presence on the net; I wrote her a letter and I realized I was writing a letter to a part of

me." . . . Online personae are objects-to-think-with when thinking about identity as multiple and decentered rather than unitary. (1997: 77)

We are accustomed to thinking of the self as unitary; the opposite of this, we may assume, is "insanity" and multiple personality disorder, in which an individual dissociates into several or many separate and distinct personalities. But there are other ways of theorizing the self. We can consider the self to exist normally in multiple states of being, expressed in various ways and, as Turkle puts it, "cycled through" (1997: 81–83).

It has always been possible to lie regarding one's physical appearance when connecting invisibly—whether via the telephone, a personal ad in a newspaper, or the Internet (for more on deception, see Chapter 5). The nature of the "lie" is now more potentially complicated than ever, as people distort a variety of personal characteristics in a variety of different ways, sometimes simultaneously, limited only by their own imaginations. They can even "mentally transgender or ungender themselves" (O'Brien 1999: 99). Surely such acts will traumatize or enrage those with rigid minds, but deception, recall, is a part of everyday life. How can we ever be sure (especially in these times of sex-change operations, plastic surgery, and digital image editing) that the person with whom we spend time *is* who we think he or she really is?

There do seem to be limits regarding how far and how fast most of us can process the alteration and multiplication of individual identity. Just as "the act of transcribing the binary may in fact reinscribe it" (O'Brien 1999: 99), it remains difficult to think about the self without using traditional categories such as those circumscribing gender and sexuality. Even when we bend these categories a bit, they only stretch so far and are still for the most part "snapped back into place" (ibid., 100). Though computers and computerized beings are becoming ever more "intelligent," taking on humanlike traits, a self still remains uniquely "embodied" in a human being who has certain types of traits.[28] We still form images of people in bodies when we connect with them. The fundamental categories we use to understand the self—gender being the primary one—are very difficult to disassemble; we can hardly think of or meaningfully connect to others without them.

This may not always be the case, however, as future connectors learn to handle ambiguity and the crossing of identity boundaries as a seemingly "natural" fact of life. Those who allow themselves to develop various aspects of their identities fluidly and creatively have the potential to develop a more highly differentiated self. If unsure how to comfortably cycle through and express these aspects, the self will have difficulty asserting and integrating itself. But if a multiplicity of selves or aspects of the self can be acknowledged and integrated, many more states of mind and manifestations of self can be considered "healthy" and within the realm of the normal (excluding those indicative of pathological and dissociative mental states, of course). The modern self might then gain much-needed validation as it struggles with the challenge of determining its own identity in a very complex world. And it—we—might even gain a kind of liberation from more rigidly conceived notions of self.

It is my contention, therefore, that the development of flexible-mindedness (for individuals and for a society) is optimal. A person whose mind is characterized by an appropriate level of flexibility is able to tolerate some ambiguity in the social world while still requiring and recognizing some structure, some boundaries. Rather than drawing hard and fast boundaries around communities (and experiences), such a person sees these boundaries as being at least somewhat permeable and movable and welcomes the access to additional mental perspectives. Mental flexibility permits the simultaneous development of a multifaceted individual and society while subverting neither to the other. It can assist in the balancing and management of the conflicts and tensions that inevitably arise in the modern world.

Rather than experiencing conflicts of social connection as a nightmare of competing obligations that force people to constantly pick and choose their alliances, the flexible minded can develop strategies to mentally shift among these contexts. Such people can reflect upon and consciously articulate their roles (and the expectations and obligations associated with them) and better learn to negotiate them. When choices must be made, they can be made more knowledgeably and freely. This enhances both growth *and* confidence, as different sides of one's self become more comfortably integrated. Ideally, previously "tangled" webs of connectedness may come to be experienced as a pleasurably diverse range of contacts.

When different aspects of one's self are permitted to emerge and are considered authentic, one can grow and change and one's self can be most fully realized. Mabel discovered this when her mother began to e-mail her from time to time:

> One day, I'm checking my e-mail, and it's mom, and I notice that she's forwarded to me this computerized version of a butt—a rear end—along with a joking comment from her. I couldn't believe it. I was incredulous. She has never been the kind of person who would joke about such a thing in person—too religious and straight-laced and motherly. And I thought—e-mail has given

her the opportunity to be the person she can't normally be in her suburban life. [Do you think that this was a genuine aspect of herself?] Oh yes. She can be more herself online—she's like a kid in a candy store. And she's becoming more liberated in real life, too, much more relaxed, and less judgmental. We both had a really great laugh about it.

As an individual becomes more flexible and aware of the positive and negative effects of connecting in a variety of ways, he or she becomes less of a conformist and thus less exploitable.[29]

We lose little, then, by considering the category of "that with which we can become bonded" flexibly (though, again, not recklessly or without some limits). To be sure, we are not used to thinking of normal selves as encompassing multiple personae or multiple states of being. Experiences and others we encounter mentally may seem unsettling, ambiguous, or unsafe—and sometimes, to be sure, they are. But modern life, with its complex role sets and webs of connectedness, challenges us to understand these new worlds, adapt to them, and live within them. In order to equip new generations with the adaptive tools they will need in a world in which technologies will only become more deeply ingrained in their lives, we may want to consider methods of *cognitive socialization* (Zerubavel 1997: 15–19) whereby we help people from youth to adulthood cultivate the mental flexibility that is so useful in the modern age.

Children need to be given clearly defined limits and to sense secure attachments—without them, they may experience a terrifying feeling of boundlessness. As the parent of any two-year-old knows, boundlessness (or a need to test the boundaries and limits of the world and of oneself) can be manifested in toddlers' simultaneous desire to cling to well-defined things and rules of order and to question and defy them. Even for the very young, there is much ambivalence and contradiction in the expression of individuality. An ongoing challenge, but one well worth undertaking, is to help young children learn exactly how to balance their need for attachment to their caretakers with their strong need for individuation.[30] This can help them think independently and more flexibly while not feeling abandoned, or feeling that they are abandoning others. When children are taught to think very rigidly (to color only within the lines, to play only with others of a particular race or gender), they learn to compartmentalize different aspects of the world into predetermined, preexisting mental "boxes." This denies all of the ambiguity and diversity that exists in the natural and social worlds, including the diversity of perspectives in a culture and a society and the "multiplicity of self" *within* ourselves.

Children need to separate from caretakers, teachers, and peers and develop their own multifaceted selves, yet know that they will still be accepted, loved, and cared for. For this to occur, we must expose children to different perspectives and encourage experimentation with boundaries and creativity while still expecting adherence to limits and rules.

When this balance is not achieved, extreme mental rigidity, or its opposite, a boundless "fuzzy" approach to life, is a likely consequence. Children may become intolerant of difference or excessively clingy or, conversely, they may develop a fear of intimacy. We must keep in mind that very young children usually are quite adaptable and can "take in" new experiences rather easily unless they are socialized not to. A balance of attachment and individuation is certainly achievable. Children can learn that the world is filled with diversity and change, yet they can feel safe exploring it and finding their own place within it (Zerubavel 1991: 47–51). And their selves can confidently develop.

As children grow older, previously established boundaries and limits become blurred. As they approach adolescence, there is an intense preoccupation with the body and the self and with belonging to peer groups. When they struggle with whether or not they will, for example, be accepted in their desired peer group, make the team, feel comfortable with their sexual orientation, or get into the college of their choice, they are struggling with the difficulty of developing (or maintaining) mental flexibility in an intensely rigid atmosphere. Facing rapid and monumental physical and social changes, adolescents may respond, as younger children do, with extreme rigidity or looseness, either compartmentalizing as many aspects of their life as possible (teasing those who are "different," joining cliques, clubs, and gangs) to bring some sense of order to a very chaotic time, or forgoing all sense of order whatsoever (and, sometimes, they do both!).

We can teach and cultivate mental flexibility in children, adolescents, and young adults, however. A clear and firm understanding of ever-changing rules, expectations, and experiences, within which space is left for dialoguing, negotiating limits, and earning the privilege of greater autonomy, is a useful approach (Shaw-Brachfeld 1998). The goal, as in young childhood, is the development of a combination of attachment and independence, but in a different ratio, one more appropriate to a given individual's age and maturity. When the attachment/independence balance is not met, these children may turn either excessively "inward" (developing an obsession with privacy and secrecy, a retreat into solitude, agoraphobia, or anorexia) or "outward" (exhibiting excessive aggression, hostility, or promiscuity—see Zerubavel 1991: 47–51). The ultimate goal, of course, is to help children draw their own distinctions and set their own limits with balance and *flexibility* in preparation for life in a highly complex world that will place great demands on them.

Excessive behavioral and mental "stiffness" or "looseness," if developed in childhood and adolescence, may persist in adulthood. Even in the adult years, though, people contain within them the ability to change their ways of thinking—and even change long-held mental models. We can stretch our "mental muscles" in new and different educational and intellectual pursuits. We can intentionally diversify our world, our experiences, and our social connections. We can challenge ourselves to master new technologies and understand different perspectives. And we can incorporate these new understandings into our definition of self. When we encounter a familiar boundary or limit, we can peek beyond it and allow ourselves to wonder without judgment or preconceived notion what life might be like "over there." And then maybe, occasionally, when we're ready, we might take a little mental trip across the boundary, a little flight of curiosity.

It is easier to write these words, I know, than to push beyond certain limits, particularly long-held mental boundaries, and to teach the very young to do so when we are not always so sure ourselves. Perhaps a reasonable first step is to try to become tolerant of what is different; the "other." Tolerance, when feasible, of whatever lies on the "other side" of a boundary is the first step in understanding it, and it need not necessarily lead to a crossing of that boundary or a full-fledged embrace of the difference. Instead, one might simply ask oneself when approaching a new situation or concept why *anyone* might be interested in such a thing or in living that particular way. One might conjure up as many responses to this as he or she can (thus really flexing the mental muscles)—and even involve other friends or family members in the exercise, making it a learning experience all the way around. New things (foods, music, hobbies, other cultures) can be tried in this way, step by step, one at a time, when it feels unthreatening to do so, and then can either be incorporated to some degree into one's own life, or not. Perhaps, at the very least, the "others" who live in different ways might come to be seen as not so completely different, not so strange, not so wrong.

But even all this is easier said than done. Attitudes and prejudices are slowly and deeply inculcated in our minds; they can be the product of decades of subtle socialization by a variety of agents. On the other hand, as we have learned, even deeply held mental models are subject to change under the right circumstances or when presented with compelling evidence (DiMaggio 1997). Our minds *allow for* flexibility. But often we must defy massive sociocultural pressures to resist rigidity. Many cultures and groups still "punish" mental flexibility in their members.

Mental flexibility, however, is very much alive: we see it every day in explorers, inventors, artists, scholars, and others who embark on the often difficult and rather brave journey to expand their mental horizons (Zerubavel 1993). Just as a child will ideally both attach to and separate from his or her parents, caregivers, and peers, the mentally flexible social member will ideally become a part of—and yet an individual who is separate from—many groups and communities. Connectedness can be felt and experienced in a multitude of ways and sites, resulting in an endless supply of mental perspectives that can be "tried on for size" and either integrated into the mind or rejected. Sociomental connectedness might then be able to be seen as just another form of connecting and just another source of connections—not so strange, not so false, not so odd. And a rich source of understanding and of connectedness can be thoughtfully incorporated into a fat, well-balanced portfolio of social connections.

As technologies become more sophisticated and more thoroughly folded into our lives, future generations of connectors will probably develop an unprecedented capacity for increasingly abstract modes of thought. They may become more flexible in envisioning, defining, and forming social bonds and their selves and may not feel compelled to force their conceptions of their selves and of others into categories that predate new modes of interaction. They will likely use technologies creatively to sustain many different aspects of the self and many types of relationships—some sociomental in origin, some face-to-face—simultaneously and easily, all of which would be framed simply, unremarkably, as authentic. In time, ours may become a more mentally flexible society in general, given to understanding, accepting, and inventing hybrid modes of thinking, behaving, and interacting.

In being exposed to a multiplicity of communities and mental perspectives, internalizing some and adapting others, flexible-minded individuals can create a fluid, highly unique identity. The limits that rigid thinking places on understanding the world eventually become limits that it places on its "self." But flexible thinkers challenge boundaries and limits when experiencing commonality with others and thus widen and deepen the process by which they develop their selves. And whole societies can be "knit together" of the varied, diverse connections that can result.

CONNECTING

None of us is used to thinking of connecting as a cognitive and emotional phenomenon. We are primed to think of the kind of interpersonal relations that do not originate in traditional settings as harbingers of an increasingly heartless world in which modern persons are hopelessly alienated from others and from themselves.[31] Indeed, feelings of community lost and social dislocation are quite real. Risks and hazards abound. But we also have the opportunity to "make visible" much more of the social fabric than has ever before been seen and studied and to help people make sense of their rapidly changing lives. We can rethink our notion of what it means to connect and to be social.

It is becoming less and less helpful, I feel, to delineate and decry the "differences" between mediated and face-to-face interaction. Both are part of the modern experience, and all communication, as we have seen, is mediated in some way, if only by the simple gesture or the spoken word. The mediated/face-to-face dichotomy owes as much to traditional systems of categorization as to intrinsic differences between these modes of connecting and hinders us in seeing the complex, composite ways in which social connections are made.[32] Rather than attempt to reconcile the differences between mediated and face-to-face communication, I suggest that we study the processes, experiences, and effects of all forms of connecting.[33] Toward this end, we might consider social connectedness to exist on a kind of "multimodal" continuum, recognizing that *all* social connections require some degree, some type, of mediation.[34]

I suggest that we begin to create this model of social connecting *not* by placing "face-to-face" and "sociomental" at opposite ends of this continuum but by considering first the perceived level of "reality" or genuineness of a connection. I suggest that we consider those connections experienced by a connector as undeniably authentic at one pole of the continuum (e.g., a heartfelt connection between infant and mother, author and reader, close Internet buddies, a god and a believer) and those that seem inauthentic (between people who only pretend to like one another, or people who are merely involved in a sales transaction) at the other pole. Each individual experience of connecting can be "placed" somewhere along this axis as we rate its "degree" or accent of reality and authenticity.

Then we can "open up the model," adding other axes and charting other properties of connectedness that have been identified here (the connection's strength, bidirectionality, and intimacy) and elsewhere along these axes. The degree of physicality inherent in a connection certainly constitutes another (very useful) axis with which to consider the nature of a connection, ranging from a high degree of face-to-face interaction to little or none. With a multidimensional model such as this, the face-to-face component can simply be seen as one aspect of the whole, one piece that intersects with others in constituting a whole relationship. Otherwise invisible, less detectable aspects of connecting can, with this model, be charted on axes right alongside that which represents degree of physicality—allowing for comparability and examination but not granting one axis primacy or superiority over another.

Of course, we can employ other models to conceptualize connecting. We might consider interactional life as a piece of music. Sociomental connections could be seen as the deep, low, ongoing "bass line" (or *baseline*) of social interaction in general, underscoring the infinite variety of melodies that can be imagined, performed, and improvised "upon" it.[35] In each melody different qualities of social connectedness would become evident at different moments, peaking at various levels. Though the bass line (sociomental connectedness) is necessary and fundamental, we would not want to conceive of music characterized only by deep, steady tones and rhythms, or only of piercing high notes. We would want to conceive of social life as a giant symphony consisting of endless movements and variations.

As the indispensable "bass line" or bedrock of interaction, sociomental connectedness can be envisioned as a kind of *mental infrastructure* for society. It underpins and makes possible many of its more visible aspects. It links us through our minds and our hearts, and it serves as the mental glue that keeps even face-to-face connections together in periods of absence. *It is in the intersection and structuring of our social connections—visible and invisible—that our societies are built.* Interlocking networks and webs of sociomental connectedness—characterized by varying levels of strength, reciprocity, authenticity, and intimacy, and by varying degrees of face-to-face interaction—undergird *all* sociation, reaching to the very core of a group and a society.

One of the most prominent characteristics of the modern age is its "tightened social framework, which has brought isolated regions and classes of a nation into society and has multiplied the degree of contact and interaction between persons through the revolutions of communication and transportation," as Daniel Bell (1973: 42) observes. As sociomental connections are numerous, with "webs" of connection widely dispersed "around" individuals, the likelihood of intergroup contact among people of very different backgrounds and types is high (Blau 1977). The mental pathways established by sociomental connectors permit information and influence to flow not only from person to person but from group to group, tying *all* members of the first structure to *all* members of the second (the "weak ties" of which Mark Granovetter speaks [1973]).[36] Weaker social connections "are indispensable to individuals' opportunities and to their integration into communities," Granovetter explains, pointing out that, in contrast, "strong ties, breeding local cohesion, lead to overall fragmentation" (ibid., 1378). Claude Fischer's research into urban networks also has demonstrated the integrative potential of the "instant" or "weak" contacts of urban dwellers, founded not on kin and tradition as much as on political and cultural interests and the like (1982). Offline and online, "weak ties are more apt than strong ties to link people with different social characteristics" (Wellman and Gulia 1999: 176), contributing mightily to the cohesion and strength of a society.

As sociomental connections are made and maintained, they help disparate parts of a society know of one another, share information and influence, and become linked, and it has never been more important that they do so. Many of the arenas in which people have traditionally "gotten together" no longer serve the same integrative purposes they once did. Neighborhoods and cities are increasingly fragmented and isolated from one another. They have become dwarfed by the size and complexity of the social (and economic) systems in which they are embedded, and their power to integrate societies is correspondingly reduced (Calhoun 1988: 239). As Rose Coser writes:

> Closely knit groups, even though they give individuals a feeling of security and a sense of belonging, have less survival value, at least in the modern world, than those that permit or encourage their members actively to pursue relations with individuals and groups on the outside and to orient themselves toward other institutions for their needs. This is because such *rigid conformity does not permit readaptation to changing circumstances and conflicting demands, which is what the modern world is all about.* (1991: 76; emphasis added)

As we continue to learn (and teach children) to understand and work with modern modes of connectedness, ideally the result will be a stronger society with members who are prepared to adapt to the many changes that they will undoubtedly encounter.

Traditional, multiplex, particularistic, *gemeinschaft* bonds are generally *ineffective* in creating opportunities for structural growth in our highly technologized world. Weak ties link people to a wider variety of others, which can open up increased opportunities. When people are a part of many groups with their roles segmented, they are "in contact with and therefore better able to understand [more of] the outside forces that [have] an immediate impact on their lives."[37] They are able to see and hear about things and learn things that they might otherwise have had little exposure to—and that might very well become critical to know. They forge the kinds of connections that can prove invaluable in the digital age.

A great deal of integrative "action" takes place on the Internet. People often demonstrate a greater willingness to respond to others' requests for help online than offline, in which they are hesitant to "get involved." The lack of status cues and the seemingly egalitarian nature of Internet life can encourage people with different social characteristics to come into a greater degree of contact than would be likely in face-to-face settings (Wellman and Gulia 1999: 176). The tightly integrated social systems that form in modernity "are only possible on the basis of sophisticated communications and transportation infrastructures which allow for the spread of indirect *relationships*," Calhoun notes.[38]

As people become more integrated into large-scale social systems, their lives become more globalized. Not only can they read and learn about distant others, they can see them via television or connect with them via the telephone or Internet. Communities with global reach formed online can foster an increase in connectedness that cuts across localities and states (Wellman 1997: 449). This can give a wider variety of people more direct contact with one another than ever before and a sweeping sense of togetherness with others a world away. It can also diminish the reach and influence of states and governments with respect to these communities.

We all make connections with absent others. Some of these are weak and some are quite strong. In reading, painting, and television viewing, in telephoning, writing to, and talking about those who are far away, we all have the potential to develop an expansive sense of togetherness with many, many people. Of course, we still crave and need the traditional mode of human connectedness. But side by side with face-to-face interaction, another way of connecting to one another has developed. Sociomental connectedness is an indispensable, defining characteristic of modern life.

In acknowledging this, and simply seeing sociomental connection as part of the everyday human experience, quite a lot can be gained. The social fabric is revealed as more densely "stitched" together; not quite so threadbare.[39] It may "be reassuring to "see" connections between us that we were once unaware of and that bond us to one another." We can question and study and value these connections and may make face-to-face contacts, in response to some of them. Simply put, we can make more thoughtful interactional choices. In time, more and more of us will likely become more flexible connectors, at ease with hybrid forms of connectedness and with the role that technology can play in our lives. With awareness and conscious intention, we can learn just how and when to—and when not to—access sociomental connections and communities: a powerful bit of knowledge to gain in a complex, technology-based society.

Individuals who are flexible and adept at sociomental connecting can, in effect, initiate connectedness and community at the touch of a button. They need to know, though, exactly what it is that they are doing, and so they should feel free to "own" and discuss such experiences, to become fully versed about hazards and benefits, and to learn the limits. Achieving a healthy balance of sociomental and face-to-face relationships at both the individual and societal levels is indeed a challenge in the Internet age. With education, demystification, and mental flexibility, though, we can take some firm strides toward this goal.

When people connect sociomentally, they will indeed be vulnerable to those who would use or encourage the creation of such connections for exploitative or dangerous purposes, but social life has always had, and will always have, exactly this element of risk. No one social form can be expected to be free of (or to heal) societal or personal ills. In exploring the potential of *all* social forms to inspire social connectedness, however, we can more knowledgeably observe both the bright and dark sides of sociation, help individuals respond to each more intelligently and, when we need to, repair and strengthen the social fabric.

Seen as a *replacement* for face-to-face interaction, purely mental "meetings" can certainly seem frighteningly futuristic, cold, and impersonal, but *there is no reason to expect that sociomental connections and communities of the mind need exist in any manifestation other than as a supplement to face-to-face forms.* Fears of "big brother" notwithstanding, humans have for millennia come together in a variety of ways, across time and great distances, and technology has made that possible. Continuing technological innovations ensure that our ability to connect with others in new and different ways will only expand. The challenge is to see that our understanding of the processes, experiences, and impact of connecting keeps pace.

In cultivating the mental flexibility necessary to conceptualize togetherness as a mental phenomenon, then, our understanding of social life is greatly enriched. We acknowledge the capacity of people to form connections in all of the "places" and ways that have meaning for them. We are more alert to the dangers. And we can begin to see our communities and societies as neither necessarily disintegrating nor prospering but as being created and recreated continuously, in endless moments of sociation and connection.

Many interesting and useful things can certainly be discovered in the study of social ties that are characterized by face-to-face contact, but hidden underneath and in the midst of these contacts, hundreds of invisible connections are made and maintained in our minds, touching our hearts and teaching us about the "other." These sociomental connections, bonds, and communities of the mind link us to one another and make us feel part of a whole even as we shroud them in darkness and mystery. It is my hope that in casting light on sociomental connections they can be seen as both commonplace and significant; an ordinary part of everyday life that can affect us more deeply than we might imagine. The most important of all human activities occur in the shared spaces of our minds: thinking, learning, caring, and connecting. As we begin to envision, examine and understand our sociomental connections, we banish some of the shadows from these spaces.

Appendix 1

Investigating the Sociomental: The Face-to-Face Interview Methodology

I used a two-pronged research methodology to investigate the sociomental phenomenon. In the primary branch of the investigation, which I outline in this appendix, I conducted fifty in-depth, semi-structured, face-to-face interviews in which I explained and gave examples of the concepts involved and then recorded all accounts of experiences of sociomental connecting. (The interview questions, along with a brief profile of these fifty individuals, follow.) It was my aim to gain the best possible qualitative "access" to people's states of mind and their feelings regarding these experiences. I supplemented these interviews with shorter, interactive question-and-answer surveys online with an additional 143 individuals in order to more completely understand the online connecting experience, which will be described in Appendix 2.

THE SAMPLE

To select the subjects I interviewed face-to-face I used a "snowball" sampling technique. This form of *strategic informant sampling* is generally used in studying very specific aspects of groups and societies. Its strength is the identification and characterization of distinct and particular social forms; its weakness is that results are not universally generalizable but rather are illustrative of concepts and constructs. In strategic informant sampling, the interviewer builds up a sample by hand selecting a small number of people to interview and then asking those initial subjects to supply names of other potential subjects. From there, the potential pool of interview subjects "snowballs." Subjects are subsequently selected for demographic and/or substantive reasons to create a group that is as diverse as possible given the needs and conditions of the study. When the data form a cohesive whole, and when criteria for the study are met, sampling ceases (see Smith 1975: 117–18). As my goal was to characterize distinct social forms and concepts that have been relatively unexamined and thus fundamentally in need of illumination and illustration, this method served my objectives well.

My priority for the sample was that it consist of people with varying levels of technological sophistication, as technology plays such a critical role in the formation and maintenance of connections when the individuals involved are not physically present to one another. Therefore, when potential subjects were referred to me, I assigned them to one of two sampling groups based upon subjects' general level of technological sophistication—what I called the "low-tech" and "high-tech" groups. I interviewed twenty-five people whose use of technology was relatively rudimentary: they were less than comfortable using emergent technologies and had not, at the time of the interview, embraced the potential of the computer as a tool of interpersonal communication (some used it merely for word processing or record keeping, and some did not use it at all).[1] I also interviewed twenty-five people whose use of communication technology was more sophisticated: they were fluent in using the most up-to-date technologies and embraced them rather easily, including using the computer to access the Internet and to make cyberspace connections (e-mail, computer messaging, chatting, gaming and/or conferencing) with other people.

I also wanted to achieve a range of gender, racial and ethnic backgrounds, ages, levels of educational attainment, marital statuses, and occupations in my sample so that the experiences people related to me would not be unduly limited in scope. As the selection of subjects progressed, I would increasingly select subjects to achieve the greatest diversity practicable in each of these categories, given the limits of strategic informant sampling (the interviewer has no demographic control over the subjects to whom he or she is referred) and the resources of the project (I was only able to study people in those regions in which I lived, worked, or could visit, and thus the sample, and the study, comprises Americans and their attitudes and lifestyles only). Within these limits, I selected the most diverse sample possible.

The sample had a gender mix of 56 percent females and 44 percent males. It had a racial mix of 52 percent Caucasian individuals and 48 percent people with backgrounds that would be considered of minority status in the United States—22 percent African American or mixed race/part-black identification, 14 percent Hispanic or Latino, 8 percent Asian, 2 percent (one individual) Native American, and 2 percent West Indian. Agewise, the sample spanned ages seventeen to sixty-eight and skewed toward the under-forty demographic—just over three-quarters (76%) of the subjects were between ages twenty-one and thirty-nine, two individuals (4%) were under twenty-one, and one-fifth (20%) were between ages forty and sixty-eight (incidentally, all six of the subjects over age forty-five fell into the "low technology" category). The median age of the sample was twenty-nine. Educational attainment ranged from the Ph.D. level (one individual—2%) to only some high school completed (also one person, 2%), with the remaining subjects distributed in this way: high school completed, 24 percent; some college completed, 6 percent; bachelor's degree completed, 50 percent (the median level); some graduate school, 6 percent; master's degree, 10 percent. 56 percent of the sample reported being unmarried, and 40 percent were married, with two individuals (4%) indicating that, although single, they cohabit in a long-term, committed relationship. Finally, a number of very different occupations are represented in the sample (see "Profiles of the Interviewees" at the end of this appendix), with no one occupation claiming four or more practitioners among the sample. In excerpting these interviews, I protect the confidentiality of each subject by assigning him or her a pseudonym (which, in all cases, is simply a first name; also, people to whom subjects refer in their discussions are either given pseudonyms or the names excised). I also report all occupations generally enough to protect subjects' identities, occasionally altering some nonessential detail of the individual's occupation or stated interests if doing so seemed important in maintaining confidentiality, and I assured subjects I would do so when reporting or publishing results.

THE INTERVIEWS

The interviews were conducted during the approximately two-year period between June 1995 and July 1997. They took place in and around the town of New Brunswick, New Jersey, where Rutgers, the State University of

New Jersey, is located, and in various towns throughout northern and central New Jersey. Sixteen interviews were conducted in Champaign, Illinois, near the University of Illinois, where I spent some time during the course of the research. Interviews lasted anywhere from approximately fifty minutes to over three hours, an average of about an hour and a half, although frequently either the interview subjects or myself would reestablish contact to follow up on one issue or another. I asked each subject the questions listed here, straying beyond the script to ask follow-up questions, to clarify responses, and to pursue interesting avenues. I spoke with people in their homes or workplaces, or, occasionally, at my home. I tape-recorded interviews with permission in all instances, took notes, and later transcribed the tapes myself, in some cases editing them lightly for publication clarity only.

I had little difficulty finding people who were willing to be interviewed. Most were extremely forthcoming and thoughtful and, as I have mentioned, declared the experience valuable, helpful, even emotional. I was asking people to look at social connectedness in a new and different way and to recognize and evaluate the strength and nature of social connections and mental processes that might have been only tacitly felt and experienced prior to the interview. This required the subject to actively consider some rather complex issues as we spoke, and they did; all but two, in fact, shared very personal thoughts, ideas, and memories. Two interviewees had somewhat more difficulty doing so.

As the following general questionnaire indicates, I asked individuals to consider various "permutations" of connectedness. I prompted them to think about social bonding more broadly and flexibly than they might have ever done before, and to think about a full spectrum of connections and bonds that could be formed in the absence of face-to-face copresence. I began to discover *whether* and *how* people experienced these ordinarily "invisible," often unrecognized connections. I also asked them some general questions about the role that they felt technology was playing in their lives to get a sense of how they were thinking about some of the larger issues involved.

I used the following questions as a guide in structuring the fifty face-to-face interviews:

I. BACKGROUND INFORMATION

What is your name, address, and phone number? What is your age, marital status, and race/ethnicity?

What is your occupation, level of schooling?

To what extent do you use technological devices in your job? Which ones? How are they used? How comfortable are you with them?

Think of some of the different broad interests and affiliations you have, whether personal or professional, serious or frivolous. These may be in the area of religion, politics, education, your job, hobbies, leisure activities, and so on. To what extent do you use technological devices as you pursue these interests? Which ones? How are they used? How comfortable are you with them?

Approximately how much do you use the following technologies, and for what purpose: computers? television? radio? magazines? newspapers? Do you read many books?

Do you tend to use each of these technologies when you are by yourself, or with others? Why?

II. GENERATING A LIST OF FACE-TO-FACE SOCIAL CONNECTIONS REPRESENTING VARYING DEGREES OF CLOSENESS

Is there someone in your life with whom you feel very close but rarely see face-to-face? Who? How do you know him or her?

Is there someone you see quite often face-to-face but do not feel particularly close to? This should *not* be someone you have any kind of intense feelings for, either positive or negative, but someone you feel fairly "neutral" toward. Does anyone like this come to mind? Who? How do you know him or her?

Is there someone you once knew well but with whom you have now broken off ties? Who? How did you know him or her?

III. QUESTIONS ABOUT EACH OF THE INDIVIDUALS NAMED ABOVE

How did you meet _____? Was it face-to-face or via mediated contact, such as the phone, e-mail, and so on? How long have you known him or her?

About how often do (did) you have contact with _____? To what extent does (did) it tend to be face-to-face and to what extent via notes, letters, phone calls, fax, computer? (Itemize)

Does (did) your contact with _____ follow any kind of routine or pattern—even loosely?

Do you tend to talk or otherwise communicate about certain topics with any consistency? What kinds of topics? Do you talk together in any special kinds of ways—do you use special words or phrases, and so on?

Do (did) you talk much about your relationship with _____ with anyone else, any "third persons"? If so, with whom, and about how often and to what extent? What kinds of things do you tend to discuss?

When you are neither in touch with _____ nor talking *about* _____, do you think about him or her very much? About how much and to what extent? What usually prompts you to think of _____?

Do you keep any photos, gifts, objects, or mementos that remind you of _____ around where you can see them on a regular basis? Are there any songs that remind you of _____? Do you dream about _____ much?

Do you feel that any of these activities perpetuate a sense of connection to _____? How so?

Can you describe your sense of connectedness to _____? How does it make you feel? What does it do for you?

Would you consider _____ and yourself to be members of any kind of community together? I am thinking of community broadly here, as a set of people with something in common that has meaning for them and that gives them a "sense of belonging" or "sense of community"—whether or not they see each other much, or at all.

How close (if at all) would you say that you and _____ are? Explain.

Would you consider this a relationship? A mutual relationship? What makes you think that?

How long do you think your connection to _____ will last? Do you expect that your degree of closeness to _____ will change?

IV. ADDITIONAL QUESTIONS SPECIFICALLY ABOUT PEOPLE WITH WHOM SUBJECT HAS BROKEN OFF TIES

How exactly did your relationship with _____ end? Was it gradual or sudden? Mutually decided or not?

Was a technological medium such as a phone, letter, or computer used? If so, how?

Did you or do you continue to know of ____ through a third person or through some other means? Explain. How much and to what extent did (do) you continue to know of ____ ?

Did you or do you continue to think about ____ ? About how often and to what extent?

Do you think you will try to reestablish the connection some day? Why or why not?

V. Generating a list of sociomental connections

Do you ever have a sense of being connected, in any way at all, to any family members who live far away and whom you have never actually met? Who?

Do you ever have a sense of still being connected to family members who have passed away? Who?

Do you ever have a sense of being connected in any way at all to any of your ancestors? Who?

Have you ever had a sense of being connected to an unborn child—either your own or someone else's—perhaps a family member or a close friend's? Who? Did that bond "continue" after the baby's birth?

Are there other people you have never met but who share the same affinity for ____ (a particular interest) that you do, and to whom you feel connected in some way? Who?

Are there people you have never met but whom you have come to feel you know as a consequence of your work? Who?

Are there any people who have lived in the past and are no longer alive but of whom you are aware of sharing the same interest for ____ (particular interest, work) that you do, and to whom you feel connected in some way? Who?

Have you ever belonged to an organization or association that gives you a feeling of fellowship among its members? Do you also feel that fellowship with members you have never met?

Have you ever felt a sense of connectedness to a television or movie actor—a sense that you perhaps kind of "know" him or her? Who? Have you felt connected to a person you have heard on the radio—either a broadcaster or caller to a talk show? To a musical performer? To an artist? To an author?

Have you ever felt connected to a fictional character in a book, TV show, or movie, so that you care about what happens to the character and feel connected to him or her?

(If applicable) Have you ever developed a connection with someone solely on the basis of e-mail or computer use? Who?

VI. QUESTIONS ABOUT EACH OF THE SOCIOMENTAL CONNECTIONS NAMED ABOVE

Can you describe this "sense of connectedness"? What does it feel like?

How did it develop?

Was technology involved in the development of the connection? How?

Do you feel that this connection is strong enough to be considered a "bond"? Explain.

About how often do you think of this connection (bond)?

Would you consider _____ and yourself members of any kind of community together? Again, I am thinking of community broadly here, as a set of people with something in common that has meaning for them and that gives them a "sense of belonging" or "sense of community," even though they may have never met.

(If possible to meet face-to-face) Why haven't you met _____ face-to-face? Do you want to? Do you think you will? Why or why not?

(If possible to have technologically mediated contact) Have you ever tried to contact _____ through a technological mediator such as a letter, phone, computer, and so on? When? How? Or, why not?

(If applicable) Do you ever read or hear about _____ in newspapers, books, magazines, newsletters, computers, or over radio and TV? Give examples.

VII. SOME GENERAL CONCLUDING QUESTIONS

How do you manage to sustain your various social connections, bonds, relationships, and social circles? Do you use technological mediators a lot?

Do you meet face-to-face a lot? Do you talk about other people and think about them a lot? Please explain.

What is your general feeling about technology and the way it affects your life? Does it make it better or worse, and in what ways? How about your relationships—do the kind of technologies we've been talking about today affect them? If so, how?

Is there anything you would like to ask me, or talk about, regarding the interview, technology, or your social connections or relationships?

Can you think of anyone you know who might like to or be willing to be interviewed by me on this topic?

PROFILES OF THE INTERVIEWEES

Here I provide a brief profile of the fifty individuals with whom I conducted in-person, face-to-face interviews. The names given here are pseudonyms, and occupations are stated generally (and in some cases, altered slightly) to ensure subjects' privacy and confidentiality. Again, I divide them into "low" and "high" technology users; there are twenty-five subjects in each category.

LOW TECHNOLOGY USERS

These individuals are, in general, less comfortable with computer technology than their counterparts in the "high technology" group, using computers (if and when they do use them) only for word processing or other applications required in a "low-tech" job. If they have used the Internet, they do so only rarely and somewhat experimentally and had not, at the time of the interview, fully integrated e-mail into their routines. Most people in this category do not use computers at all.

Anita, 22, single, Hispanic. She has a bachelor's degree and intends to attend graduate school and become a social services worker. Anita loves Spanish and English soap operas and regularly reads a Spanish language magazine that helps her feel connected to the Hispanic community. She is not very comfortable with most technologies—even VCRs.

Bill, 40, single, African American. He has a bachelor's degree and works in the broadcasting industry. Bill enjoys using technology in general—radio, TV, magazines, newspapers, books, and computers for word processing—but has not gotten involved in e-mailing or using the Internet due to being "too busy to learn now."

Brian, 25, single, Caucasian. He is currently attending graduate school in mathematics. He considers himself a moderate television viewer and reader and uses advanced technologies primarily in mathematics and in pursuing his interest in astronomy.

Caitlin, 32, married, Caucasian. She has a degree in nursing and works as a nurse in a hospital. She is only comfortable with technology at work and does not want to keep a computer around the house—"I'm afraid of what the kids could get into." She watches a lot of television and reads and writes letters occasionally.

Carlos, 24, single, Hispanic. Carlos has a master's degree in social work and works as a college administrator. He is a big fan of sports radio, talk radio, jazz, and health and fitness and simply has not yet become involved in Internet technologies.

Claire, 34, married, Caucasian. A high school graduate, Claire works as a typist. She is not very comfortable with technology, though she must use a computer at work, but she says, "We haven't had the need for one at home, and then there's the expense." She enjoys watching TV shows at night with her husband and following her strong interest in music through the radio and recordings.

Eddie, 37, married, Caucasian. He is a high school graduate who works as a municipal clerk. He and his wife watch television with their family a lot in the evenings, and he also enjoys listening to the radio during the day— talk radio mostly. He is not interested in the computer, he says; he likes to write "with his hands."

Elizabeth, 17, single, Caucasian. Elizabeth is a high school student who enjoys using computers at school but has not had a chance to learn how to go on the Internet yet. She prefers TV and radio to print media and also goes to the movies a lot.

Gerard, 65, married, Caucasian. He is a high school graduate and retired contractor. The radio and newspapers are his favorite media, especially to follow his interests in the world of music. He sees no use for computer technology in his life.

Grace, 22, single, African American. Grace is a college graduate looking for work as a model to finance graduate school in the future. She reads magazines and books "all the time," listens to the radio much more than she watches TV, and is comfortable with computers but has just begun learning about and using the Internet.

Howard, 68, married, Caucasian. He graduated from high school and is a retired farmer, who enjoys television, radio, and newspapers and does not intend to learn about computers.

Janice, 56, married, Caucasian. She attended some college, did not graduate, and works as a secretary. Janice loves movies, books, writing letters, and traveling to see her friends face-to-face. She just got a computer and plans to learn to use the Internet "when I have time."

Joanne, 22, single, African American. She has a master's degree and is a teacher. She uses computers for work but has not felt ready to "take the plunge" and dive into the Internet. Joanne is comfortable with other technologies and uses them all moderately, including writing letters fairly often.

Joe, 27, single, African American. He has a bachelor's degree and works as an accountant. He uses technology mostly to follow sports on TV, radio, and print media. He does not use the Internet because he "doesn't really have the time."

Kara, 35, married, Caucasian. A college graduate, she is a radio talk show host who keeps up with current events via television, radio, magazines, and newspapers "constantly." She has not yet begun to use the Internet to help her stay informed but plans to do so some day.

Keith, 41, married, Native American. A high school graduate, Keith works in air conditioning and heating repair. He is not a big technology, computer, or electronic/print media user; he watches some TV but only "occasionally and spontaneously" and prefers to get together with friends.

Kim, 46, married, Asian. She graduated from high school and did not go on to college. Kim cleans people's homes for a living. She likes staying active and prefers "doing things" to sitting around watching TV or using a computer. She likes to read, though.

Linda, 40, married, Caucasian. She is a high school graduate who owns her own day care center. Linda's favorite medium is television, but she does not overindulge; she prefers staying active and being with people face-to-face. She is planning to buy a computer to help her organize her business but is still deciding what she needs it to do.

Louise, 36, married, Caucasian. She is a high school graduate who is a foster parent and does not have a job outside of the home. Louise loves to read and write stories and letters, and she watches some TV and listens to the radio "a bit." She cannot currently afford a computer with Internet access, she says, nor can she afford the service.

Nicole, 29, single, Caucasian. Nicole has a master's degree and works as a counselor. She enjoys watching her favorite television shows and listening to National Public Radio, likes reading books, and does a lot of reading for work. She sees no immediate need for "complicated" computer technology in her life.

Nora, 64, married, Caucasian. A high school graduate, Nora is a homemaker and a former cosmetician. She loves books and listening to music on the radio, and she travels to see her family in Ireland as often as possible. She sees little reason to become computer literate.

Randy, 39, single, Caucasian. Randy is a college graduate who is a high school athletic coach. He watches approximately four to five hours of television a day and enjoys reading books and publications related to his job and his interest in aviation. He has tried e-mail twice but does not currently have "the money or the inclination" to become more computer sophisticated; he plans to "get into it" someday, and in the meantime, he writes a lot of letters longhand.

Roger, 36, married, Caucasian. He is a high school graduate and construction worker. He loves watching sports on television and his favorite shows with his family, and he listens to sports radio a lot. He considers the computer too expensive to be feasible to own and use.

Rosa, 22, single, Hispanic. She is a college graduate who is working as a paralegal. She loves listening to the radio, watching TV talk shows, and enjoys Hispanic/Latina magazines and actresses and singers, and she is not comfortable with any kind of sophisticated technologies, including computers.

Sally, 68, married, Caucasian. She is a high school graduate who is a homemaker. Sally enjoys watching television, especially shows about painting or arts and crafts, and listening to music, on the radio or on her stereo. She will not be learning to use a computer and does not need to, she insists.

HIGH TECHNOLOGY USERS

These individuals are very comfortable in general with computer technology. E-mail is an integral part of their communication system, and they are comfortable using the Internet and digital technology for work, leisure, or both.

Alicia, 39, married, African American. A college graduate, Alicia owns her own day care center. Alicia loves technology—she plays computer games to relax, listens to the radio about an hour a day and calls in to talk shows when she feels passionately about the topic, reads magazines and responds through letters to them as well, and has had an "e-mail pen pal." She says that the television is constantly on in her home, "no matter what I'm doing; I fall asleep with it on in the background," but she rarely just sits and watches it.

Annie, 30, single, Asian. She is a graduate student in psychology who works in a counseling center. She uses computers much more for work than for fun, and "when I get the chance, I watch TV as much as possible." She is a big believer in e-mail and does not have the time to use most other media at all.

Bruce, 30, married, Caucasian. He has a Ph.D. and is a college dean. Bruce thoroughly enjoys using the Internet, especially for e-mail and news groups, and he loves to "follow" his interest in music with the computer, TV, radio, magazines and newspapers, and by playing recordings at home. He also watches "a great deal" of TV news and sports, listens to a lot of talk radio, and likes to read.

Cindy, 33, single, Caucasian. She has two master's degrees and is working in the computer industry, using computers "90 percent of the time at work." She also uses the Internet for fun, reads books and magazines a great deal, and watches some television.

E.J., 21, single, of mixed race. He is a college graduate who writes and illustrates an "underground" newsletter. He used to enjoy video games but now prefers surfing the Internet and watching television (especially on weekends). He also listens to the radio much of the day and has little interest in "mainstream" print media. He uses a computer to lay out and prepare portions of his publication.

Elise, 26, single and engaged to be married, Caucasian. Elise has a master's degree and works as a lab technician. She has weaned herself off of extensive Internet use (she once spent many hours a day on a MUD) but still enjoys e-mailing and surfing the 'Net. She considers herself a moderate user of other electronic and print media.

Gino, 29, married, Caucasian. He is a college graduate who works as a research analyst. Gino uses electronic technological devices "all day long," he says, including a lot of radio, television, computer, and video games; "I even prefer electronic music to acoustic."

Jeremy, 23, single and engaged to be married, Caucasian. He has a bachelor's degree and is attending medical school. The Internet is the primary technological "filler" for what little leisure time Jeremy has, spending an hour or two a day on the 'Net and watching little TV (he mostly watches the news). He also reads a few magazines weekly and occasionally reads books; he listens to the radio only in the car.

Jessica, 21, single, of mixed race. She is a college graduate who is working in retail sales. Jessica watches two to three hours of television a day and listens to radio more than three hours a day (she prefers the music stations). She only "flips through" magazines and newspapers. She is completely comfortable with computer technology and also enjoys reading books a great deal.

Jose, 23, single, Hispanic. He is a recent college graduate who is looking for work in management. Jose likes using the computer (but not for "chatting"), enjoys about an hour a day of television news and talk shows, and loves to watch basketball games on TV over the weekend. He does not read much, except for work and school purposes.

Ken, 29, single and engaged to be married, Asian. He has a master's degree and works as a management consultant. He watches television and listens to the radio a couple of hours a day each and reads much less (except when work related). He uses computers in most aspects of his life.

Ling, 22, single, Asian. She has a bachelor's degree and is hoping to attend graduate school in the sciences soon; she now works part time in a chemical lab. She often uses sophisticated technologies in the lab and has come to love technological "gadgets" of all kinds. She watches television most nights and has the radio on all day, and though she feels very comfortable with computers and e-mailing, she wants to learn much more about computers.

Lucas, 44, married, Caucasian. He has a college degree and is a vice president of marketing for a large company. He uses the Internet, video conferencing, and other computer technologies for almost all aspects of his job, and he enjoys using computers during his leisure time as well.

Luis, 22, single, Hispanic. A recent college graduate, Luis is looking for work in the recording industry. He is skilled in the use of music and recording technology (including using computers for this purpose), uses the Internet frequently (especially e-mail), "loves" TV (it is on "all weekend"), and listens to a lot of radio and music via recordings. He does not use print media nearly as much; "I'd have to be really interested in something."

Mabel, 25, single and living with a partner in a long-term relationship, Caucasian. A college graduate, Mabel works as a freelance writer and researcher. She is an almost constant user of technology and the media. Her television is on "almost continuously" at home, she says, often while the stereo is on *and* she is spending time on the Internet as well. She enjoys e-mailing, chatting, and visiting different Web sites, reads a newspaper every day and magazines "all the time," and adores reading books.

Maria, 29, married, Hispanic. She has a college degree, is currently studying for her master's in social work, and is an office manager. She uses computers for work and leisure, watches television two hours a day, listens to the radio in the car, and enjoys books and Hispanic magazines, but she does not read the newspaper much: "It's too depressing."

Rashima, 23, single, African American. She has a bachelor's degree and is working as a sales representative. She does not watch much television, listens to the radio "more so than TV," and enjoys reading magazines and books from time to time. She is not completely comfortable with computer technology but has made extensive use of e-mail over the last couple of years.

Roy, 28, single, Caucasian. Roy is a college graduate who works in a library. He is extremely fluent in computer use, loves to read all print media, and enjoys television as well. He also takes part in a fantasy football league, the progress of which he uses various media to track.

Rebecca, 28, single, Caucasian. A college graduate, Rebecca is a secondary school teacher who uses computers to design CD-ROM games for her students. She also loves television, movies, and surfing the 'Net, especially to follow her favorite sport, football.

Rhonda, 23, single, of mixed race. A college graduate, Rhonda is currently looking for work in the field of communications. She knows how to use computers, participates in Internet groups, and uses e-mail, though she prefers the telephone. She watches five hours of television a day, listens to music on the radio "all day," and subscribes to about ten magazines. She also loves books, especially fiction, and reads newspapers.

Ricky, 24, single, Hispanic. He has a bachelor's degree and he works as a college administrator. Ricky enjoys using computers, though not for "chatting," and he works so many hours that he has little time for television or surfing the 'Net. He listens to the radio mostly in the car and likes to read.

Tapashi, 19, single, West Indian. Currently a college student, Tapashi loves using the computer for schoolwork, research, and fun, enjoys e-mailing and chatting over the Internet, and watches "too much TV," she says—up to three hours a day. She does not read many magazines or newspapers but does love to read novels.

Tom, 25, single and living with a partner in a long-term relationship, Caucasian. Tom has a college degree and is a news editor. He follows and tracks most of his interests on the Internet and generally makes full use of computer technology, including e-mail and the "chat" and Usenet features. He watches television for a couple of hours a day, reads magazines, newspapers, and books often, and enjoys music or politically oriented talk shows on the radio.

Tonya, 25, single, African American. Tonya has a master's degree and is a social services worker. She enjoys e-mailing and using the Internet and also watches television, listens to the radio, goes to movies, and reads books and magazines— "No *National Enquirers*, though."

Ugo, 21, single, African American. He has completed some college and is currently working part time in a UPS-type mailing and shipping organization, and is looking for work with a newspaper. Ugo watches three to six hours of television a day, listens to music on the radio three or four hours each day, and browses through newspapers every day and magazines nearly every day. He enjoys the Internet, including the chat rooms, and loves reading books.

Appendix 2

Cyberspace Connecting:
The Online Survey Methodology

In order to understand more completely the process of connecting via the Internet, I familiarized myself with six different types of online discussion groups (also called bulletin boards, message boards, news groups, forums, or list serves).[1] I was concerned with discovering how people create connections and communities online, how they define and experience them, and the impact on the individual participating in them. In each group I observed the nature of the interactions, elicited subjects to describe and explain the phenomenon of cyberspace connecting (especially within the group) to me, and noted responses, relevant comments, and "threads" of discussion.

I found that online research has both benefits and drawbacks. On the positive side, large numbers of people can be easily reached in a way that is both cost-effective and user-friendly. Generally nonintrusive—no one's dinner is interrupted by an unwelcome phone call—responses can be given at leisure and are purely voluntary. A team of interviewers need not be hired and trained. One has access to individuals who otherwise might be difficult to recruit, and respondents often are especially honest in their anonymity and even feel good about participating, according to Steve Cook, senior vice president for Greenfield Online Research Center in Westport, Connecticut. "We don't get a lot of pattern answers, which indicates that people take the time to think about the questions," he observes. "And we get incredible open-ended comments" (Edmondson 1997: 12). Online surveying, however, does not lend itself to long, complex surveys, cannot be assumed to be representative of non-Internet users, and does not allow for the verification of visible aspects of subjects' identity.[2]

I used online research, therefore, in a secondary sense to complement my primary face-to-face interview method and to tell me more about the high-tech "end" of sociomental connecting. I used short surveys to obtain specific information about cyberspace connecting and technology use. And I sought to achieve a sample which, like my primary sample, was as diverse as possible.

THE GROUPS

Of the countless groupings that form on the Internet, I chose six rather different types. My primary criteria was that they center around interests about which people feel strongly in order to enhance the possibility that some kind of connections would be formed within them (which I could then observe and analyze). I also chose groups with disparate demographic and qualitative profiles to span the spectrum of the online (and general) social world as best as possible. I decided on soap operas, sports, science, religion, literature, and age groups. These seemed sufficiently different from one another so that various dimensions of social life would likely be included in the overall sample.[3]

All online subjects were surveyed anonymously. Though some individuals chose to share with me what they claimed were their names, ages, gender, and other background information, I do not report these, as I had no way to verify such information face-to-face and because it is critical to respect the anonymity and social experience of subjects in cyberspace.[4] It is just as important to maintain confidentiality in cyberspace as in literal space; it shows respect for "social reality of cyberspace" (Paccagnella 1997). I also provide only a general description of the chosen groups, and I do not identify them specifically to further protect subjects' identities and sense of freedom online.

To elicit subjects, I inquired within the six groups whether members might be interested in answering a few questions about online connecting and their online groups, and I attached the short survey that follows. I followed up with additional questions in private e-mail exchanges and observed and "tracked" relevant discussions and postings. In all, I was able to gather data online from a total of 143 individuals, encompassing all six groups. I conducted most of my online research during the fourteen-month period between September 1997 and November 1998.

I found the groups that I would study in various ways. I heard about an online group that exchanged ideas about the soap opera *Guiding Light* from my sister, and I determined that this group would serve my purposes after "lurking" passively on it for about a week. The soap opera genre tends to elicit powerful feelings among fans and a strong desire to talk about it.[5] The Internet serves this desire well and is perfectly suited to following a daily, serialized television program (in fact, some fictionalized, dramatic serials are offered solely on the Internet). The participants in this group mostly identified themselves as women, with a broad age range, though at least twelve people identified themselves proudly (and even somewhat "loudly," as it were) as males in their teens and twenties. Some people used names from which gender could not be inferred (SoapFan, etc.). During the time I spent with this group, I saw it coalesce to a striking extent—I saw group members begin to get to know one another along numerous dimensions unrelated to soap opera viewing, sharing information such as: "Do you live in the city or country?" "What are your favorite junk foods?" "What are your phobias or weird/eccentric habits?" and "Do you roll your toilet paper and paper towels under or over?" Eventually, a subgroup of individuals on this message board started their own message board in order to exchange messages solely about one another's lives, having little or nothing to do with *Guiding Light* (their initial common interest)! This lively group became highly interested in my research and contributed much to my understanding of sociomental connecting. Forty-eight people from this group contributed to this study.

I chose a sports message board to capture the online "fan" community experience with individuals of a likely different demographic profile than the soap opera group I had already found (specifically in gender; I wanted to include more men in my sample than I suspected were on the soap opera board). I decided on one oriented toward baseball—comprising fans of the New York Mets—because my familiarity with the sport and the team would enable me, I hoped, to follow the discussions as knowledgeably as possible. Also, at the time of this research, the Mets were experiencing a mini-renaissance of sorts—a rare (for the mid-1990s) "good year"—which was attracting much interest and traffic to the group. I thought that this would increase my chances of obtaining subjects *and* useful responses; instead of spending their energy bemoaning a losing season and dissecting the reasons for it (a favorite activity of sports fans), group members might, I hoped, be more inclined to spend some time helping a sociologist with her research. The group did take its sports and the team's relatively "good" season very seriously, however, and discussed it busily; my research inspired less interest here than on some of the other boards. (Soap opera viewers,

I should add, also dissected and discussed nearly every aspect of their program in exhaustive detail—much as sports fans did with each game—yet responded strongly to my research as well.) I did receive ten insightful, helpful responses from this group, though.

I wanted to include some followers of a specialized "hard" science so that I could study yet another likely demographic: a group whose members would necessarily be highly concentrated among the well educated. I selected physics—and the subfield of relativity—because it fit these criteria and because I found I could keep up with the discussion better than with any of the other hard science-oriented groups. The exchanges on this board were abstruse and intellectually ambitious. Ten members, whose user names suggested that they might be mostly male, responded to my topic with some extremely thoughtful analyses of social connecting and bonding.

I decided to survey members of an online group devoted to religious discussion because I wanted to see if communal bonding with regard to religious ideas and phenomena would translate to a non-face-to-face setting. Religious bonding tends to be communal by definition. Would it translate to cyberspace? I found that nearly every communal interest—or certainly every interest that I could imagine—seems to translate somehow to cyberspace. I selected a group devoted to Christianity and to considering the effects of the mass media on living Christian lives, as I thought my topic might be welcomed by this group and would likely prompt some discussion. I received only eight direct responses from this group, though I witnessed many passionate, emotional discussions on the topic of the Church and the media.

I actually found the most emotional and lengthy discussion threads formed within the literature discussion group. I wanted to survey a group devoted to literature because the love of books and reading—particularly of *series* of books—had proved to evoke strong sociomental bonds in many of the people with whom I had already conducted primary interviews. I knew literature would serve as a strong rallying point for an Internet community of the mind, and after "surfing" through several groups, I found one devoted to reading and discussing a classic series of books. This group, which seemed to be almost entirely composed of women, formed attachments to their common interest in literature *and* to one another, which were thoughtfully, often movingly expressed. Thirty-seven people from this group contributed to the study, often posting and discussing issues relevant to my work among themselves.

Finally, I examined an "age group" called Generation X. As we look to others of our age as a "reference group," they can strongly influence the way in which we make sociomental connections (see Chayko 1993a; Shibutani 1955). I decided to survey a group of "Generation Xers," or people who were roughly in their twenties during the 1990s, because I noticed that many of their discussions seemed to center around their feelings of group identity and of whether or not they *were* a community. It also was one of the only groups I studied that seemed to be rather obviously gender and racially mixed (as their responses to their remembered experiences and favorite symbols indicated). Thirty "Gen-Xers" contributed to this research.

THE SURVEY

In each of the six online discussion groups I surveyed, I observed and "tracked" subject matter relevant to the study. I also inquired via a posted message (either to the whole group or some clearly interested subset) whether individuals might be interested in responding to a short survey about the experience of online connecting. I then sent to people who agreed to participate the survey that follows, with the request that they respond to any or all of its questions to help me understand the impact of technology and the mind on social connectedness. I invited respondents to feel free to respond privately to my e-mail address or to respond to and discuss any of these issues publicly on the board. I assured them that results would be reported and published anonymously, and that the identity of the group would be kept confidential as well, and that if they had any questions or comments about this survey, they could contact me at my e-mail address.

1. Do you feel connected to others in this group? If so, can you describe how it feels—what it "does" for you? If not, can you share with me why not?

2. Why, exactly, do you take time out of your day to post and read messages? If you enjoy it, can you state specifically what is so enjoyable about it for you?

3. What is your general feeling about technology (e.g., the Internet) and the way it affects your life? Does it make it better or worse, and in what ways? How about your relationships—does going on the Internet affect them? If so, how?

4. Is "the rest of your life" any different since you started going online? If so, how? If not, why do you think it is not?

Notes

CHAPTER 1

1. As Horton and Wohl (1956), Walther (1996), Rheingold (1995, 1993), Barlow (1995), Lombard (1995), Lombard and Ditton (1997), Rafaeli (1990), Parks and Floyd (1996), Merton (1946), Nordlund (1978), Beniger (1987), Meyrowitz (1985: 118–24), Perse and Rubin (1989), Caughey (1984), and Cerulo, Ruane, and Chayko (1992) have demonstrated.

2. Term conceived in collaboration with Eviatar Zerubavel (see Zerubavel 1993).

3. In order to underscore the social reality of connections and communities formed and maintained in the mind and the validity of the experience of forming them, I do not describe them as "virtual," "imaginary," or "para-social." To be sure, people who examine virtual reality (Chayko 1993b), imagined communities (Anderson 1983), or para-social interaction (Horton and Wohl 1956) are speaking of a phenomenon similar to or overlapping that which I detail in this book. Still, I feel that to call social connections "virtual," "imaginary," or "para-social" implies that they may be something less than real, less than fully social, a position with which I disagree and do not wish to unintentionally promulgate through the use of potentially misleading terminology.

4. To date, most research on social connection does not focus on mental or technologically mediated forms of connectedness, assuming, instead, the inherent advantage and superiority of face-to-face interaction, as Cerulo, Ruane, and Chayko (1992), Cerulo (1997), Purcell (1997: 102), Flanagin and Metzger (2001), and Rafaeli (1990) point out.

5. I consider *all* connections formed with "others" who are not physically present *sociomental connections.* I use the term *sociomental bond* more narrowly than I do *connection* to indicate a connection of somewhat greater strength and durability that is still, however, created and maintained in the absence of face-to-face copresence. When three or more people create and share a structure of social connections and a common identity without all of them ever having face-to-face contact with one another, I consider it a *community of the mind* (see Tonnies 1963 [1887]). Sociomental bonds and communities of the mind, then,

are subsets of the larger set of sociomental connections, which in turn is a subset of the universe of *all* of the ways in which people can be connected.

6. See Appendixes 1 and 2 for more detailed descriptions of the research methods used.

7. As the term *tie* (or *social tie*) has been largely appropriated by social network theorists to denote the presence of a connection grounded in face-to-face interaction between two people in a social network, I avoid the use of the term in conceptualizing connections in this book in order to emphasize the not necessarily physical nature of social connectedness.

8. Although it is possible that these two individuals indeed had not formed any sociomental connections that they could recall, given the prevalence and commonality of such connections I believe that it is more likely that these individuals could not make the conceptual leap to envisioning, categorizing, or speaking of such phenomena as real and legitimate and thus openly acknowledging them.

9. According to attachment theory, people's primary motivation in life is to be connected to other people because it is essential for survival (Johnson 1994: 35; see also Ainsworth 1978 and Bowlby 1973, 1979, 1981, 1988). Davis (1973: 31) further details some of the reasons that impel people to seek out others: the impulses to receive stimulation, express emotions, assert themselves, and enhance their enjoyment of various activities. Elias (1974: xxviii) and Mazlish (1989) also provide interesting perspectives on the human need for connectedness.

CHAPTER 2

1. See Cerulo and Ruane (1998) for a detailed typology of social connectedness that encompasses these and other dimensions.

2. Mental flexibility is a mode of thinking characterized by the ability to "think outside" rigidly defined conceptual boundaries. See Zerubavel (1991: 115–22, 1995: 1098–1102) for a discussion of his concept of the "flexible mind."

3. In this book, I use the term *modern* to denote the era of human existence in which mass technologies of communication and transportation are becoming part of virtually all people's lives, which roughly coincides with widespread industrialism. A reasonable approximation of this period would be from the mid-1800s to the present. I do not further break down this time period into such distinctions as "postmodern," "postindustrial," "late modern," "information age," or some other division, as the very presence (or absence) of widespread mass technologies has the most striking influence on my analysis. Further subdivisions add little, if anything, to my conceptualization of these issues.

4. DeFleur and Ball-Rokeach (1975: 154). See Durkheim (1984 [1893]: 129–31) for the original articulation of the argument.

5. I use and expand on the ideas of Murray Davis (1973: xxii) here.

6. See, for example, Postman (1993), McLuhan (1964), Ong (1982), Meyrowitz (1985), and Marx and Engels (1978 [1845]).

7. As Schramm and Porter (1982: 14–15) demonstrate. See also Altheide (1995), Altheide and Snow (1991), Habermas (1969), Febvre and Martin (1976), Postman (1993), Westrum (1991) and Ong (1982).

8. See Horton and Wohl (1956), Beniger (1987), Meyrowitz (1985: 118–21), Cerulo and Ruane (1998), Cerulo, Ruane, and Chayko (1992), Walther (1996), Walther, Slovacek, and Tidwell (2001), Flanagin and Metzger (2001), Perse and Rubin (1989), and Parks and Floyd (1996).

9. Cerulo and Ruane (1996) provide numerous examples of how "death comes alive" in the modern era through technological means.

10. As Klinger (1990), Giambra (1974), Singer (1975), and Kim and Biocca (1997) note. Kubey and Csikszentmihalyi (1990: 101) conceive of television viewing, which also constitutes a significant portion of most people's waking hours, as a special kind of daydreaming, where rather than fantasizing on their own people tap into other people's ideas and fantasies—and can then, I might add, incorporate those fantasies into their own.

11. As TenHouten (1997: 3) presents the ideas of Cacioppo and Berntson. See also Varela (1992: 329).

12. See Zerubavel (1997) for a definitive treatment of this issue.

13. See Schutz and Luckmann (1973: 103–11) and Durkheim (1965 [1912]: 30, 1984 [1893], 1973 [1914]).

14. A "status characteristic" is a quality around which individuals (or social types of them) are evaluated and seen as being different from one another. The central notion of a theory of mental organizational processes, it can apply to any externally or internally identified personal quality from race, sex, age, or occupation to physical attractiveness, kindness, or intelligence, even including specific skills and talents such as mathematical or athletic ability (Berger et al. 1977: 5). A status characteristic is most often seen as an "axis" of differentiation, on the basis of which individuals, social types, and groups tend to be stereotyped and then stratified—given "status"—in a society. See also Webster (1970), Webster, Roberts, and Sobieszek (1972), Webster and Sobieszek (1973, 1974), and Berger and Fisek (1974). On the formation and stratification of "taste publics" representing different cultural tastes, see Gans (1974).

15. Shibutani (1955) and Mead (1934) expound in greater detail about exactly how people come to assume the social attitudes of a group.

16. As Zerubavel (1991: 76), Leach (1976: 33–34), and Gerson and Peiss (1985) explain.

17. See Zerubavel (1991, esp. pp. 74–80) for an elegant argument and bountiful examples of this.

18. For more examples and discussions of this idea, see Varela (1992: 330), Goffman (1961: 19–26), Bateson (1972 [1955]: 127), Jakobson (1978 [1942]: 69–87), Tversky (1977: 329), and Zerubavel (1991: 77–78).

19. This idea is elaborated further in Wittgenstein (1953), Rosch (1973), Rosch et al. (1976), Rosch and Mervis (1975), McCloskey and Glucksberg (1978), and Durkheim and Mauss (1963 [1903]).

20. Some (e.g., Merleau-Ponty [1963]) would say that *none* do, that phenomena cannot even be said to exist outside of our perceptions of them.

21. To our knowledge, no human culture has habitually viewed the world as a wholly random process, even if its inhabitants consider the causes of certain events beyond their power (Dunbar 1989: 49).

22. Some theorists propose that this type of mental organization is best thought of simply as evidence of patterns of mental activation, and that "schemata," per se, do not necessarily exist (Collins and Loftus 1975; Rumelhart and McClelland 1986; see also Basil 1994: 182). Concepts such as "mental models," "schemata," and "mental maps" are, of course, constructs used to help us understand the inner workings of the mind. I find them useful constructs, though, which at the very least can help us understand how patterns of mental activity serve to organize our experience in an extremely structured, "maplike" way.

23. See Lakoff (1987: 13), DiMaggio (1997), Douglas (1966), Carley and Palmquist (1992), and Johnson-Laird (1983).

24. For additional examples and a more detailed discussion, see Devine (1989), Schneider (1991), Berger et al. (1980), and DiMaggio (1997).

25. As Whorf (1956 [1940]), Vygotsky (1962, 1978), Luria (1981), and Cicourel (1974) argue.

26. As an example, Danziger (following Mannheim's formulation) has identified five different thought styles that predominated in mid-twentieth-century South Africa: the Conservative, Technicist, Catastrophic, Liberal, and Revolutionary (Danziger 1958, 1963).

27. Several theories of the construction of a psychological "inner space" (see Lewin 1936: 14–74) and a social or sociocultural space (see Bourdieu 1985; Feldman and Tilly 1960; Sorokin 1964 [1927]; Stein 1987) have been put forth. I have combined ideas of space as a mental construction from the former, and a way of conceiving of it as intersubjectively constructed from the latter group, in conceptualizing a socially and mentally "mapped" sociomental space.

28. See Rice and Aydin (1991), Valacich et al. (1993: 254), and Monge and Kirste (1980).

29. See Loomis (1992), Kim and Biocca (1997), Lombard and Ditton (1997), Steuer (1992), Paul (1991), and Tuan (1982: 133). For an overview of social presence theory and the ways in which it can help us understand how people who communicate with one another by computer create and recreate social presence in text, see Walther, Slovacek, and Tidwell (2001: 106–8).

30. For more on the ability of print to "transport" people mentally, see Gerrig (1993), Radway (1991), Kim and Biocca (1997), and Lombard and Ditton (1997).

31. See also Morley and Robins (1995: 132), Lombard and Ditton (1997), Kim and Biocca (1997), Barbatsis, Fegan, and Hansen (1999), and Schwartz (1981).

32. As Jones (1995: 17) put it, and as Garton, Haythornthwaite, and Wellman (1997), Parks and Floyd (1996), and Seabrook (1995) also note.

33. As Gould and White (1974: 52) have found. For more on the uses of mental maps, see Downs and Stea (1977: 1–47) and Leach (1976: 33–41, 51–54).

34. See Barsalou (1992: 185) and Downs and Stea (1977).

35. On this, see Gould and White (1974: 52), Downs and Stea (1977: 24–26), and Stein (1987: 49–80).

36. For examples and representations of the ways people in different social groups and cultural categories mentally map the world similarly, see Gould and White (1974) and Downs and Stea (1977).

CHAPTER 3

1. Depictions of community abstracted from sociological analyses of communal life indicate, collectively, that these are essential "communal" qualities. I have considered definitions and views of community and social groupings espoused by the following: Tonnies (1963 [1887]), Durkheim (1984 [1893]), Shibutani (1955), Simmel (1950 [1908]), Cooley (1964 [1922]), Hillery (1968), Nisbet (1953, 1966), Bell and Newby (1974), Scherer (1972), Otterbein (1972), Lisitzky (1956), Suttles (1972), Kanter (1972), Goffman (1963), Mazlish (1989), Stacey (1974), Gottschalk (1975), Minar and Greer (1975), Fischer (1982), Hewitt (1989: 128–48), Erikson (1966), Bellah et al. (1985), Wolfe (1989), Hunter (1974), Anderson (1983), Morris (1968), Bourdieu (1985), Keller (1988), Campbell (1958), Tajfel (1981), Lasch (1991: 120–67), and Berne (1966).

2. For discussions of this distinction, see Hillery (1968: 1–20), Bell and Newby (1974), Martindale (1964), Elias (1974), Scherer (1972), Suttles (1972: 3–18), Stacey (1974: 13–25), Gottschalk (1975: 2–33), Minar and Greer (1975, intro.), Hunter (1974: 95–139), and Hewitt (1989: 128–48).

3. See also Shibutani (1955), Mead (1934), and Goffman (1974: 499–500).

4. I thank Eviatar Zerubavel for suggesting this term.

5. See also Bower (1972: 52, 1981), Bower and Cohen (1982), Lang and Friestad (1993), Bradley et al. (1992), Fiske (1982), Loftus and Burns (1982), and Scheier and Carver (1982).

6. Hancock and Dunham (2001: esp. 326–28) provide an excellent overview of this research and an analysis of the breadth and intensity of the impressions formed in computer-mediated communication. See also Walther (1996) on selective self-presentation, Spears and Lea (1992), and Lea and Spears (1992) on the ways in which people use stereotypes and overattribution in making inferences about absent others, and Walther, Slovacek, and Tidwell (2001) on the impact of photographic images on the creation of affinity among Internet connectors.

7. Sudnow (1967). See Baker (1991) for an extensive argument and additional examples of this.

8. Greeley (1987). Similar results have been obtained by Olson et al. (1985) and Haraldsson (1985), as discussed in Baker (1991: 544–45).

9. As Frazer (1966), Rosenblatt, Walsh, and Jackson (1976), and Baker (1991: 545) note.

10. On envisioning computers as human, see Turkle (1984, 1995), Nass and Steuer (1993: 509), Nass et al. (1995), and Reeves, Nass, and O'Toole (1995: 8).

11. See Berger et al. (1977), Park (1925, 1928), Park and Burgess (1921), and Hughes (1945, 1952).

12. As Baym (1995: 138–39, 145–48) has demonstrated. Also see Parks and Floyd (1996) and Hancock and Dunham (2001).

13. As determined by Baym (1995: 130), Turner, Grube, and Meyers (2001: 231–32), Parks and Floyd (1996), Rafaeli and Sudweeks (1997), and Garton, Haythornthwaite, and Wellman (1997).

14. Harrington and Bielby (1995), Bagdikian (1987), Schiller (1989), Kellner (1990), and McCracken (1988) discuss how clusters of interest are created in a variety of contexts.

15. See Weiss (1988) for a sociological analysis of geodemographic clusters, and see Meyrowitz and Maguire (1993) for a discussion of their potential social impact.

16. Much human behavior, it should be noted, is *not* consciously directed but more automatistic. See Thayer (1990: 324–25) and Petri and Mishkin (1994: 30–32).

17. Greek philosopher Pythagoras believed in a universal kinship or sympathy among things (Miller 1990: 360).

18. See Storr (1992) and Gates (1992).

19. See Chayko (1991, 1993a), Cerulo, Ruane, and Chayko (1992), Meyrowitz (1985), Quindlen (1991), and McCarthy (1991).

20. See Cerulo and Ruane (1996) and Baker (1991).

21. See Thompson (1991).

22. See Cerulo (1995: 96–100) and Dayan and Katz (1992).

23. See Chayko (1993b), Steuer (1992), Kim and Biocca (1997), and Lombard and Ditton (1997).

24. See Zerubavel (1981, 1982, 1985, esp. p. 65).

25. See also Nisbet (1966) and Burkitt (1997).

26. As Kubey and Csikszentmihalyi (1990: 175), McHugo, Smith, and Lanzetta (1982: 382–83), Greenfield (1984: 50), Ekman, Friesen, and Ancoli (1980), and Zuckerman et al. (1981) demonstrate.

27. For more on network theory and its conceptualization of social connectedness, see Wellman (1988), Wellman, Carrington, and Hall (1988), Garton, Haythornthwaite, and Wellman (1997), Uehara (1990), Nadel (1957), Walker, Macbride, and Vachon (1977), Fischer et al. (1977), Fischer (1982), Barnes (1972), and Burt (1980).

28. I draw from and extend Simmel's "web of group affiliations" (1962 [1908]) in conceptualizing networks of sociomental connections as taking the shape of a "web." I also acknowledge the influence of Zerubavel (1997: 1–22) on the "web of sociomental affiliations," Bates and Peacock (1989: 567) on the usefulness of structural models in specifying how parts of a social unit are joined or connected in a "web of relationships" forming a bounded whole, Gilligan (1985) on webs of connections, and Mazlish (1989: 261–62) on the difference between a "chain" and a "web" of connections.

29. For examples of this, see Harrington and Bielby (1995), Cerulo, Ruane, and Chayko (1992), Chayko (1991), and Intintoli (1984).

CHAPTER 4

1. There is an elaborate and a detailed store of sensory/perceptual information in an individual's long-term memory (Sparks et al. 1995: 4). Our mental models assist us in retrieving and processing information from long-term memory (DiMaggio 1997; Barsalou 1992).

2. As Fischer et al. (1977), Cerulo and Ruane (1998), Mitchell (1995), and Turkle (1995) all claim.

3. See Cerulo (1995), Cerulo, Ruane, and Chayko (1992), Krain (1977), Kanter (1972: 169–75), Stein (1987: 57), Lewis (1975: 3–12), Landecker (1960), and Davies (1982: 1036–50).

4. See Cerulo, Ruane, and Chayko (1992), Brown (1989), Perse and Rubin (1989), Fiske (1988), Brundson (1984), Austin, Roberts, and Nass (1990), and Rosen (1986).

5. See also Kubey and Csikszentmihalyi (1990: 182–84), Gitlin (1980), and Tuchman (1978).

6. As Gans (1980: 56–57), Kubey and Csikszentmihalyi (1990: 171–73), and Finn and Gorr (1988: 139–41) have found.

7. See Caughey (1984: 31–76), Meyrowitz (1985), Wenner and Gantz (1989: 43), Kubey and Csikszentmihalyi (1990: 220), and Schwartz (1981: 55–65).

8. For more on this, see Berger and Luckmann (1967: 92–105, 149–51), Kubey and Csikszentmihalyi (1990: 7–9, 182–90), and Cohen (1989: 51–54).

9. On the process of collective remembering, see Halbwachs (1980 [1950]: 60–68, 136–57) and Freud (1967 [1922]); see also McDougall (1920) on the "group mind."

CHAPTER 5

1. As Couch (1992: 125), Sehested (1975), and Weiland (1975) detail.

2. See Cerulo and Ruane (1998), Walther, Slovacek, and Tidwell (2001), Wellman and Gulia (1999), and Walther (1996).

3. On the relationship between cognition and emotion, see Lazarus (1982: 1019), Clark (1993: 302), Zajonc (1979), and Schachter and Singer (1962).

4. For other examples of sociomental connections between celebrities and fans that have resulted in a face-to-face relationship, see Harrington and Bielby (1995: 58–67).

5. This claim is supported by Wellman (1997: 447), Mitchell (1995), and Rheingold (1993).

6. Loftus, cited in Neimark (1995: 85). See also Roediger and McDermott (1995) on the creation of "false" memories.

7. Horton and Wohl (1956: 215, emphasis added). See also Nordlund (1978), Beniger (1987), Meyrowitz (1985: 118–24), and Perse and Rubin (1989).

8. I will reiterate here that there is certainly a *physical* difference in response and impact between face-to-face and sociomental connections.

9. On the realness of "knowing" such others, see Goffman (1961), Singer (1980: 46), Meyrowitz (1985: 119), Perse and Rubin (1989), Bargh (1988), and Caughey (1984).

10. Schwartz (1981: 53, 1974), Goffman (1974), Nass and Steuer (1993), and Nass et al. (1995).

11. See Chayko (1993b), Zerubavel (1991), Goffman (1974), Bateson (1972 [1955]), and Fine (1983).

12. Harrington and Bielby (1995: 105). See also Jenkins (1992) and Chayko (1993b).

13. Of course, pathological fan obsession does exist and is a serious concern, but it is far less common than ordinary sociomental connectedness. See Jensen (1992) and Harrington and Bielby (1995).

14. Harrington and Bielby (1995: 124); see Fine (1983: 5), Radway (1991), and Modleski (1982).

15. Harrington and Bielby (1995: 124–25), Kaplan (1986: 153), and Jensen (1992).

16. As discussed in Harrington and Bielby (1995: 134). See Winnicott (1971).

17. Wellman and Gulia (1999: 178–81) provide an overview of literature demonstrating this. See, especially, Cerulo and Ruane (1998) and Reid (1995).

18. See Miller (1976), Chodorow (1978), and Gilligan (1985).

19. Gerstel (1988); see Caldwell and Peplau (1982), Davidson and Duberman (1982), Fox et al. (1985), and Rubin (1985).

20. As Reid (1995: 173), Walther, Slovacek, and Tidwell (2001), Kiesler and Sproull (1986: 1498), and Kiesler, Siegel, and McGuire (1984: 1129) demonstrate.

21. Walther (1996); see also Wellman and Gulia (1999: 180) and Baym (1995).

CHAPTER 6

1. Bell (1973), Giddens (1990, 1991), and Ritzer (2000) all discuss the impact of rapid social change.

2. On multiple realities and the different types of reality that can be experienced, see Berger and Luckmann (1967: 19–28), Goffman (1974), Davis (1983: 1–11), Caughey (1984: 119–240), James (1983 [1890]: 917–20), Shibutani (1955: 566), and Singer, who describes the reality that television generates as "in itself, a small social world. It provides 'company' for the solitary viewer and peoples his or her world, at least temporarily" (1980: 47).

3. See Berger and Luckmann (1967), Bateson (1972 [1955]), Garfinkel (1967), and Giddens (1990).

4. Thayer (1990) discusses this idea in greater depth (see, esp., p. 328).

5. See Jones (1995, esp. p. 30), Ross (1990), Cavanaugh (1997), and Pursell (1995).

6. Those who have written and spoken about the loss of community include thinkers as diverse as philosophers Jean-Jacques Rousseau and Edmund

Burke, writers William Wordsworth, Thomas Carlysle, Elizabeth Gaskell, Benjamin Disraeli, and George Eliot, and classical and contemporary social critics Ferdinand Tonnies, Karl Marx, Friedrich Engels, Robert Bellah, and Christopher Lasch (as Mazlish [1989: 3–127, esp. 56–57] details in an excellent overview).

7. See Putnam (1995) and Reeves (2001).

8. This is why Socrates did not write down his lectures, a task taken on by Plato, who must have appreciated the significance of preserving Socrates' words. See Cooke (1992) and Postman (1993: 3–20).

9. The belief that television has a negative influence on children seems to "satisfy some need among educated people," says Daniel Anderson, the coauthor of a report funded by the U.S. Department of Education in 1989. The report concluded that the prevailing social attitude that television is dangerous trickled down from academia to the public and was based upon academic research that was slipshod or biased, and in large part came from unrefereed sources, unpublished conference papers, and journals with minimal scientific review (in Cooke 1992). See also Beniger (1987) and Ong (1982).

10. See Fischer (1997, 1985: 286–89) for a more complete articulation of these ideas and additional examples.

11. As has been demonstrated by Flanagin and Metzger (2001). See also Walther, Slovacek, and Tidwell (2001), Perse and Courtright (1993), Katz, Haas, and Gurevitch (1997), Kayany, Wotring, and Forrest (1996), Rice (1993), Hiltz and Turoff (1978), and Walther (1997).

12. For various approaches to this, see Heath (1997), Adoni (1995), Reid (1995), Baym (1995), Kubey and Csikszentmihalyi (1990: 109), Davis (1994: 24), Perrolle (1987: 113–14), Wenner and Gantz (1989: 134–35), Rheingold (1993), Fischer (1997), Postman (1993), and Stoll (1995: 41).

13. As Lievrouw and Finn (1990: 42), Contractor et al. (1996: 455), and Culman and Marcus (1987) note. Walther (1996) explains that in some circumstances in which computer-mediated communication is "hyperpersonal," it can be even more rewarding than face-to-face communication. See Turner, Grube, and Meyers (2001: 232) for more on this concept.

14. See Ritzer (2000) for more on our ever-increasing demand for efficiency in all things in what he calls the "McDonaldization of Society."

15. I reiterate that outcomes associated with human sociation can *never* be guaranteed—an element of risk and uncertainty is always involved.

16. For examples of this, see Rafaeli (1990: 172–73), Pacheco (1990), Mitchell (1995), Turkle (1995), Rheingold (1995, 1993), Bruckman (1992), Lazarsfeld, Berelson, and Gaudet (1944), Katz and Lazarsfeld (1955), Riley and Riley (1951), Schramm, Lyle, and Parker (1961), Bostian and Ross (1965), Kuroda

(1966), Donohew (1967), Atkin (1972, 1973), Chaffee (1972, 1982), and McQuail, Blumler, and Brown (1972).

17. See Kubey and Csikszentmihalyi (1990), Katz and Foulkes (1962), Nordlund (1978), and Chaffee (1982).

18. See Rakow (1994: 1694), Giddens (1984) on the structurationist conception of agency, particularly under social and material constraints, and Cohen's discussion of this (1989: 9–55, 197–231).

19. See Mazlish (1989: 22) and McLuhan (1964).

20. Goffman (1961: 80). See also Goffman (1974) and Berger and Luckmann (1967).

21. For more on these uses and the potential effects of technology, see Flanagin and Metzger (2001), Turner, Grube, and Meyers (2001), Rheingold (1995), Finn (1997), Nell (1988), Parks and Floyd (1996), Bock (1994), Chayko (1993b), Kanaley (1995), and Walther (1996).

22. Mazlish (1989: 28). As an example of this mythology, Scherzer notes that preindustrial community life in New York between 1830 and 1875 was much less geographically bound than is usually assumed; there were few homogeneous neighborhoods and great mobility, and "for the most part, attachment to space remained weak throughout the period for all classes" (Scherzer 1992: 159–60).

23. In two separate studies a mere seventeen years apart, Oscar Lewis "found" widespread fear, envy, and distrust in the same Mexican village that Robert Redfield "found" to be unified, well integrated, smoothly functioning, and cooperative (in Elias 1974: xiv). One plausible explanation of this disparity is that one's preconceived notions about what community is can certainly color what one looks for, sees, and "finds" in a social situation. This example also illustrates the complexity that exists in any reasonably long-standing group or community. A community will always "contain" more complexity than "meets the eye." See also Mazlish (1989) and Gans (1988: 98–120).

24. As Campbell claims (1990: 140). See also Wellman (1979).

25. As Lisitzky (1956), Otterbein (1972, esp. 24–29), Hall (1969: 178), Bell and Newby (1974), and Elias (1974) detail.

26. As Geertz (1973), Tuan (1982), Rosen (1984), and White and Kirkpatrick (1985) detail. See also Gergen (1991: 8–13).

27. James (1983 [1890]). See also Goffman (1981) and Turkle (1995, 1997).

28. For a discussion and a timeline of milestones in the development of machines and computers with the ability to "think"—*artificial intelligence*—see Maney (2001). For additional perspectives on and manifestations of this, see Kurzweil (2000) and Cohen (2000).

29. See Coser (1991: 17–25, 156–59), Merelman (1984: 31), and Hewitt (1989).

30. As Ainsworth (1978) and Bowlby (1988, 1981, 1979) discuss in great detail.

31. This sense of alienation is discussed more thoroughly by Lasch (1977), Marx (1978 [1844]: 70–81), Marcuse (1962), Braverman (1974: 57), and Hochschild (1983).

32. To date, research tends not to explore "composite forms of interaction that do not assume the displacement of interpersonal forms of communication by their mass media descendants" (Purcell 1997: 102). Efforts to explore the interplay among different media and various forms of communication have been made, however, by Flanagin and Metzger (2001), Walther, Slovacek, and Tidwell (2001), Cerulo and Ruane (1998), and Rafaeli and Sudweeks (1997).

33. I echo suggestions that we study processes of connecting common face-to-face and mediated interaction made by Ruben and Lievrouw (1990: 5), Cerulo (1997), Cerulo and Ruane (1996), Cerulo, Ruane, and Chayko (1992), Meyrowitz (1985), and Purcell (1997).

34. Rafaeli (1990) has proposed a similar type of continuum, encompassing face-to-face and mediated interaction in what he calls a continuum of "interactivity."

35. Many thanks to Christena Nippert-Eng for the analogy.

36. Wellman (1988: 44) and Granovetter (1973) provide descriptions of the process with regard to more traditionally conceived social networks; Wellman and Gulia (1999: 175–76) specifically discuss its application to online networks.

37. Coser (1991: 88). See also Coser (1974), Granovetter (1973), and Wellman and Gulia (1999).

38. Calhoun (1988: 239, emphasis added). See also Calhoun (1986, 1991) and Wellman (1997).

39. Many thanks to Ira Cohen for this analogy.

APPENDIX 1

1. The personal computer and the Internet were just emerging as widespread technologies during the time of this study (the mid- to late 1990s). One can assume that if this study had been performed during an earlier (or a later) period, a difference would be evident in regard to whether certain technologies would be viewed as "low" or "high" tech.

APPENDIX 2

1. Many formats facilitate the "posting" and "receiving" of messages in differently themed Internet message groups. They all provide a form of "one-to-many"

communication; the distinctions between the formats are not critical for these purposes.

2. Edmondson (1997) and Krasilovsky (1996). See also Paccagnella (1997).

3. Of course, Internet users are likely to be drawn from society's better educated and higher socioeconomic strata, as Fineman (1995) and Jackson (1994) note. See also Hoffman, Novak, and Schlosser (2000).

4. It is easier to invent a persona and to disguise one's age, gender, race, and so on online than in person (see O'Brien 1999; Turkle 1997). The nature of the topics I chose did not seem to inspire outrageous levels of deception, however, as these topics encompass fairly common interests. People can easily disguise their actual identities online, substituting different user names for their actual names when making cyberspace connections, but the exchange of views on soaps, sports, science, literature, religion, and on being in a specific age group, does not seem to require extensively disguising one's personal characteristics.

5. As Harrington and Bielby (1995), Brown (1989), Ang (1985), and Intintoli (1984) all demonstrate.

References

Adoni, H. 1995. "Literacy and Reading in a Multimedia Environment." *Journal of Communication* 45:2:162–74.

Ainsworth, M. 1978. *Patterns of Attachment*. Hillsdale, N.J.: Erlbaum.

Allman, W. F. 1993. "Pioneering the Electronic Frontier." *U.S. News and World Report* 115:22:56–63.

Altheide, D. 1995. *An Ecology of Communication: Cultural Formats of Control*. Hawthorne, N.Y.: Aldine de Gruyter.

———— 1997. "The News Media, the Problem Frame, and the Production of Fear." *Sociological Quarterly* 38:4:647–68.

Altheide, D. L., and R. P. Snow. 1991. *Media Worlds in the Postjournalism Era*. Hawthorne, N.Y.: Aldine de Gruyter.

Anderson, B. 1983. *Imagined Communities*. London: Thetford Press.

Ang, I. 1985. *Watching Dallas: Soap Opera and the Melodramatic Imagination*. New York: Methuen.

Atkin, C. K. 1972. "Anticipated Communication and Mass Media Information Seeking." *Public Opinion Quarterly* 35:188–89.

————. 1973. "Instrumental Utilities and Information Seeking." Pp. 205–242 in *New Models for Mass Communication Research*, ed. P. Clarke. Beverly Hills, Calif.: Sage.

Austin, E., D. Roberts, and C. Nass. 1990. "Influences of Family Communication on Children's Television Interpretation Processes." *Communication Research* 18:238–259.

Babbie, E. 1989. *The Practice of Social Research*. Belmont, Calif. Wadsworth.

Badham, R. 1986. *Theories of Industrial Society*. New York: St. Martin's Press.

Bagdikian, B. H. 1987. *The Media Monopoly*. Boston: Beacon Press.

Baker, P. M. 1991. "Socialization after Death: The Might of the Living Dead." Pp. 539–551 in *Growing Old in America*, ed. B. Hess and E. W. Markson. New Brunswick, N.J.: Transaction.

201

Ball, D. W. 1967. "Toward a Sociology of Toys: Inanimate Objects, Socialization, and the Demography of the Doll World." *Sociological Quarterly* 9:447–58.

Baran, S. J., and D. K. Davis. 1995. *Mass Communication Theory: Foundations, Ferment, and Future.* Belmont, Calif.: Wadsworth.

Barbatsis, G., M. Fegan, and K. Hansen. 1999. "The Performance of Cyberspace: An Exploration into Computer-Mediated Reality." *Journal of Computer-Mediated Communication.* Available online at http://www.ascusc.org/jcmc/vol5/issue1/barbatsis.html.

Bargh, J. A. 1988. "Automatic Information Processing: Implications for Communication and Affect." Pp. 9–32 in *Communication, Social Cognition, and Affect,* ed. Donohew, A. E. Sypher and E. T. Higgins. Hillsdale, N.J.: Erlbaum.

Barlow, J. P. 1995. "Is There a There in Cyberspace?" *Utne Reader* (March–April): 52–56.

Barnes, J. A. 1972. *Social Networks.* New York: Addison-Wesley.

Barsalou, L. W. 1992. *Cognitive Psychology.* Hillsdale, N.J.: Erlbaum.

Barth, F. 1969. *Ethnic Groups and Boundaries.* Boston: Little, Brown.

Basil, M. D. 1994. "Multiple Resource Theory I: Application to Television Viewing." *Communication Research* 21:2:177–207.

Bates, F. L., and W. G. Peacock. 1989. "Conceptualizing Social Structure: The Misuse of Classification in Structural Modeling." *American Sociological Review* 54:565–77.

Bateson, G. 1972 [1955]. "A Theory of Play and Phantasy." Pp. 177–193 in *Steps to an Ecology of Mind.* New York: Ballantine.

Baym, N. K. 1995. "The Emergence of Community in Computer-Mediated Communication." Pp. 138–163 in *Cybersociety,* ed. S. G. Jones. Thousand Oaks, Calif.: Sage.

Becker, H. 1976. "Art Worlds and Social Types." Pp. 41–57 in *The Production of Culture,* ed. R. Peterson. Beverly Hills, Calif: Sage.

Begley, S. 2001. "Memory's Mind Games." *Newsweek* (July 16): 52–54.

Bell, C., and H. Newby. 1974. *The Sociology of Community.* London: Frank Cass and Company.

Bell, D. 1973. *The Coming of Post–Industrial Society.* New York: Basic Books.

Bellah, R. N., R. Madsen, W. M. Sullivan, A. Swidler, and S. M. Tipton. 1985. *Habits of the Heart.* New York: Harper & Row.

Beniger, J. 1986. *The Control Revolution.* Cambridge: Harvard University Press.

———. 1987. "Personalization of Mass Media and the Growth of Pseudo-Community." *Communication Research* 14:3:352–71.

Berger, J., and M. H. Fisek. 1974. "A Generalization of the Status Characteristics and Expectation States Theory." Pp. 163–205 in *Expectation States Theory: A Theoretical Research Program*, ed. J. Berger, T. L. Conner, and M. H. Fisek. Cambridge, Mass.: Winthrop.

Berger, J., M. H. Fisek, R. Z. Norman, and M. Zelditch. 1977. *Status Characteristics and Social Interaction*. New York: Elservier.

Berger, J., S. J. Rosenholtz, and M. Zelditch. 1980. "Status Organizing Processes." *Annual Review of Sociology* 6:479–508.

Berger, P., and T. Luckmann. 1967. *The Social Construction of Reality*. Garden City, N.Y.: Doubleday.

Berne, E. 1966. *The Structure and Dynamics of Organizations and Groups*. New York: Grove Press.

Berscheid, E. 1983. "Emotion." Pp. 110–168 in *Close Relationships*, ed. H. H. Kelley et al. New York: W. H. Freeman and Company.

Berscheid, E., and L. A. Peplau. 1983. "The Emerging Science of Relationships." Pp. 1–19 in *Close Relationships*, ed. H. H. Kelley et al. New York: W. H. Freeman and Company.

Best, S. 1989. "The Commodification of Reality and the Reality of Commodification: Jean Baudrillard and Post-Modernism." *Current Perspectives in Social Theory* 9:23–51.

Biocca, F., and M. Levy. eds. 1995. *Communication in the Age of Virtual Reality*. Hillsdale, N.J.: Erlbaum.

Blau, P. M. 1977. *Inequality and Heterogeneity*. New York: Free Press.

Blau, P. M., and J. Schwartz. 1984. *Cross-Cutting Social Circles*. New York: Academic Press.

Bock, P. 1994. "He's Not Disabled in Cyberspace." *Seattle Times*. (February 21): A1–2

Boorstin, D. 1961. *The Image: A Guide to Pseudo-Events in America*. New York: Harper & Row.

Bostian, L. R., and J. E. Ross. 1965. "Functions and Meanings of Mass Media for Wisconsin Farm Women." *Journalism Quarterly* 42:69–76.

Bourdieu, P. 1985. "The Social Space and the Genesis of Groups." *Theory and Society* 14:723–44.

Bower, G. H., and P. R. Cohen. 1982. "Emotional Influences in Memory and Thinking: Data and Theory." Pp. 291–331 in *Affect and Cognition*, ed. M. S. Clark and S. T. Fiske. Hillsdale, N.J.: Erlbaum.

Bower, G. H. 1972. "Mental Imagery and Associative Learning." *Cognition in Learning and Memory*, ed. L. W. Gregg. New York: Wiley.

Bower, G. H. 1981. "Mood and Memory." *American Psychologist* 36:2:129–48.

Bowlby, J. 1973. *Child Care and the Growth of Love.* 2d ed. Baltimore: Penguin.

———. 1979. *The Making and Breaking of Affectional Bonds.* London: Tavistock.

———. 1981. *Attachment and Loss.* New York: Basic Books.

———. 1988. *A Secure Base.* New York: Basic Books.

Bradley, M. M., M. K. Greenwald, M. C. Petry, and P. J. Lang. 1992. "Remembering Pictures: Pleasure and Arousal in Memory." *Journal of Experimental Psychology: Learning, Memory, and Cognition* 18:2:379–90.

Bramson, L. 1961. *The Political Context of Sociology.* Princeton, N.J.: Princeton University Press.

Braverman, H. 1974. *Labor and Monopoly Capital.* New York: Monthy Review Press.

Browder, S. 1997. "When Infertility Treatment Works Too Well." *New Woman* (June): 120–28.

Brown, M. E. 1989. "Soap Opera and Women's Culture." Pp. 161–90 in *Women's Communication,* ed. K. Carter and C. Spitzak. Norwood, N.J.: Ablex.

Bruckman, A. 1992. "Identity Workshop: Emergent Social and Psychological Phenomena in Text-based Virtual Reality." Unpublished manuscript. Cambridge, MA: M.I.T. Media Laboratory.

Brundson, C. 1984. "Writing about Soap Opera." Pp. 82–87 in *Television Mythologies,* ed. L. Masterson. London: Comedia.

Burkitt, I. 1997. "Social Relations and Emotions." *Sociology* 31:1:37–56.

Burnkrant, R., and A. Sawyer. 1983. "Effects of Involvement and Message Content on Information Processing Intensity." Pp. 43–64 in *Information Processing Research in Advertising,* ed. R. Harris. Hillsdale, N.J.: Erlbaum.

Burt, R. 1980. "Models of Network Structure." *Annual Review of Sociology* 6:79–141.

Caldwell, M. A., and L. A. Peplau. 1982. "Sex Differences in Same-Sex Friendship." *Sex Roles* 8:721–33.

Calhoun, C. 1986. "Computer Technology, Large-Scale Social Integration, and the Local Community." *Urban Affairs Quarterly* 22:329–49.

———. 1988. "Populist Politics, Communications Media, and Large-Scale Societal Integration." *Sociological Theory* 6:219–41.

———. 1991. "Imagined Communities and Indirect Relationshps: Large-Scale Social Integration and the Transformation of Everyday Life." Pp. 95–120 in *Social Theory for a Changing Society,* ed. P. Bourdiueu and J. S. Coleman. New York: Russell Sage Foundation.

Campbell, D. T. 1958. "Common Fate, Similarity, and Other Indices of the Status of Aggregates of Persons As Social Entities." *Behavioral Science* 3:14–25.

Campbell, K. E. 1990. "Networks Past: A 1939 Bloomington Neighborhood." *Social Forces* 69:1:139–55.

Carley, K., and M. Palmquist. 1992. "Extracting, Representing, and Analyzing Mental Models." *Social Forces* 70:3:601–36.

Carlin, P. 1993. "The Jackpot in Television's Future." *New York Times Magazine* (February 28): 36–41.

Carter, B. 1996. "Feel Good!" *New Woman* (September): 14.

Carter, B. et al. 1983. "Radio's Gabfest." Pp. 322–325 in *Mass Media and Popular Culture*, ed. F. Rissover and D. Birch. New York: McGraw-Hill.

Caughey, J. 1984. *Imaginary Social Worlds*. Lincoln: University of Nebraska Press.

Cavanaugh, K. 1997. "Input Overload." *The Star-Ledger* (May 26): 17, 20.

Cerulo, K. 1995. *Identity Designs: The Sights and Sounds of a Nation*. New Brunswick, N.J.: Rutgers University Press.

——— 1997. "Re-framing Sociological Concepts for a Brave New (Virtual?) World." *Sociological Inquiry* 67:1:48–58.

Cerulo, K., and J. Ruane. 1996. "Death Comes Alive: Technology and the Re-Conception of Death." *Science As Culture* 28:1:444–66.

———. 1998. "Coming Together: New Taxonomies for the Analysis of Social Relations." *Sociological Inquiry* 68:398–425.

Cerulo, K., J. Ruane, and M. Chayko. 1992. "Technological Ties That Bind: Media-Generated Primary Groups." *Communication Research* 19:1:109–29.

Chaffee, S. H. 1972. "The Interpersonal Context of Mass Communication." Pp. 95–120 in *Current Perspectives in Mass Communication Research*, ed. F. G. Kline and P. J. Tichenor. Beverly Hills: Sage.

———. 1982. "Mass Media and Interpersonal Channels: Competitive, Convergent, or Complementary?" Pp. 62–80 in *Inter/Media: Interpersonal Communication in a Media World*. 2d ed., ed. G. Gumpert and R. Cathcart. New York: Oxford University Press.

Chayko, M. 1991. "The Electronic Community: Creating Social Ties and Communities in Mass Media Use." Paper presented at the annual meetings of the American Sociological Association, August 25, 1991, Cincinnati.

———. 1993a. "How You 'Act Your Age' When You Watch TV." *Sociological Forum* 8:4:573–93.

———. 1993b. "What Is Real in the Age of Virtual Reality? 'Reframing' Frame Analysis for a Technological World." *Symbolic Interaction* 16:2:171–81.

Chodorow, N. 1978. *The Reproduction of Mothering*. Berkeley: University of California Press.

Cicourel, A. 1974. *Cognitive Sociology*. New York: Free Press.

Clark, C. 1993. "Review Essay: 'Emotions and Social Bonds,' on Emotions and Violence: Shame and Rage in Destructive Conflicts, by Thomas J. Scheff and Suzanne M. Retzinger." *Social Psychology Quarterly* 56:4:300–4.

Cohen, A. 2000. "The Machine Nurturer." *Time* (December 4): 112–14.

Cohen, I. 1989. *Structuration Theory*. New York: St. Martin's Press.

Collingwood, H. 1997. "X Marks the Spot." *Working Woman* 22:5:25–31.

Collins, A. M., and E. F. Loftus. 1975. "A Spreading-Activation Theory of Semantic Processing." *Psychological Review* 82:407–28.

Comisky, P., and J. Bryant. "Factors Involved in Generating Suspense." *Human Communication Research* 9:49–58.

Contractor, N. S., D. R. Seibold, and M. A. Heller. 1996. "Interactional Influence in the Structuring of Media Use in Groups." *Human Communication Research* 22:4:451–81.

Cooke, P. 1992. "TV or Not TV." *In Health* (December–January): 33–43.

Cooley, C. 1964 [1922]. *Human Nature and the Social Order*. New York: Schocken.

Coser, L. 1974. *Greedy Institutions*. New York: Free Press.

Coser, R. 1991. *In Defense of Modernity*. Stanford, Calif.: Stanford University Press.

Couch, C. J. 1992. "Toward a Formal Theory of Social Processes." *Symbolic Interaction* 15:2:117–34.

Coughlin, K. 2001. "Cyber-Predators Lie in Wait for Children." *The Star-Ledger* (June 20): 3.

Culnan, M. J., and M. L. Markus. 1987. "Information Technologies." Pp. 420–443 in *Handbook of Organizational Communication*, ed. F. M. Jablin, L. L. Putman, K. H. Roberts, and L. W. Porter. Newbury Park, Calif.: Sage.

Curtis, P. 1992. "Mudding: Social Phenomena in Text-Based Social Realities." Pp. 48–68 in *DIAC-92: Directions and Implications of Advanced Computing*, ed. D. Schuler. Palo Alto, Calif.: Computer Professionals for Social Responsibility.

D'Andrade, R. 1995. *The Development of Cognitive Anthropology*. New York: Cambridge University Press.

Danziger, K. 1958. "Self-Interpretations of Group Differences of Values (Natal, South Africa)." *Journal of Social Psychology* 47:2:317–25.

———. 1963. "Ideology and Utopia in South Africa: A Methodological Contribution to the Sociology of Knowledge." *British Journal of Sociology* 14:1:63.

Davidson, L. R., and L. Duberman. 1982. "Friendship: Communication and Interactional Patterns in Same-Sex Dyads." *Sex Roles* 8:809–22.

Davies, C. 1982. "Sexual Taboos and Social Boundaries." *American Journal of Sociology* 87:1032–63.

Davis, M. 1973. *Intimate Relations*. New York: Free Press.

———. 1983. *Smut*. Chicago: University of Chicago Press.

Davis, N. M. 1994. "CyberFacts." *Presstime* (October): 24–25.

Dayan, D., and E. Katz. 1992. *Media Events: The Live Broadcasting of History*. Cambridge: Harvard University Press.

DeFleur, M., and S. Ball-Rokeach. 1975. *Theories of Mass Communication*. New York: Longman.

de Grazia, S. 1964. *Of Time, Work, and Leisure*. New York: Anchor Books.

D'Emilio, J. 1983. *Sexual Politics, Sexual Communities*. Chicago and London: University of Chicago Press.

Devine, P. G. 1989. "Stereotypes and Prejudices: Their Automatic and Controlled Components." *Journal of Personality and Social Psychology* 56:5–18.

Dewey, J. 1915. *Democracy and Education*, New York: Mac Millan.

DiLauro, J. 1995. "The Gossip—West Coast." *Soap Opera Weekly* (May 23): 17.

DiMaggio, P. 1997. "Culture and Cognition." *Annual Review of Sociology* 23:263–87.

Dominguez, V. R. 1986. *White By Definition*. New Brunswick, N.J.: Rutgers University Press.

Donohew, L. 1967. "Communication and Readiness for Change in Appalachia." *Journalism Quarterly* 44:679–87.

Dossey, L. 1995. "The Body As Music." *Utne Reader* (March–April): 80–81.

Douglas, M. 1966. *Purity and Danger*. New York: Praeger.

Downs, R. N., and D. Stea. 1977. *Maps in Minds*. New York: Harper & Row.

Dunbar, R. 1989. "Common Ground for Thought." *New Scientist* 7:48–50.

Durkheim, E. 1965 [1912]. *The Elementary Forms of Religious Life*. New York: Free Press.

———. 1966 [1897]. *Suicide*. New York: Free Press.

———. 1973 [1914]. "The Dualism of Human Nature and Its Social Conditions." Pp. 149–63 in *On Morality and Society*, ed. R. N. Bellah. Chicago: University of Chicago Press.

———. 1984 [1893]. *The Division of Labor in Society*. New York: Free Press.

Durkheim, E., and M. Mauss. 1963 [1903]. *Primitive Classification*. Chicago: University of Chicago Press.

Easton, M. S., and R. LaRose. 2000. "Internet Self-Efficacy and the Psychology of the Digital Divide." *Journal of Computer-Mediated Communication.* Available online at http://www.ascusc.org/jcmc/vol6/issue1/easton.html.

Eco, U. 1986. *Travels in Hyperreality.* Orlando: Harcourt, Brace, Jovanovich.

Edmondson, B. 1997. "The Wired Bunch." *American Demographics* 19:6:10–15.

Edwards, M. L. 1995. "Coffee with a Friend." *New Woman* (January): 16.

Ekman, P., W. V. Friesen, and S. Ancoli. 1980. "Facial Signs of Emotional Experience." *Journal of Personality and Social Psychology* 39:1125–34.

Elias, N. 1974. "Towards a Theory of Communities." Pp. ix–xxxix in *The Sociology of Community*, ed. C. Bell and H. Newby. London: Frank Cass and Company.

Ellul, J. 1964. *The Technological Society.* New York: Alfred A. Knopf.

Emerson, R. W. 1906 [1841]. Essays. New York: Dutton.

Erikson, E. H. 1985. *Childhood and Society.* New York: Norton.

Erikson, K. 1966. *Wayward Puritans.* New York: John Wiley & Sons.

Febvre, L., and H. Martin. 1976. *The Coming of the Book.* New York: Verso.

Feld, S. L. 1981. "The Focused Organization of Social Ties." *American Journal of Sociology* 86:101–35.

———. 1991. "Why Your Friends Have More Friends Than You Do." *American Journal of Sociology* 96:6:1464–77.

Feldman, A. S., and C. Tilly. 1960. "The Interaction of Social and Physical Space." *American Sociological Review* 25:877–84.

Fentress, J., and C. Wickham. 1992. *Social Memory.* Oxford: Blackwell.

Fiebert, M. S., and K. S. Wright. 1989. "Midlife Friendships in an American Faculty Sample." *Psychological Reports* 64:1127–30.

Fine, G. A. 1983. *Shared Fantasy.* Chicago: University of Chicago Press.

Fineman, H. 1995. "The Brave New World of Cybertribes." *Newsweek* (February 25): 30–34.

Finholt, T., and L. S. Sproull. 1990. "Electronic Groups at Work." *Organizational Science* 1:1:41–64.

Finn, S. 1997. "Origins of Media Exposure: Linking Personality Traits to TV, Radio, Print and Film Use." *Communication Research* 24:507–29.

Finn, S., and M. Gorr. 1988. "Social Isolation and Social Support As Correlates of Television Viewing Motivations." *Communication Research* 15:2:135–58.

Fischer, C. S. 1982. *To Dwell among Friends.* Chicago: University of Chicago Press.

———. 1985. "Studying Technology and Social Life." Pp. 284–300 in *High Technology, Space, and Society*, ed. M. Castells. Beverly Hills, Calif.: Sage.

Fischer, C. S. 1992. *America Calling*. Berkeley: University of California Press.

———. 1997. "Technology and Community: Historical Complexities." *Sociological Inquiry* 67:1:113–18.

Fischer, C. S., R. M. Jackson, C. A. Stueve, K. Gerson, and L. M. Jones. 1977. *Networks and Places*. New York: Free Press.

Fiske, J. 1986. "Cagney and Lacey: Reading Character Structurally and Politically." *Communication* 13:4:399–426.

———. 1988. *Television Culture*. New York: Routledge.

Fiske, S. T. 1982. "Schema Triggered Affect: Applications to Social Perception." Pp. 55–78 in *Affect and Cognition*, ed. M. Clark and S. Fiske. Hillsdale, N.J.: Erlbaum.

Flanagin, A. J., and M. J. Metzger. 2001. "Internet Use in the Contemporary Media Environment." *Human Communication Research* 27:1:153–81.

Fleck, L. 1981 [1935]. *Genesis and Development of a Social Fact*. Chicago: University of Chicago Press.

Foucault, M. 1973 [1966]. *The Order of Things*. New York: Vintage Books.

Fox, M., M. Gibbs., and D. Auerbach. 1985. "Age and Gender Dimensions in Friendship." *Psychology of Women Quarterly* 9:489–502.

Frankl, V. 1984 [1959]. *Man's Search for Meaning*. New York: Simon and Schuster.

Frazer, J. G. 1966. *The Fear of the Dead in Primitive Religion*. New York: Biblio and Tannen.

Freud, S. 1967 [1922]. *Group Psychology and the Analysis of the Ego*. New York: Liveright.

Gans, H. 1962. "Urbanism and Suburbanism As Ways of Life." Pp. 625–648 in *Human Behavior and Social Processes*, ed. A. M. Rose. Boston: Houghton Mifflin.

———. 1974. *Popular Culture and High Culture*. New York: Basic Books.

———. 1980. "The Audience for Television—and in Television Research." Pp. 55–81 in *Beyond Violence and Children*, ed. S. B. Withey and D. B. Abeles. Hillsdale, N.J.: Erlbaum.

———. 1988. *Middle American Individualism*. New York: Free Press.

Garfinkel, H. 1967. *Studies in Ethnomethodology*. Englewood Cliffs, N.J.: Prentice Hall.

Garton, L., C. Haythornthwaite, and B. Wellman. 1997. "Studying Online Social Networks." *Journal of Computer-Mediated Communication* 3:1. Available online at http://207.201.161.120.jcmc.

Gates, D. 1992. "Getting to the Heart of Music." *Newsweek* (December 28): 58.

Geertz, C. 1973. *The Interpretation of Cultures*. New York: Basic Books.

Gelernter, D. 2000. "Will We Have Any Privacy Left?" *Time* (June 26): 155:25:74–75.

Gergen, K. J. 1991. *The Saturated Self*. New York: Basic Books.

Gerrig, R. J. 1993. *Experiencing Narrative Worlds*. New Haven, Conn.: Yale University Press.

Gerson, J. M., and K. Peiss. 1985. "Boundaries, Negotiation, Consciousness: Reconceptualizing Gender Relations." *Social Problems* 32:317–31.

Gerstel, N. 1988. "Divorce, Gender, and Social Integration." *Gender & Society* 2:3:343–67.

Giambra, L. M. 1974. "Daydreaming across the Lifespan: Late Adolescent to Senior Citizen." *International Journal of Aging and Human Development* 5:115–40.

Giddens, A. 1979. *Central Problems in Social Theory*. London: Macmillan.

———. 1984. *The Constitution of Society*. Berkeley: University of California Press.

———. 1990. *The Consequences of Modernity*. Stanford, Calif.: Stanford University Press.

———. 1991. *Modernity and Self-Identity*. Stanford, Calif.: Stanford University Press.

Gilligan, C. 1985. *In a Different Voice*. Cambridge: Harvard University Press.

Gitlin, T. 1980. *The Whole World is Watching: Mass Media in the Making and Unmaking of the New Left*. Berkeley, Calif: Univ. of California Press.

Goffman, E. 1959. *The Presentation of Self in Everyday Life*. Garden City, N.Y.: Anchor.

———. 1961. *Encounters*. Indianapolis: Bobbs-Merrill.

———. 1963. *Behavior in Public Places*. New York: Free Press.

———. 1974. *Frame Analysis*. New York: Harper Colophon.

———. 1981. *Forms of Talk*. Philadelphia: University of Pennsylvania Press.

———. 1983. "Presidential Address: The Interaction Order." *American Sociological Review* 48:1–17.

Goldfarb, B. 1990. "Computer Modems As a Mainstream Meeting Place." *USA Today* (October 30): 4D.

Gottschalk, S. S. 1975. *Communities and Alternatives*. Cambridge, Mass.: Schenkman.

Gould, P., and R. White. 1974. *Maps in Minds*. Baltimore: Penguin.

Granovetter, M. 1973. "The Strength of Weak Ties." *American Journal of Sociology* 78:1360–80.

Greeley, A. M. 1987. "Hallucinations among the Widowed." *Sociology and Social Research* 71:4:258–63.

Greenfield, P. M. 1984. *Mind and Media*. Cambridge: Harvard University Press.

Grunig, J. 1982. "The Message-Attitude-Behavior Relationship: Communication Behavior of Organizations." *Communication Research* 9:163–200.

Guthrie, W. K. C. 1962. *A History of Greek Philosophy: Vol. 1*. Cambridge: Cambridge University Press.

Gutman, A. 1986. *Sports Spectators*. New York: Columbia University Press.

Habermas, J. 1989. *The Structural Transformation of the Public Sphere*. Trans. Michael Burger. Cambridge: MIT Press.

Hacker, H. M. 1951. "Women As a Minority Group." *Social Forces* 30:60–69.

Halbwachs, M. 1980 [1950]. *The Collective Memory*. New York: Harper.

Hall, E. T. 1969. *The Hidden Dimension*. Garden City, N.Y.: Anchor Books.

Hancock, J. T., and P. J. Dunham. 2001. "Impression Formation in Computer-Mediated Communication Revisited: An Analysis of the Breadth and Intensity of Impressions." *Communication Research* 28:3:325–47.

Handlin, O. 1964. "Comments on Mass and Popular Culture," Pp. 105–112 in *Culture for the Millions? Mass Media in Modern Society*, ed. N. Jacobs. Boston: Beacon Press.

Hannigan, S. L., and M. T. Reinitz. 2001. *Journal of Experimental Psychology* 27:4:931–40.

Haraldsson, E. 1985. "Representative National Survey of Psychic Phenomenon." *Journal of the Society for Psychic Research* 53:145.

Harrington, C. L., and D. D. Bielby. 1995. *Soap Fans*. Philadelphia: Temple University Press.

Heath, R. P. 1997. "In So Many Words: How Technology Shapes the Reading Habit." *American Demographics* (March): 39–43.

Heritage, J. 1984. *Garfinkel and Ethnomethodology*. Cambridge: Polity.

Hernes, G. 1991. "Comments." Pp. 121–126 in *Social Theory for a Changing Society*, ed. P. Bourdieu and J. S. Coleman. New York: Russell Sage Foundation.

Hewitt, J. P. 1989. *Dilemmas of the American Self*. Philadelphia: Temple University Press.

Hiebert, R., D. Ungurait, and T. Bohn. 1979. *Mass Media II*. New York: Longman.

Higginbotham, E. B. 1992. "African-American Women's History and the Meta-language of Race." *Signs* 17:2:251–76.

Hillery, G. A. 1968. *Communal Organizations*. Chicago: University of Chicago Press.

Hiltz, S. R., and M. Turoff. 1978. *The Network Nation*. Reading, Mass.: Addison-Wesley.

Hinckley, D. 1995. "Computer-Generated Radio: The Wave of the Future?" *New York Daily News* (April 13): 48.

"His TV Mirror Image." 1992. *USA Weekend* (February 14–16): 16.

Hochschild, A. R. 1983. *The Managed Heart*. Berkeley: University of California Press.

Hoffman, D. L., T. P. Novak, and A. E. Schlosser. 2000. "The Evolution of the Digital Divide: How Gaps in Internet Access May Impact Electronic Commerce." *Journal of Computer-Mediated Communication* 3 (March). Available online at http://www.ascusc.org/jcmc/vol5/issue3/hoffman.html.

Horton, D., and R. Wohl. 1956. "Mass Communication and Para-Social Interaction: Observations on Intimacy at a Distance." *Psychiatry* 19:3:215–29.

Hughes, E. C. 1945. "Dilemmas and Contradictions of Status." *American Journal of Sociology* 50:353–59.

———. 1952. "Status and Identity." Pp. 100–115 in *Where Peoples Meet*, ed. E. C. Hughes and H. M. Hughes. Glencoe, Ill.: Free Press.

Humphrey, N. 1997. *A History of the Mind*. New York: Simon & Schuster.

Hunter, A. 1974. *Symbolic Communities*. Chicago: University of Chicago Press.

Intintoli, J. 1984. *Taking Soaps Seriously: The World of Guiding Light*. New York: Praeger.

Isaacson, N. 1996. "The Fetus-Infant: Changing Classifications of In Utero Development in Medical Texts." *Sociological Forum* 11:3:457–80.

Jackendoff, R. 1994. *Patterns in the Mind*. New York: Basic Books.

Jackson, D. S. 1994. "Battle for the Soul of the Internet." *Time* (July 25): 50–56.

Jacobson, D. 1997. "New Frontiers: Territory, Social Spaces, and the State." *Sociological Forum* 12:1:121–33.

Jakobson, R. 1978 [1942]. *Six Lectures on Sound and Meaning*. Cambridge: MIT Press.

James, W. 1983 [1890]. *Principles in Psychology*. Cambridge: Harvard University Press.

Jary, D., and J. Jary. 1991. *The Harper-Collins Dictionary of Sociology*. New York: Harper-Collins.

Jenkins, H. 1992. *Textual Poachers: Television Fans and Participatory Culture*. London: Routledge Press.

Jensen, J. 1992. "Fandom As Pathology: The Consequences of Characterization." Pp. 9–29 in *The Adoring Audience*, ed. L. A. Lewis. New York: Routledge.

John, R. R. 1997. *Spreading the News*. Cambridge: Harvard University Press.

Johnson, S. 1994. "Love: The Immutable Longing for Contact." *Psychology Today* (March–April): 32–37, 64–66.

Johnson-Laird, P. N. 1983. *Mental Models*. Cambridge: Harvard University Press.

Jones, S. G. 1995. "Understanding Community in the Information Age." Pp. 10–35 in *Cybersociety*, ed. S. G. Jones. Thousand Oaks, Calif.: Sage.

Kadi, M. 1995. "Welcome to Cyberia." *Utne Reader* (March–April): 57–59.

Kahwaty, D. H. 1991. "Guiding Light." *Soap Opera Digest* (July 9): 24–28.

Kando, T. 1980. *Leisure and Popular Culture in Transition*. St. Louis: C. V. Mosby.

Kanaley, R. 1995. "Seizing an On-line Lifeline: The Disabled and the Net." *Philadelphia Inquirer.* (July 8): A1, A8.

Kanter, R. M. 1972. *Commitment and Community*. Cambridge: Harvard University Press.

Kaplan, C. 1986. "The Thorn Birds: Fiction, Fantasy, Femininity." Pp. 142–66 in *Formations of Fantasy*, ed. V. Burgin, J. Donald, and C. Kaplan. New York: Methuen.

Katz, E., and D. Foulkes. 1962. "On the Use of the Mass Media As 'Escape': Clarification of a Concept." *Public Opinion Quarterly* 26:377–88.

Katz, E., H. Haas, and M. Gurevitch. 1997. "20 Years of Television in Israel: Are There Long-Run Effects on Values, Social Connectedness, and Cultural Practices?" *Journal of Communication* 47:2:3–20.

Katz, E., and P. F. Lazarsfeld. 1955. *Personal Influence*. New York: Free Press.

Katz, J. 1962. *Exclusiveness and Tolerance*. New York: Schocken.

Kayany, J. M., C. E. Wotring, and E. J. Forrest. 1996. "Relational Control and Interactive Media Choice in Technology-Mediated Communication Situations." *Human Communication Research* 22:3:399–421.

Keller, S. 1988. "The American Dream of Community: An Unfinished Agenda." *Sociological Forum* 3:2:167–83.

Kellner, D. 1990. *Television and the Crisis of Democracy*. Boulder: Westview Press.

Kiesler, S. and L. Sproull. 1986. "Response Effects in the Electronic Survey." *Public Opinion Quarterly* 50:402–413.

Kiesler, S., J. Siegel and T. W. McGuire. 1984. "Social Psychological Aspects of Computer-Mediated Communication." *American Psychologist* 39:1123–34.

Kim, T., and F. Biocca. 1997. "Telepresence via Television: Two Dimensions of Telepresence May Have Different Connections to Memory and Persuasion." *Journal of Computer-Mediated Communication* 3:2. Available online at http://207.201.161.120.jcmc.

Klapper, J. 1960. *The Effects of Mass Communication.* New York: Free Press.

Klein, F. G. 1971. "Media Time Budgeting As a Function of Demographics and Lifestyle." *Journalism Quarterly* 48:211–21.

Klinger, E. 1990. *Daydreaming: Using Waking Fantasy and Imagery for Self-Knowledge and Creativity.* Los Angeles: Tarcher.

Kolbert, E. 1992. "Test-Marketing a President." *New York Times Magazine* (August 30): 18–21, 68, 72.

Kornet, A. 1997. "The Truth about Lying." *Psychology Today* (May–June): 30:3:52–57.

Krain, M. 1977. "A Definition of Dyadic Boundaries and an Empirical Study of Boundary Establishment in Courtship." *International Journal of Sociology of the Family* 7:107–23.

Krasilovsky, P. 1996. "Surveys in Cyberspace." *Marketing Tools* (November–December): 18–23.

Kubey, R., and M. Csikszentmihalyi. 1990. *Television and the Quality of Life.* Hillsdale, N.J.: Erlbaum.

Kuroda, Y. 1966. "Political Role Attributions and Dynamics in a Japanese Community." *Public Opinion Quarterly* 29:602–13.

Kurzweil, R. 2000. "The Virtual Thomas Edison." *Time* (December 4): 116–18.

Ladd, E. C. 1999. *The Ladd Report.* New York: Free Press.

Lakoff, G. 1987. *Women, Fire, and Dangerous Things.* Chicago: University of Chicago Press.

Landecker, W. S. 1960. "Class Boundaries." *American Sociological Review* 25:868–77.

Lang, A., and M. Friestad. 1993. "Emotion, Hemispheric Specialization, and Visual and Verbal Memory for Television Messages." *Communication Research* 20:5:647–70.

Langer, S. 1957. *Philosophy in a New Key.* Cambridge: Harvard University Press.

Lasch, C. 1991. *The True and Only Heaven.* New York: Norton.

———. 1977. *Haven in a Heartless World.* New York: Basic Books.

Lazarsfeld, P. F., B. Berelson, and H. Gaudet. 1944. *The People's Choice.* New York: Columbia University Press.

Lazarus, R. S. 1982. "Thoughts on the Relations between Emotion and Cognition." *American Psychologist* 37:9:1019–24.

Lea, M., and R. Spears. 1992. "Paralanguage and Social Perception in Computer-Mediated Communication." *Journal of Organizational Computing* 2:321–42.

Leach, E. 1976. *Culture and Communication.* Cambridge: Cambridge University Press.

Leakey, R. 1995. "The Art that Sounded out the Dark." *Utne Reader* (March–April): 85.

LeBon, G. 1920. *The Crowd: A Study of the Popular Mind.* New York: Penguin Books.

Lemonick, M. D. 1995. "Glimpses of the Mind." *Time* 146:3:44–52.

Lever, J., and S. Wheeler. 1993. "Mass Media and the Experience of Sport." *Communication Research* 20:1:125–43.

Lewin, K. 1936. *Principles of Topological Psychology.* New York: McGraw-Hill.

Lewis, B. 1975. *History—Remembered, Recovered, Invented.* Princeton, N.J.: Princeton University Press.

Lewis, H. B. 1976. *Psychic War in Men and Women.* New York: New York University Press.

Lievrouw, L. A., and T. A. Finn. 1990. "Identifying the Common Dimensions of Communication: The Communication Systems Model." Pp. 37–66 in *Mediation, Information, and Communication,* vol. 3, ed. B. D. Ruben and L. A Lievrouw. New Brunswick, N.J.: Transaction.

Lindesmith, A. R., A. L. Strauss and N. K. Denzin. 1977. *Social Psychology.* New York: Holt, Rinehart and Winston.

Lisitzky, G. 1956. *Four Ways of Being Human.* New York: Viking Press.

Loftus, E. F., and T. E. Burns. 1982. "Mental Shock Can Produce Retrograde Amnesia." *Memory and Cognition* 10:318–23.

Lombard, M. 1995. "Direct Responses to People on the Screen: Television and Personal Space." *Communication Research* 22:3:288–324.

Lombard, M., and T. Ditton. 1997. "At the Heart of It All: The Concept of Presence." *Journal of Computer-Mediated Communication* 3:2. Available online at http://www.ascusc.org/jcmc/vol3/issue 2/lombard.html.

Long, L. H. 1976. "The Geographical Mobility of Americans." *Current Population Reports.* Special Studies, Ser. P-23, 64. Washington, D.C.: U.S. Bureau of the Census.

Loomis, J. M. 1992. "Distal Attribution and Presence." *Presence* 1:1:113–18.

Lopata, H. Z. 1976. "Review Essay: Sociology." *Signs* 2:165–76.

Lukacs, L. 1997. "The Information Society and the Church." *Internet Research: Electronic Networking Applications and Policy* 7:1:16–26.

Luria, A. R. 1976. *Cognitive Development: Its Cultural and Social Foundations.* Cambridge and London: Harvard University Press.

———. 1981. *Language and Communication.* New York: John Wiley & Sons.

Lyons, J. O. 1978. *The Invention of the Self.* Carbondale: Southern Illinois University.

Maney, K. 2001. "Artificial Intelligence Isn't Just a Movie." *USA Today* (June 20): 1A–2A.

Mannheim, K. 1936. *Ideology and Utopia.* New York: Harvest.

Marcuse, H. 1962. *Eros and Civilization.* New York: Vintage Books.

Markus, H., and P. Nurius. 1986. "Possible Selves." *American Psychologist* 41: 954–69.

Marsh, D. 1987. *Glory Days.* New York: Pantheon.

Marvin, C. 1988. *When Old Technologies Were New.* New York: Oxford University Press.

Marx, K. 1939. *Grundrisse.* Harmondsworth: Pelican.

———. 1978 [1844]. "Economic and Philosophic Manuscripts of 1844." Pp. 66–125 in *The Marx-Engels Reader,* 2d ed., ed. R. C. Tucker. New York: Norton.

Marx, K., and F. Engels. 1978 [1845]. "The German Ideology." Pp. 146–200 in *The Marx-Engels Reader,* 2d ed., ed. R. C. Tucker. New York: Norton.

Mazlish, B. M. 1989. *A New Science.* New York: Oxford University Press.

McCarthy, M. J. 1991. "TV Coverage Heightens Stress of War By Keeping Viewers in Constant Touch." *The Wall Street Journal* (January 24): B1, B4.

McCloskey, M. E., and S. Glucksberg. 1978. "Natural Categories: Well Defined or Fuzzy Sets?" *Memory and Cognition* 6:4:462–72.

McCracken, G. 1988. *Culture and Consumption.* Bloomington: Indiana University Press.

McDougall, W. 1920. *The Group Mind.* New York: Arno Press.

McHugo, G., C. Smith, and J. Lanzetta. 1982. "The Structure of Self-Reports of Emotional Responses to Film Segments." *Motivation and Emotion* 6:4:365–84.

McKibben, B. 1992. "Why Even the New Seems Like Deja Vu." *New York Times* (April 5): H1, 35.

McLuhan, M. 1964. *Understanding Media.* New York: McGraw-Hill.

McQuail, D., J. G. Blumler, and J. R. Brown. 1972. "The Television Audience: A Revised Perspective." *Sociology of Mass Communications,* ed. D. McQuail. Middlesex, UK: Penguin.

Mead, G. H. 1934. *Mind, Self, and Society.* Chicago: University of Chicago Press.

Merelman, R. M. 1984. *Making Something of Ourselves.* Berkeley: University of California Press.

Merleau-Ponty, M. 1962. *Phenomenology of Perception.* Trans. C. Smith. New York: Humanities Press.

———. 1963. *The Structure of Behavior.* Trans. A. Fisher. Boston: Beacon Press.

Merton, R. 1946. *Mass Persuasion*. New York: Harper & Row.

Meyrowitz, J. 1985. *No Sense of Place*. New York: Oxford University Press.

———. 1990. "Mediated and Unmediated Behavior." Pp. 67–94 in *Mediation, Information, and Communication*, vol. 3, ed. B. D. Ruben and L. A. Lievrouw. New Brunswick, N.J.: Transaction.

———. 1993. "Images of Media: Hidden Ferment—and Harmony—in the Field." *Journal of Communication* 43:3:55–66.

———. 1994. "The Life and Death of Media Friends: New Genres of Intimacy and Mourning." *American Heroes in a Media Age*, ed. R. Cathcart and S. Drucker. Boston: Hampton Press.

Meyrowitz, J., and J. Maguire. 1993. "Media, Place, and Multiculturalism." *Social Science and Modern Society* 30:5:41–48.

Mickey Mantle Foundation. 1995. *Letters to Mickey*. New York: Harper Collins.

Miller, G. L. 1990. "Resonance and the Energy of Intelligence." Pp. 349–364 in *Mediation, Information, and Communication*, vol. 3, ed. B. D. Ruben and L. A. Lievrouw. New Brunswick, N.J.: Transaction.

Miller, J. B. 1976. *Toward a New Psychology of Women*. Boston: Beacon Press.

Minar, D. W., and S. Greer. 1975. *The Concept of Community*. Chicago: Aldine.

Mitchell, J. C., ed. 1969. *Social Networks and Urban Situations*. Manchester: Manchester University Press, Institute of Social Research, Zambia.

Mitchell, W. J. 1995. *City of Bits*. Cambridge: MIT Press.

Modleski, T. 1982. *Loving with a Vengeance*. London: Methuen.

Monge, P. R., and K. M. Kirste. 1980. "Measuring Proximity in Human:Organizations." *Social Psychology Quarterly* 43:110–15.

Morley, D., and K. Robins. 1995. *Spaces of Identity*. London: Routledge.

Morris, H. S. 1968. "Ethnic Groups." Pp. 167–172 in *International Encyclopedia of the Social Sciences*, vol. 5. New York: Macmillan and Free Press.

Morris, P. E., and P. J. Hampson. 1983. *Imagery and Consciousness*. London: Academic Press.

Munch, R. 1988. *Understanding Modernity*. New York: Routledge.

Munsterberg, H. 1916. *The Photoplay: A Psychological Study*. New York: Appleton.

Nadel, S. F. 1957. *The Theory of Social Structure*. London: Cohen and West.

Nass, C., M. Lombard, L. Henriksen, and J. Steuer. 1995. "Anthropocentrism and Computers." *Behavior and Information Technology* 14:4:229–38.

Nass, C., and J. Steuer. 1993. "Voices, Boxes, and Sources of Messages: Computers and Social Actors." *Human Communication Research* 19:4:504–27.

Neimark, J. 1995. "It's Magical. It's Malleable. It's Memory." (January–February) *Psychology Today* 28:1:44–49, 80–85.

Nell, J. 1988. *Lost in a Book*. New Haven, Conn.: Yale University Press.

Newhagen, J. E., J. W. Cordes, and M. R. Levy. 1995. "Nightly@nbc.com: Audience Scope and the Perception of Interactivity in Viewer Mail on the Internet." *Journal of Communication* 45:3:164–75.

Newhagen, J. E., and S. Rafaeli. 1996. "Why Communication Researchers Should Study the Internet: A Dialogue." *Journal of Computer-Mediated Communication* 1:4. Available online at http://www.ascusc.org/jcmc/vol1/issue4/vol1no4.html.

Nietzke, A. 1978. "Getting It On with Gunsmoke." *Human Behavior* (June): 63–67.

Nippert-Eng, C. 1995. *Home and Work*. Chicago: University of Chicago Press.

Nisbet, R. A. 1953. *The Quest for Community*. New York: Oxford University Press.

———. 1966. *The Sociological Tradition*. New York: Basic Books.

Nordland, R., and J. Bartholet. 2001. "The Web's Dark Secret." *Newsweek* (March 19): 44–51.

Nordlund, J. 1978. "Media Interaction." *Communication Research* 5:2:150–75.

O'Brien, J. 1999. "Writing in the Body." Pp. 76–104 in *Communities in Cyberspace*, ed. M. A. Smith and P. Kollock. New York: Routledge.

Oden, G. C. 1977. "Fuzziness in Semantic Memory: Choosing Exemplars of Subjective Categories." *Memory and Cognition* 5:198–204.

Olafson, P. 1993. "Plug into User-Friendly Friendships." *New York Daily News* (April 18): City Lights Section, Pp. 2–3.

Olson, P., J. Suddeth, P. J. Peterson, and C. Egelhoff. 1985. "Hallucinations of Widowhood." *Journal of the American Geriatric Society* 33:543.

Ong, W. J. 1982. *Orality and Literacy*. London: Methuen.

Onians, R. B. 1951. *The Origin of European Thought*. Cambridge: Cambridge University Press.

Otterbein, K. 1972. *Comparative Cultural Analysis*. New York: Holt, Rinehart, and Winston.

Paccagnella, L. 1997. "Getting the Seat of Your Pants Dirty: Strategies for Ethnographic Research on Virtual Communities." *Journal of Computer Mediated Communication* 3:1. Available online at http://www.asusc.org/cmc/vol3/issue1/paccagnella html.

Pacheco, P. 1990. "Fan Clubs—From Engelbert to Mr. Ed." *New York Times* (November 4): 2:1, 20–21.

Palombo, S. R., and H. Bruch. 1964. "Falling Apart: The Verbalization of Ego Failure." *Psychiatry* 27:248–58.

Park, R. E. 1925. "The Concept of Position in Sociology." *American Sociological Review* 20:1–14.

———. 1928. "The Bases of Race Prejudice." *Annals* 140:11–20.

Park, R. E., and E. Burgess. 1921. *Introduction to the Science of Sociology*. Chicago: University of Chicago Press.

Parks, M., and K. Floyd. 1996. "Making Friends in Cyberspace." *Journal of Computer-Mediated Communication* 1:4. Available online at http://www.ascuse.org/jcmc/vol1/issue 4/vol1no4.html.

Paul, F. 1991. "E-Mail Comes of Age." *Omni* 13:7:35.

Pauling, L. 1948. *The Nature of the Chemical Bond*. 2d ed. Ithaca, N.Y.: Cornell University Press.

Perrolle, J. A. 1987. *Computers and Social Change*. Belmont, Calif.: Wadsworth.

Perse, E. M., and J. A. Courtright. 1993. "Normative Images of Communication Media: Mass and Interpersonal Channels in the New Media Environment." *Human Communication Research* 19:485–503.

Perse, E. M., and R. B. Rubin. 1989. "Attribution in Social and Personal Relationships." *Communication Research* 16:1:59–77.

Petri, H. L., and M. Mishkin. 1994. "Behaviorism, Cognitivism, and the Neuropsychology of Memory." *American Scientist* 82:30–37.

Petty, R., and J. Cacioppo. 1986. *Communication and Persuasion: Central and Peripheral Routes to Attitude Change*. New York: Springer-Verlag.

Postman, N. 1993. *Technopoly*. New York: Vintage Books.

Purcell, K. 1997. "Towards a Communication Dialectic: Embedded Technology and the Enhancement of Place." *Sociological Inquiry* 67:1:101–12.

Pursell, C. 1995. *The Machine in America*. Baltimore: Johns Hopkins University Press.

Putnam, R. D. 1995. "Bowling Alone." *Journal of Democracy* 6:1:65–78.

Quindlen, A. 1991. "The Back Fence." *New York Times* (January 20): E:19.

Radway, J. A. 1991. *Reading the Romance*. Chapel Hill: University of North Carolina Press.

Rafaeli, S. 1990. "Interacting with Media: Para-Social Interaction and Real Interaction." Pp. 125–183 in *Mediation, Information, and Communication*, vol. 3, ed. B. D. Ruben and L. A. Fievrouw. New Brunswick, N.J.: Transaction.

Rafaeli, S., and R. J. LaRose. 1993. "Electronic Bulletin Boards and 'Public Goods' Explanations of Collaborative Mass Media." *Communication Research* 20:2:277–97.

Rafaeli, S., and F. Sudweeks. 1997. "Networked Interactivity." *Journal of Computer-Mediated Communication* 2:4. Available online at http://ascuse.org/jcmc/vol2/issue4/rafaeli.sudweeks.html.

Rakow, L. 1994. "Book Review: America Calling." *American Journal of Sociology* 99:6:1693–95.

Rawls, A. W. 1989. "Language, Self, and Social Order: A Reformulation of Goffman and Sacks." *Human Studies* 12:147–72.

Reeves, B., and C. Nass. 1996. *The Media Equation*. Cambridge: Cambridge University Press.

Reeves, B., C. Nass, and K. O'Toole. 1995. "Is My Computer a Person?" *USA Weekend* (March 10–12): 8.

Reeves, R. 2001. "We Bowl Alone, but Work Together." *New Statesman* (April 2): 14:650:23–24.

Reich, R. B. 1991. "Secession of the Successful." *New York Times Magazine* (January 20): 16–17, 42–45.

Reid, E. 1995. "Virtual Worlds: Culture and Imagination." Pp. 164–183 in *Cybersociety*, ed. S. G. Jones. Thousand Oaks, Calif.: Sage.

Restak, R. M. 1988. *The Mind*. New York: Bantam Books.

Rheingold, H. 1993. *The Virtual Community*. Reading, Mass.: Addison-Wesley.

———. 1995. "The Virtual Community." *Utne Reader* (March–April): 61–64.

Rice, R., and C. Aydin. 1991. "Attitudes Toward New Organizational Technology: Network Proximity As a Mechanism for Social Information Processing." *Administrative Science Quarterly* 36:627–47.

Rice, R. E. 1992. "Using Network Concepts to Clarify Sources and Mechanisms of Social Influence." Pp. 43–52 in *Progress in Communication Sciences*, vol. 12, ed.W. Richards Jr. and G. Barnett. Norwood, N.J.: Ablex.

———. 1993. "Media Appropriateness: Using Social Presence Theory to Compare Traditional and New Organizational Media." *Human Communication Research* 19:451–84.

Riley, M. W., and J. W. Riley. 1951. "A Sociological Approach to Mass Communication Research." *Public Opinion Quarterly* 15:444–50.

Ritzer, G. 2000. *The McDonaldization of Society*. Thousand Oaks, Calif.: Pine Forge Press.

Roediger, H. L., and K. B. McDermott. 1995. "Creating False Memories: Remembering Words Not Presented in Lists." *Journal of Experimental Psychology: Learning, Memory, and Cognition* 21:4:803–14.

Rogers, E. M. 1986. *Communication Technology: The New Media in Society*. New York: Free Press.

Roloff, M. E., and D. H. Solomon. 1989. "Sex Typing, Sports Interests, and Relational Harmony." Pp. 290–311 in *Media, Sports, and Society*, ed. I. Wenner. Newbury Park, Calif.: Sage.

Rosch, E. 1973. "On the Internal Structure of Perceptual and Semantic Categories." Pp. 111–144 in *Cognitive Development and the Acquisition of Language*, ed. T. E. Moore. New York: Academic Press.

Rosch, E., and C. B. Mervis. 1975. "Family Resemblances: Studies in the Internal Structure of Categories." *Cognitive Psychology* 7:573–605.

Rosch, E., C. B. Mervis, W. D. Gray, D. M. Johnson, and P. Boyes-Braem. 1976. "Basic Objects in Natural Categories." *Cognitive Psychology* 8:382–439.

Rose, A. M., and C. B. Rose. 1969. *Sociology—The Study of Human Relations*. New York: Alfred A. Knopf.

Rosen, R. 1986. "Soap Operas: Search for Yesterday." Pp. 42–67 in *Watching Television*, ed. T. Gitlin. New York: Pantheon.

Rosenberg, B. 1971. "Mass Culture Revisited." Pp. 3–12 in *Mass Culture Revisited*, ed. B. Rosenberg and D. W. White. New York: Free Press.

Rosenblatt, P. C., R. P. Walsh, and D. J. Jackson. 1976. *Grief and Mourning in Cross-Cultural Perspective*. Minneapolis: HRAF Press.

Roser, C., and M. Thompson. 1995. "Fear Appeals and the Formation of Active Publics." *Journal of Communication* 45:1:102–21.

Ross, A. 1990. "Hacking Away at the Counterculture." *Postmodern Culture* 1:1:1–43.

Rothenbuhler, E. W. 1988. "The Living Room Celebration of the Olympic Games." *Journal of Communication* 38:4:61–81.

Rothschild, M., and M. Houston. 1980. "Individual Differences in Voting Behavior: Further Investigations of Involvement." Pp. 655–658 in *Advances in Consumer Research* 7, ed. J. Olson. Ann Arbor, Mich.: Association for Consumer Research.

Ruben, B. D. 1975. "Intrapersonal, Interpersonal, and Mass Communication Processes in Individual and Multi-Person Systems." Pp. 164–190 in *General System Theory and Human Communication*, ed. B. D. Ruben and J. Y. Kim. Rochelle Park, N.J.: Hayden.

Ruben, B. D., and L. A. Lievrouw. 1990. "Introduction." Pp. 3–8 in *Mediation, Information and Communication*, vol. 3, ed. B. D. Ruben and L. A. Lievrouw. New Brunswick, N.J.: Transaction.

Rubenstein, C. 1981. "Who Calls In? It's Not the Lonely Crowd." *Psychology Today* 15:12:90.

Rubin, L. 1985. *Just Friends*. New York: Harper & Row.

Rumelhart, D. E., and J. L. McClelland. 1986. *Parallel Distributed Processing*, vol. 1. Cambridge: MIT Press.

Saunders, C. S., D. Robey, and K. A. Vaverek. 1994. "The Persistence of Status Differentials in Computer Conferencing." *Human Communication Research* 20:443–72.

Schachter, S., and J. Singer. 1962. "Cognitive, Social, and Physiological Determinants of Emotional State." *Psychological Review* 69:5:379–99.

Scheier, M., and C. Carver. 1982. "Cognition, Affect, and Self-Regulation." *Affect and Cognition*, ed. M. Clark and S. Fiske. Hillsdale, N.J.: Erlbaum.

Scherer, J. 1972. *Contemporary Community: Sociological Illusion or Reality?* London: Tavistock.

Scherzer, K. A. 1992. *The Unbounded Community*. Durham, N. C.: Duke University Press.

Schiller, H. I. 1989. *Culture, Inc.* New York: Oxford University Press.

Schluchter, W. 1981. *The Rise of Western Rationalism*. London: University of California Press.

Schneider, D. J. 1991. "Social Cognition." *Annual Review of Psychology* 42:527–61.

Schramm, W. 1954. "How Communication Works." Pp. 3–26 in *The Process and Effects of Mass Communication*, ed. W. Schramm. Urbana: University of Illinois Press.

Schramm, W., J. Lyle, and E. B. Parker. 1961. *Television in the Lives of Our Children*. Stanford, Calif.: Stanford University Press.

Schramm, W., and W. Porter. 1982. *Men, Women, Messages, and Media*. New York: Harper & Row.

Schutz, A. 1951. "Making Music Together: A Study in Social Relationship." *Social Research* 18:76–97.

———. 1962 *Collected Papers*. The Hague: Martinus Hijholf.

———. 1973 [1945]. *Collected Papers*, vol. 1. The Hague: Martinus Hijhoff.

Schutz, A., and T. Luckmann. 1973. *The Structures of the Life-World*. Evanston, Ill.: Northwestern University Press.

Schwartz, T. 1974. *The Responsive Chord*. Garden City, N. Y.: Anchor Press.

———. 1981. *Media: The Second God*. New York: Random House.

Seabrook, J. 1995. "Home on the Net." *The New Yorker* (October 16): 66–76.

Sehested, G. J. 1975. "The Evolution of Solidarity." *Constructing Social Life*, ed. C. J. Couch and R. A. Hintz Jr. Champaign, Ill.: Stipes.

Seinfeld, J. 2001. "Why I Miss You, Too." *TV Guide* (June 30): 49:26:19.

Sennett, R. 1978. *The Fall of Public Man*. New York: Vintage Books.

Shakespeare, W. 1981. "Macbeth." *Selected Plays*. Franklin Lakes, Penn.: Franklin Library, 511–84.

Shaw-Brachfeld, J. 1998. "The Psychosocial Aspects of Puberty." *Child: St. Barnabus Hospital Medical Center Department of Pediatrics* (spring): 1, 5.

Shibutani, T. 1955. "Reference Groups As Perspectives." *American Journal of Sociology* 60:562–69.

Shilling, C. 1997. "Emotions, Embodiment, and the Sensation of Society." *Sociological Review* 45:2:195–219.

Shore, B. 1991. "Twice-Born, Once Conceived: Meaning Construction and Cultural Cognition." *American Anthropologist* 93:9–25.

Simmel, G. 1950 [1908]. *The Sociology of Georg Simmel*, ed. K. Wolff. New York: Free Press.

———. 1962 [1908]. *Conflict and the Web of Group Affiliations*. New York: Free Press.

Singer, J. L. 1975. *The Inner World of Daydreaming*. New York: Harper & Row.

———. 1980. "The Power and Limitations of Television: A Cognitive-Affective Analysis." Pp. 31–64 in *The Entertainment Functions of Television*, ed. P. Tannenbaum. Hillsdale, N.J.: Erlbaum.

Smith, H. W. 1975. *Strategies of Social Research*. Englewood Cliffs, N.J.: Prentice Hall.

Smolan, R., and J. Erwitt. 1996. *24 Hours in Cyberspace*. New York: Macmillan.

Sollors, W. 1986. *Beyond Ethnicity*. New York: Oxford University Press.

Sorokin, P. A. 1964 [1927]. *Sociocultural Causality, Space, Time*. New York: Russell and Russell.

Sparks, G. G., C. W. Sparks, and K. Gray. 1995. "Media Impact on Fright Reactions and Belief in UFOs." *Communication Research* 22:1:3–23.

Spears, R., and M. Lea. 1992. "Social Influence and the Influence of the 'Social' in Computer-Mediated Communication." Pp. 30–65 in *Contexts of Computer-Mediated Communication*, ed. M. Lea. London: Harvester-Wheatsheaf.

Sperry, R. W. 1952. "Neurology and the Mind-Brain Phenomenon." *American Scientist* 40:291–312.

Stacey, M. 1974. "The Myth of Community Studies." Pp. 13–26 in *The Sociology of Community*, ed. C. Bell and H. Newby. London: Frank Cass and Company.

Stahl, L. 2001. "Lesley Stahl: The History of a Reader." *O Magazine* (July): 175–76.

Stein, H. F. 1987. *Developmental Time, Cultural Space*. Norman: University of Oklahoma Press.

Steuer, J. 1992. "Defining Virtual Reality: Dimensions Determining Telepresence." *Journal of Communication* 42:4:73–93.

Stoll, C. 1995. "The Internet? Bah!" *Newsweek* (February 27): 41.

Stone, A. R. 1990. "Virtual Systems." Pp. 408–625 in *Incorporations*, ed. J. Crary and S. Kwinter. New York: Zone.

———. 1992. "Will the Real Body Stand Up? Boundary Stories about Virtual Cultures." Pp. 81–118 in *Cyberspace: First Steps*, ed. M. Benedikt. Cambridge: MIT Press.

Stone, C. S. 1974. *Should Trees Have Standing?* Los Altos, Calif: William Kaufman.

Storr, A. 1992. *Music and the Mind*. New York: Free Press.

Sudnow, D. 1967. *Passing On: The Social Organization of Dying*. Englewood Cliffs, N.J.: Prentice Hall.

Suttles, G. D. 1972. *The Social Construction of Communities*. Chicago: University of Chicago Press.

Svetkey, B. 1990. "Nick's Knack." *Entertainment Weekly* (June 29): 35–37.

Tajfel, H. 1981. *Human Groups and Social Categories*. Cambridge: Cambridge University Press.

Taylor, M. 1984. *Erring: A Postmodern A/Theology*. Chicago: University of Chicago Press.

TenHouten, W. D. 1997. "Neurosociology." Paper presented at the 1997 annual meetings of the American Sociological Association, August 12, Toronto, Canada.

Thayer, L. 1990. "Tropes and Things." Pp. 323–348 in *Mediation, Information, and Communication*, vol. 3, ed. B. D. Ruben and L. A. Lievrouw. New Brunswick, N.J.: Transaction.

Thomas, K. 2001. "Most Teens Ignore Web's Sexual Solicitations." *USA Today* (June 20): 1D.

Thomas, W. I., with D. S. Thomas. 1928. *The Child in America*. New York: Knopf.

Thompson, S. 1991. "1–900-Don't Touch Me: Techno-Sex and Emotional Attachments." Paper presented at the annual meetings of the Eastern Sociological Society, Providence, Rhode Island.

Thorne, B. 1981. "Gender . . . How Is It Best Conceptualized?" *Readings in Sex and Gender*, ed. L. Richardson and V. Taylor. Washington, D. C.: Heath and Company.

Toffler, A. 1970. *Future Shock*. New York: Bantam Books.

Tonnies, F. 1963 [1887]. *Community and Society.* New York: Harper.

Total Research Corporation. 1991. *Report on Market Clusters and Quality Attributes.* Princeton, N.J.

Tuan, Y. 1982. *Segmented Worlds and Self.* Minneapolis: University of Minnesota Press.

Tuchman, G. 1978. *Making News.* New York: Free Press.

Turkle, S. 1984. *The Second Self.* New York: Simon and Schuster.

———. 1995. *Life on the Screen.* New York: Simon and Schuster.

———. 1997. "Multiple Subjectivity and Virtual Community at the End of the Freudian Century." *Sociological Inquiry* 67:1:72–84.

Turner, J. W., J. A. Grube, and J. Meyers. 2001. "Developing an Optimal Match within Online Communities: An Exploration of CMC Support Communities and Traditional Support." *Journal of Communication* 5:2:231–51.

Tversky, A. 1977. "Features of Similarity." *Psychological Review* 84:327–52.

Uehara, E. 1990. "Dual Exchange Theory, Social Networks, and Informal Social Support." *American Journal of Sociology* 96:3:521–57.

Uems, A., J. Coupland, A. Folwell, and L. Sparks. 1997. "Talking about Generation X: Defining Them As They Define Themselves." *Journal of Language and Social Psychology* 16:3:251–77.

Valacich, J. S., D. Paranka, J. F. George, and J. E. Nunamaker. 1993. "Communication Currency and the New Media." *Communication Research* 20:2:249–76.

Vanek, J. 1978. "Household Technology and Social Status." *Technology and Culture* 19:361–75.

Van Gennep, A. 1960 [1908]. *The Rites of Passage.* Chicago: University of Chicago Press.

Varela, F. J. 1992. "The Reenchantment of the Concrete." Pp. 320–343 in *Incorporations*, ed. J. Crary and S. Kwinder. New York: Zone.

Viewers for Quality Television newsletter. 1990. (September–October): 34.

Vygotsky, L. S. 1962. *Thought and Language.* New York: Wiley.

———. 1978. *Mind in Society.* Cambridge: Harvard University Press.

Walker, K., A. Macbride, and M. Vachon. 1977. "Social Support Networks and the Crisis of Bereavement." *Social Science and Medicine* 11:35–41.

Walther, J. B. 1992. "Interpersonal Effects in Computer-Mediated Interaction." *Communication Research* 19:1:52–90.

———. 1994. "Anticipated Ongoing Interaction versus Channel Effects on Relational Communication in Computer-Mediated Interaction." *Human Communication Research* 20:4:473–501.

Walther, J. B. 1996. "Computer-Mediated Communication: Impersonal, Interpersonal, and Hyperpersonal Interaction." *Communication Research* 23:1:3–43.

———. 1997. "Group and Interpersonal Effects in International Computer-Mediated Collaboration." *Human Communication Research* 23:3:342–69.

Walther, J. B., and J. K. Burgoon. 1992. "Relational Communication in Computer-Mediated Interaction." *Human Communication Research* 19:1:50–88.

Walther, J. B., C. L. Slovacek, and L. C. Tidwell. 2001. "Is a Picture Worth a Thousand Words? Photographic Images in Long-Term and Short-Term Computer-Mediated Communication." *Communication Research* 28:1:105–34.

Warner, W. L. 1959. *The Living and the Dead.* New Haven, Conn.: Yale University Press.

Weber, M. 1958. *The Protestant Ethic and the Spirit of Capitalism.* New York: Charles Scribner's Sons.

———. 1978. *Economy and Society.* Berkeley: University of California Press.

Webster, M. A. 1970. "Status Characteristics and Sources of Expectations." *Report No. 82.* Center for Study of Social Organization of Schools. Baltimore: Johns Hopkins University.

Webster, M. A., L. Roberts, and B. I. Sobieszek. 1972. "Accepting 'Significant Others': Six Models." *American Journal of Sociology* 78:576–98.

Webster, M. A., and B. I. Sobieszek. 1973. *Sources of Self-Evaluation.* New York: Wiley-Interscience.

———. 1974. "Sources of Evaluations and Expectation States." Pp. 115–158 in *Expectation States Theory: A Theoretical Research Program,* ed. J. Berger, T. L. Conner, and M. H. Fisek. Cambridge, Mass., Winthrop.

Weiland, M. W. 1975. "Forms of Social Relations." *Constructing Social Life,* ed. C. J. Couch and R. A. Hintz Jr. Champaign, Ill.: Stipes.

Weiss, M. J. 1988. *The Clustering of America.* New York: Harper & Row.

Weitman, S. R. 1970. "Intimacies: Notes toward a Theory of Social Inclusion and Exclusion." *Archives Eurpoeennes de Sociologie* 11:348–67.

Wellman, B. 1979. "The Community Question: The Intimate Networks of East Yorkers." *American Journal of Sociology* 84:1201–31.

———. 1988. "Structural Analysis: From Method and Metaphor to Theory and Substance." Pp. 19–61 in *Social Structures,* ed. B. Wellman and S. D. Berkowitz. Cambridge: Cambridge University Press.

———. 1997. "The Road to Utopia and Dystopia on the Information Highway." *Contemporary Sociology* 26:4:445–49.

Wellman, B., P. J. Carrington, and A. Hall. 1988. "Networks As Personal Communities." Pp. 130–184 in *Social Structures,* ed. B. Wellman and S. D. Berkowitz. Cambridge: Cambridge University Press.

Wellman, B., and M. Gulia. 1999. "Virtual Communities As Communities: Net Surfers Don't Ride Alone." New York. Pp. 163–190 in *Communities in Cyberspace*, ed. M. A. Smith and P. Kollock. New York: Routledge.

Wenner, L. 1989. "Overviews: The Research Agenda." Pp. 13–48 in *Media, Sports, and Society*, ed. L. Wenner. Newbury Park, Calif.: Sage.

Wenner, L., and W. Gantz. 1989. "The Audience Experience with Sports on Television." Pp. 241–269 in *Media, Sports, and Society*, ed. L. Wenner. Newbury Park, Calif.: Sage.

Westrum, R. 1991. *Technologies and Society*. Belmont, Calif.: Wadsworth.

White, G., and J. Kirkpatrick, eds. 1985. *Person, Self, and Experience*. Berkeley: University of California Press.

Whorf, B. L. 1956 [1940]. *Language, Thought, and Reality*. Cambridge: MIT Press.

Willey, M. M., and S. A. Rice. 1993. *Communication Agencies and Social Life*. New York: McGraw-Hill.

Williams, R. 1990. *Hierarchical Structures and Social Value*. Cambridge: Cambridge University Press.

Winnicott, D. W. 1971. *Playing and Reality*. London: Tavistock.

Witten, M. G. 1992. "The Transformed Self: Images of Human Nature and Human Need in the Conversion-Talk of Contemporary Protestant Sermons." Princeton University, unpublished paper.

———.1993. *All Is Forgiven*. Princeton, N.J.: Princeton University Press.

Wittgenstein, L. 1953. *Philosophical Investigations*. Oxford: Blackwell.

Wolfe, A. 1989. *Whose Keeper? Social Science and Moral Obligation*. Berkeley: University of California Press.

Wolff, K., ed. 1950. *The Sociology of Georg Simmel*. New York: Free Press.

Wright, R. 1995. "The Evolution of Despair." *Time* (August 28): 50–57.

Wuthnow, R. 1998. *Loose Connections: Joining Together in America's Fragmented Communities*. Cambridge, Mass: Harvard University Press.

Zadeh, L. A. 1965. "Fuzzy Sets." *Information and Control*. 8:338–353.

Zajonc, R. B. 1979. "Feeling and Thinking: Preferences Need No Inferences." Paper presented at the September 2 meeting of the American Psychological Association, New York.

Zerubavel, E. 1981. *Hidden Rhythms*. Chicago: University of Chicago Press.

———. 1982. "The Standardization of Time: A Sociohistorical Perspective." *American Journal of Sociology* 88:1:1–23.

———. 1985. *The Seven Day Circle*. New York: Free Press.

Zerubavel, E. 1991. *The Fine Line*. New York: Free Press.

———. 1993. "Horizons: On the Sociomental Foundations of Relevance." *Social Research* 60:2:397–413.

———. 1995. "The Rigid, the Fuzzy, and the Flexible: Notes on the Mental Sculpting of Academic Identity." *Social Research* 62:4:1093–1106.

———. 1997. *Social Mindscapes*. Cambridge: Harvard University Press.

Zuckerman, M., R. Klorman, D. T. Larrance, and N. H. Spiegel. 1981. "Facial, Autonomic, and Subjective Components of Emotion: The Facial Feedback versus the Externalizer-Internalizer Distinction." *Journal of Personality and Social Psychology* 41:929–44.

Index

Academia and social connectedness,
    4–5, 41, 54, 140
Accountants, 22
Acoustics, 66
Actors, connections to, ix, 3, 33, 58,
    62, 76, 109–110, 116–117 (*see also*
    under specific actors, soap opera
    actors, media figures)
Adolescence (*see* age and social
    connectedness, adolescence)
Advertising, marketing and public
    relations/promotions, 33, 62–66,
    77–78, 93, 133
Age and social connectedness, 5, 18,
    23, 35, 53; adulthood, 27, 52 , 86,
    118, 131, 135, 154; childhood, 3, 15,
    20–21, 27, 50, 51–52, 60, 65, 86, 94,
    118, 124, 128, 129, 131–135,
    153–157; adolescence, 21, 154–155;
    elderly, 25, 141; "Generation X"
    online community, 5, 64–66,
    184–185; infancy, 39, 106, 117;
    teenage years, 25, 65
Alcott, Louisa May, ix
Allison, Jay, 106–107
American Revolution (*see also* nation,
    politics), 12
Amish, 76
Anderson, Daniel, 196n. 9
Animals and social connectedness, 39,
    51–52, 80, 124
Arsenio Hall Show, 74
Art, 67–68, 83–84, 156; premodern,
    7–10, 68; world, 76

The A-team, 65
Athletes, connections to, ix, 16, 17, 92
    (*see also* under specific athlete, sports)
Audiences, 46, 62–62, 76–78, 109–111,
    116–117, 140
Authenticity of connections (*see* reality)
Authors and writers, connections to, ix,
    1, 2, 3, 12–13, 44, 47, 60, 63, 68–69,
    91, 92, 108–109, 111, 142–143, 157
    (*see also* under specific author,
    literature, language)

Baker, P. Morgan, 50
Bank teller, banking, 128, 138
Barlow, John Perry, 120
Beatles, 81
Becker, Howard, 76
Bee Gees, 64
Begley, Sharon, 113
Bell, Alexander Graham, 137
Bell, Daniel, 158
Benefits (satisfactions) of sociomental
    connecting, anxiety reduction, 82,
    95–96; being understood, 53–61,
    66–67, 109, 142; comfort, solace, 45,
    82, 95, 106–109, 119–121, 140–141;
    convenience and accessability to
    others, 32–34, 80, 140–141, 161;
    defense or protection of one's group,
    105–108; emotional ties (*see*
    emotion); expanded social self, 104,
    151–156; flexibility (see mental
    flexibility); identification with others,
    53–66, 67–70, 104–108; increased

knowledge of others, 53–61, 67–70, 74, 104; increased face-to-face sociability, 125, 137–138; intimacy (*see* intimacy); enhanced sense of closeness, 87–89, 105–110; enhanced sense of community, 61–66, 70–73, 90–138–146, 104–110, 119–122, 140–142, 160–161; feeling less lonely, 81, 91, 97–100, 106–109, 119–121, 138–142; feeling "plugged in" and not "cut off," 70–73, 106–108, 140–142; pleasure, 142, 53–61, 74, 85–86, 91, 103–105; remembering others, 80–83, 89, 96–97; resonance with others (*see* resonance); social support, 97, 106–108, 119–121, 138–139; validation, 4–6, 55, 59, 142–143, 152

Beniger, James, 31, 122

Berscheid, Ellen, 118

Berenstain Bears, 51

Berg, Elizabeth, 108–109

Beverly Hills, 90210, 90

Bidirectionality (reciprocity) of connections, 101–102, 108–119, 126, 157–158

Biology, field of, 66

The Bionic Woman, 65

Boundaries, blurring and permeability of, 16, 19, 27, 77, 116–118, 148–156; social distinctions and divisions, 15, 23, 25, 83–84, 102, 108, 118, 127, 129–131, 147–156

Bourdieu, Pierre, 108

The Brady Bunch, 83

Breaking (severing) a connection, 48, 79, 83, 98–100, 104, 123–125

Broadcasting (*see* media, radio)

Brundson, Charlotte, 93

Bunker, Archie, ix

Business and social connectedness (*see* financial aspects of connectedness)

Byrne, Martha, 95

Cab drivers, 50

Calhoun, Craig, 62, 137–138, 144, 159, 160, 198n. 38

"Carrying" the other within, 96–100, 109

Carter, Betsy, 97

Categorization and classification, 20–28, 33, 39, 40, 52, 67, 113, 115–118, 129–131, 147, 150–157 (*see also* boundaries)

Caughey, John, 2, 16, 49, 56, 115

Cavalconte, Paul, 82

Celebrities (*see* under specific celebrity, type of celebrity)

Cerulo, Karen, x, 53, 67, 70, 111, 141, 188n. 1

Cerulo and Ruane, 53, 67, 188n. 1

Characters, fictional (*see* fictional characters)

Children and social connectedness (*see* age and social connectedness, childhood)

Chayko, Mary, 23, 42, 45, 61, 72–73, 77, 117, 131, 141

Cheech and Chong, 64

Chemistry, field of, 66–67

Clancy, Tom, 91

Clark, Candace, 43

Class, socioeconomic, and social connectedness, 23, 27, 30, 35, 53, 62, 105, 146, 147, 160 (*see also* dangers); marginalized or threatened groups, 105–108

Classification (*see* categorization, boundaries)

Cleaning personnel, 50

Clusters of connections, 40, 62–66, 73–78, 192n. 14, 192n. 15

Cobain, Kurt, 1

Cognitive (*see also* mental), capacities, 6, 11, 21, 30, 42–43, 136, 161; cohesion, 67, 69–70; development, 11, 20, 42–52, 122; involvement, 44, 59, 89–96, 102–126, 141–143; processes in connecting, general, 8, 19–37, 42–52, 79–100, 102–126 (*see also* mental impressions, orientation, perception, sensation); social foundations of cognition, 3, 19–37, 41–78, 112–126; socialization, 153–156; sociology, x, 22, 62

Cohen, Ira, x, 194n. 8, 197n. 18
Cole, Nat King, 19; Natalie, 19
Commonality (*see also* culture,
  community), common ground, 8, 10,
  13, 17, 25, 29, 39, 53–60, 70–78,
  85–100, 104, 112; common
  experiences, 25, 26, 29, 32–35,
  53–73, 83–84; common language (*see*
  language, common); common stock
  of knowledge, 26; common world,
  26, 76, 112, 124; "hub," 60–66, 75,
  103–104
Communication, field of, 8–19, 43,
  66–67, 84–85 (*see also* media,
  technology)
Community, 9, 30, 35, 37, 40, 42, 48,
  83–84; cyberspace (*see* online
  community); definitions and forms
  of, 40–41, 59, 135, 144–146;
  electronic, 72–73, 181–185; face-to-
  face, 40–41, 73, 122, 138, 146, 154;
  global, 62, 160; importance of, 20,
  21, 27, 46, 56, 70, 120, 135,
  144–146; Internet (*see* online
  community); of the mind, 2, 5, 6, 24,
  25, 35–37, 39–41, 60–78, 81, 85,
  93–95, 102–126, 130–162, 163–171,
  181–185; online (*see* online
  community); sense of, 28, 40–41,
  54–55, 62, 64–66, 70–73, 77, 104,
  111, 120, 139–141; soap opera (*see*
  soap opera community); structure,
  40–41, 42, 60–63, 73–78, 100, 103,
  115 (*see also* networks)
Complementary differentiation, 59–62
Computers and computerization,
  15–19, 43, 52, 63, 73, 106, 114, 117,
  122–123, 128, 133, 138, 140, 151
  (*see also* media, technology, Web
  sites, Internet, online); Microsoft
  Windows, 34
Comte, Auguste, 139
Conjoined twins, 3
Conscience collective, 22, 40
Cook, Steve, 181
Cooley, Charles, 31, 46, 48–49, 148
Coser, Rose, 159, 198n. 37

Crocker, Frankie, 104
Cronin, Rich, 32
Cronkite, Walter, 1
Cult, 76, 105
Culture (*see also* language, symbols, sex
  and gender, race and ethnicity, sexual
  orientation, age, class, family and the
  home, nations and nationalism,
  politics, religion); backgrounds and
  contexts, 5, 21–37, 52, 58, 122–126,
  129–131, 152–156; cultural
  framework (*see* mental lens); cultural
  experiences, shared, 17–18, 21–28,
  36, 46, 55, 64–66, 74–78; cultural
  knowledge, 2, 34–36, 39, 75; fans
  (*see* fans); popular, 17–19, 64–65,
  89–96; production of, 15, 33, 76;
  subcultures, 24, 28, 29, 35, 83,
  123–126, 129; tastes and interests,
  16–19, 23–24, 53–66, 83, 89–94,
  104–106, 140–146, 189n. 14
Curtis, Pavel, 44
Cyberspace (*see* space, cyberspace; *see
  also* Internet, online, sociomental
  space, mental space)

Dallas Cowboys, 53
Danes, Claire, 58
Dangers (hazards) of sociomental
  connectedness, abuse, 60, 132–133,
  145; alienation, 156–157, 198n. 31;
  antagonism, 143–144; deception,
  125–126, 151–152;
  depersonalization, 88, 102–103,
  122–123, 138; deterioration of face-
  to-face relationships, 98, 136–138;
  delusion, 129–132, 134; exploitation,
  132–134, 153; frustration, 144;
  hacking, 133; hate crimes, 143;
  identity theft, 133; laziness, 138;
  manipulation, 133; obsession, 95,
  129–131, 195n. 13; pedophilia,
  132–133; privacy, 133–134;
  propoganda, 133; psychosis,
  129–131, 134, 150; violence, 144
Davis, Murray, 7, 30, 53, 85, 119, 129,
  189n. 5

Daydreaming and fantasy, 20, 34, 49, 79, 84, 96, 116, 129, 136

Days of Our Lives, 17–18

Danziger, Kurt, 190n. 26

Deceased, connections to, ix, 1, 2, 3, 11, 19, 47–52, 70, 82–83, 96–100, 108, 120–121, 129–131 (*see also* family, ghosts)

DeFleur and Ball-Rokeach, 188n. 4

Delany, Dana, 104

D'Emilio, John, 108

The Depression, 145

Detroit Pistons, 53

Dewey, John, 84

Diana, Princess of Wales, 1, 112

Digital divide, 133

DiPaulo, Bella, 125–126

Distance (*see* space, distance)

Don't Tell Mom, the Babysitter's Dead, 58

Douglas, Mary, 23, 28

Downs and Stea, 35–36

Dreams (*see also* daydreaming), 98–99, 129

Durkheim, Emile, 3, 7–8, 22, 40, 47, 69, 70, 80, 101, 145

Durability of connections, 5, 7, 39, 70, 76, 79–100, 118–126

Dylan, Bob, 71

Easton Press, 63

Education and social connectedness, 4, 9, 12, 14, 23, 45, 53–55, 62, 64, 128, 133, 148, 161

Edwards, M.L., 109

Effervescence, 69–73

Electronic community (*see* community, electronic)

E-mail (*see also* online, Internet, computer), connections, 69, 86–88, 102, 120, 123, 134, 142, 152; pals, 2, 14, 102

Emerson, Ralph Waldo, 68–69

Emotion, 36, 53, 56, 86, 110, 146 (*see also* intimacy), and cognition, 2, 21, 43, 104, 115, 156–157; and social connectedness, 2, 4, 5, 8, 43, 49, 70,

74, 93–96, 101, 103, 106–108, 118–126, 127–132, 138, 141; emoticons, 83–84, 129; social aspects of, 4, 26, 43, 68–69, 71, 73, 104, 112–114

The Enlightenment, 12

Erikson, Erik, 117

Estefan, Gloria, 58

Ethics (*see* morality and ethics)

Face-to-face contact or copresence, 34, 61 (*see also* space, literal; space, distance); as component of social connection, 2, 3, 5, 7, 9, 11, 13, 41, 43, 44–53, 73–74, 79–80, 86–89, 101, 111–114, 119–126, 157–158; importance of, relative to sociomental, 6, 18, 29, 40, 45–47, 67, 75, 98–100, 106–108, 114, 127–132, 137–146, 157–162; in communities (*see* community, face-to-face); in premodern society, 7, 11, 148

Family and the home and social connectedness, 11, 15, 16–17, 22, 34, 47–48, 50–51, 53, 56–63, 69, 70, 73–74, 80–82, 85–89, 93–100, 102, 104, 106, 117, 119–125, 127–129, 136–138, 144, 148, 152–153

Fans, fan clubs (*see also* culture), 17, 46, 58, 63–65, 70, 77, 90–96, 104, 106, 109–111, 114–116, 138, 194n. 4, 195n. 13

Fantasy (*see* daydreaming and fantasy)

Feminism, 12

Fetuses and social connectedness, 5, 50–51

Fictional characters, connections to, ix, 1, 4, 13, 29, 47–52, 56–66, 69–71, 90–91, 92–96, 108, 114, 115–117, 129–131 (*see also* specific characters, soap opera characters)

Financial aspects of connectedness, 12, 60, 62–65, 76–78, 111, 114, 133, 146, 157

Fischer, Claude, 14, 136–137, 139, 159, 196n. 10

Flanagin and Metzger, 16, 18, 139, 142, 196n. 11
Fleck, Ludwik, 22
Flexibility (*see* mental flexibility)
Forrest Gump, 19
Foxx, Redd, 74
Frankl, Viktor, 35
Friends, friendship, 8, 17–19, 47, 56–60, 61, 63, 73, 79–83, 91–100, 106–107, 110, 114–116, 119–123, 138, 143
Fuzzy sets, 27

Gates, David, 81
Gelernter, David, 133–134
Gemeinschaft bonds, 39, 159
Gender and social connectedness, 23, 27, 28, 35, 52, 53, 62, 117, 121, 127, 150–151
General Hospital, 110
Gergen, Kenneth, 147
Gerstel, Naomi, 195n. 19
Gerson, Judith, x, 189n. 16
Ghosts, 49–52, 131
Gibson, William, 33
Giddens, Anthony, 28, 96, 149
Goebbels, Joseph, 133
Goffman, Erving, 42, 45, 46, 49, 89, 125, 131, 142, 149, 197n. 20
Gould and White, 191n. 33, 191n. 35
Grahn, Nancy Lee, 110
Granovetter, Mark, 158–159
Grant, Bob, 91
Greeley, Andrew, 192n.8
Griffin, W.E.B., 91
Grisham, John, 91
Guiding Light, 18, 57, 76, 93, 115–116, 119–122, 183 (*see also* soap opera online communities)
Gutenberg, Johannes, 11–12, 137 (*see also* media, premodern)

Hamlet, 49
Hancock and Dunham, 44, 54, 192n. 6
Harnessing interaction, 143
Harrington and Bielby, 111, 116, 118, 130, 194n. 4, 195n. 14, 195n. 15

Health and social connectedness, 15, 19, 23, 26, 105–107, 137, 141, 142, 151–154 (*see also* technology, medical); anorexia, 154; asthma, 82; AIDS, 17; cancer, 1
Hernes, Gudmond, 145
Higginbotham, Evelyn Brooks, 107
Hill, Anita, 71
Hinckley, David, 71
History, 8–14, 64–65, 68–69, 85, 107–108, 132, 144–146, 147–149
Home Shopping Club, 63
Homer, 147
Horton and Wohl, 115, 194n. 7
Humanity, 8–19, 25–26, 39–52, 53–62, 66–73, 79–100, 128–131, 137–146, 147–156

Identity (*see* Self and Identity)
Intellectual interaction, 22
Internet, ix, 33, 77, 90, 137, 160 (*see also* e-mail, computer); "age," 2, 6, 159; America Online, 95; chat rooms, 7, 18, 34, 59, 67, 69, 85–86, 119, 142, 144; communities, discussion boards, message boards (*see* online communities); connections, connecting (*see* online connections); MUDs, 59, 83–84, 123–125, 150; Web sites, 17, 18, 32, 34, 46, 59, 67, 141
Intersubjectivity, 20, 25, 30, 102
Interviews for this study (*see* methodology)
Intimacy, 56, 79, 88, 101–102, 118–126, 129, 141, 154, 157–158

James, William, 197n. 27
Jesus Christ (*see also* religion), 24
Joel, Billy, 81
Johnson, Lyndon B., 94
Johnson, Magic, 17

Kadi, M., 59
Kecskemeti, Charles, 111
Keillor, Garrison, 33

Kennedy, Jacqueline (Onassis), ix, 16; John F., ix, 1; John Jr., 1; Robert, 1
Kenworthy, Jonathon, 68
Kevles, Daniel, 145
King, Martin Luther, 1, 112
Kornet, Allison, 125–126

Lake Wobegon Days, 33
Lakoff, George, 26–27
Land of the Lost, 65
Langer, Suzanne, 81
Language, 39, 42 (*see also* culture, media, technology, symbols, commonality, talk); abstract, 9–10, 39; common, 26, 28–29, 30, 39, 84; preliterate, 9–10, 32, 68, 147; social foundations of, 22, 28–29; writing, 10–15, 26, 32, 34, 44, 83–84, 108–109, 122–126, 136–137
Leach, Edmund, 35
Leakey, Richard, 10
Leave it to Beaver, 32
Legitimacy of sociomental connections (*see* reality, social)
Lennon, John, 1
Letters (*see* postal system)
Lewin, Kurt, 30–31, 190n. 27
Like-mindedness, 1, 20, 29, 54–76, 86, 142
Limbaugh, Rush, 71, 84
The Lion King, 51
Literal space (*see* space, literal; face-to-face)
Literature and social connectedness, ix, 1, 5, 11–13, 47, 49, 56–57, 63, 68–70, 89–92, 104, 142–143 (*see also* authors, media, language, technology); online community, 5, 19, 97, 103, 121, 141
Little Women, ix
Loftus, Elizabeth, 113, 194n. 6
Los Angeles Lakers, 53, 105

Macbeth, 113
Mandela, Nelson, 17
Mannheim, Karl, 22, 25, 36
Mantle, Mickey, 92

March, Jo, ix
Marketing (*see* advertising)
Marsh, Dave, 110
Mazlish, Bruce, 195–196n. 6, 197n. 22
McBride, Martina, 58
The McDonaldization of Society, 196n. 14
McLuhan, Marshall, 10, 139
Mead, George Herbert, 20, 21, 26, 40, 42, 147, 148
"Meathead," 1
Mechanical solidarity, 7, 145
Media, mass media (*see also* technology, Internet, online), actors (*see* actors and under specific actors); books, 4, 16, 47, 49, 56–57, 63, 90–92, 94, 104, 115, 140 (*see also* literature and under specific authors); characters (*see* fictional characters); comic strips and cartoons, 16, 51, 65; digital, 15–16; electronic (in general), 14–19, 32, 72–73, 124, 146; figures, celebrities, 2, 29, 33–34, 46, 62, 65–66, 69–70, 104, 110, 117, 131, 140 (*see also* under specific celebrity); film and movies, 15, 16, 19, 32, 49, 51, 62, 64–65, 88, 90, 92, 115, 136, 138–139; music, records, CDs and audiotapes (*see also* musicians and under specific musicians), 15, 18–19, 27, 51, 53, 55, 58, 64–68, 71–72, 76, 81–82, 110–111, 140, 158; newpapers and magazines, 12, 16, 17, 46, 58, 93, 94, 140; newsletters, 13, 46, 140; photography, 15, 34, 44, 52, 80–81, 85; premodern, 7–12; print (in general), 12–14, 16; radio, 15, 46, 65, 67, 71–72, 82, 84, 91, 94, 104, 111, 114, 136, 138, 140; use, 45, 70–71, 84, 90–95, 116, 129, 138–146, 140; television, ix, 1, 9, 16, 17, 18, 32–34, 42, 46, 54, 57–59, 61, 64–66, 70–74, 92–95, 102–104, 109–110, 115, 136–138, 140, 160; video taping, games, cameras and conferencing, 13, 15, 18, 19, 34, 51, 67, 94, 146; virtual reality,

simulations, 67, 117, 123–126; Web
sites (*see* Internet Web sites)
Mediator (technological) and
mediation, 8–9, 12–19, 37, 40, 42,
85–89, 90, 104, 115, 123, 126, 141,
157
Medical, medicine (*see* technology,
medical; health)
Meeting of the minds, 1–6, 29–30, 31,
37, 41, 67, 109, 161
Mechanical solidarity, 7
Mensa, 45
Mental (*see also* cognitive, sociomental),
act, action, 19–21, 29, 67, 99, 117;
bond (*see* sociomental bond);
connection (*see* sociomental
connection); community (*see*
community of the mind);
environment (*see* space, mental);
field, 30–37; flexibility, 7, 24, 52, 76,
117, 122–126, 129–132, 146–162;
glue, 41, 158; image, impression,
43–59, 68–73, 80–84, 96–100,
112–118; infrastructure, 158–159;
lens, 23–28; map, 31–37, 190n. 22,
190n. 27; model, 20, 28–29,
30–39, 53, 100, 132, 155;
networks (*see* networks,
mental); orientation, 42–52, 61, 77,
85; pathways (see networks,
mental); perspective, 21–23, 66,
115, 123, 148–150, 153, 156;
reference group, 23, 42, 63–66,
148–149; schemata (*see* mental
model); similarity, 8, 19–37, 54, 56,
58, 59, 67–78, 104–108, 112–123
(*see also* mental model, like-
mindedness, oneness); space (*see*
space, mental); world, 76, 91, 112,
116, 123–125, 140–141
Merelman, Richard, 127, 148–149
Merton, Robert, 114
Methodology of this study, and
confidentiality, 165, 171, 182, 185;
components of, 3, 163; interviewees,
profiles of, 171–179; interviews,
description of, 4, 163–171; online

groups, description of, 182–185;
online surveys, description of, 4, 5,
181–182
Meyrowitz, Joshua, 9, 32, 36–37, 116,
136
Mind (*see* cognitive, mental,
community of the mind, meeting of
the minds, sociomental bond,
sociomental connection)
Mister Rogers' Neighborhood, 33
Mobility, 6, 34
Modleski, Tania, 95
Monroe, Marilyn, 1
Morality and ethics, 3, 22–25, 134
Morgan, Lorrie, 58
Mr. Ed, 32
MUDs (*see* Internet, MUDs)
Multiplexity of connections, 5, 7,
119–121, 159
Musicians, connections to, ix, 55,
64–65, 71–72, 76, 81, 110–111 (*see
also* under specific musician)
My So-Called Life, 58
My Three Sons, 32

Nations (states) and nationalism and
social connectedness, 12, 14, 23,
26, 34–35, 41, 58, 61, 62, 67,
70–72, 83, 85, 87, 105, 107,
133, 158, 160; military, 23, 35,
62, 72–73, 91, 104
Natural phenomena and social
connectedness, 51–53, 131
Neighborhood (*see* space as
neighborhood)
Neimark, Jill, 96, 113–114
Networks, mental, 31–34, 40, 61–62,
73–78, 93, 108–112, 140, 158–160;
network theory, 119, 193n. 27, 198n.
36; topological, 30
Neuropsychology (*see* psychology)
Neuroscience, 113
Newhagen and Rafaeli, 15
New York Jets, 45
New York Mets, ix, 61, 106, 183
New York Yankees, 22, 92
Nippert-Eng, Christena, x, 16, 21, 23

Objects and social connectedness,
   51–53, 80–83, 117–118, 123–125,
   131
O'Brien, Jodi, 43, 150, 151
Oklahoma, 145
Oneness, 54–76, 78
Online (*see also* under specific online
   groups studied, Internet),
   communities, 1, 5, 18, 34, 41, 46,
   59, 61, 65, 67, 69, 83, 90, 95, 103,
   106–108, 121, 140–146;
   connections, 44, 59, 69, 85–89,
   106–108, 119–126, 123–126,
   140–146, 160; personae, 150–152;
   surveys (*see* methodology)
Ontological security, 96
Organic solidarity, 8, 145
Organizations, social connectedness in,
   9, 12, 45, 61, 63, 76–77, 90, 128,
   133–135
Others, ix, 10, 14, 16, 17, 20, 21,
   29–30, 41–52, 148, 155, 160–161;
   generalized, 24, 41, 140; particular,
   24, 41–52, 56, 61, 77, 147; typified,
   types, 26, 28, 42–52, 53–56, 65, 77,
   147

Parker, Charlie, ix
Pauling, Linus, 67
Pen pals, 1, 2, 4, 14, 109 (*see also* e-mail
   pals, postal system, telephone pals)
Perception, 19, 36–37, 39, 43, 49, 54,
   60, 67, 102, 112–115, 125–126 (*see
   also* cognitive, mental),
Perse and Rubin, 104
Physicality and social connectedness
   (*see* face-to-face)
Physics, field of, 66, 184
Pink Floyd, 65
Plato, 68
Politics and social connectedness, 1, 9,
   12, 13, 16, 45, 54, 62–63, 70–71,
   76–78, 84, 134, 140, 145 (*see also*
   under specific political leader);
   Democrats, 22; Republicans, 84
"Portfolio" of connections, 6, 11,
   128, 156

Postal system, mail and letters, 13–14,
   86–88, 92, 108–109, 123, 137 (*see
   also* pen pals)
Postman, Neil, 9
Presence (*see* space, presence in)
Presley, Elvis, 1
Protestant Reformation, 12 (*see also*
   religion)
Proximity (*see* space, proximity)
Psychic phenomena, 49–55, 89, 131
   (*see also* ghosts)
Psychology, 19–21, 40–43, 66, 89–90,
   113, 128, 147–149, 150 (*see also*
   under specific psychologist);
   neuropsychology, 20; psychobiology,
   89
Purcell, Kristin, 46, 70, 198n. 32
Putnam, Robert, 135
Pythagoras, 66

QVC, 110
Quasi-synchronization (*see*
   synchronization)
Quindlen, Anna, 72

Race and ethnicity and social
   connectedness, 23, 25, 28, 35, 45,
   52, 53, 58–59, 62, 105, 107, 143,
   150
Rafaeli, Sherif, 15, 198 n. 34
Reality, continuum of, 117–118,
   157–159; genuineness of the mental
   image and mental life, 41–53,
   112–118, 122–126, 132, 161;
   genuineness of sociomental
   connectedness, 1–2, 5, 15, 40, 58,
   73, 101–102, 112–118, 141,
   157–162, 157–158; social reality, 3,
   4, 20, 28, 39, 42, 45–53, 79–80,
   89–100, 101–108, 113–118,
   123–126, 129–132
Reciprocity of connections (*see*
   bidirectionaility)
Reese, Della, 74
Reeves, Nass and O'Toole, 115
Reeves, Richard, 135
Reid, Elizabeth, 83–84, 123–125

Reification, 129, 131

Reference group (*see* mental reference group)

Region and social connectedness, 23, 30, 125

Reincarnation, 47–50

Religion and social connectedness, 9, 23, 39–40, 41, 49, 52, 54, 62, 104, 119, 129, 131–132, 145, 147, 148, 152, 157; Bible, 12; Catholic, 22, 75–76; Christianity, 24, 75–75, 119; online community, 5, 114, 119, 146, 184; Protestant, 12, 75–76; televangelism, 123

Resonance, 2, 14, 29, 66–73, 77, 114

Rheingold, Howard, 107–107, 144

Rigidity (*see* mental flexibility)

Rituals, 70–71, 80, 88–96, 100, 103, 124

Ritzer, George, 196n. 14

Rosen, Ruth, 93

Ross, Bob, 17

Rubenstein, Carin, 91

Santa Barbara, 93

Saturday Night Fever, 64

Saturday Night Live, 84

Schedules and calendars, 67

Schoolhouse Rock, 64

Schramm and Porter, 11–12, 189n. 7

Schramm, Wilbur, 11–12, 66–67, 189n. 7

Schutz, Alfred, 25–26, 66, 67, 130

Science and social connectedness, 156 (*see also* Biology, Chemistry, Physics, acoustics, and under specific scientists); online community, 5, 34, 103, 122, 184; scientific thought collective, 22

Seinfeld, Jerry, 71, 84, 109–110

Seinfeld, 84, 109–110

Self and identity, 31, 69, 128, 142, 147–156; group identity, 25, 28, 40, 54, 59, 60–66, 72–73, 83–86, 103, 115; multiplicity of, 147–156; possible selves, 147; postmodern vs. modern, 132, 147–148; social self,

50, 132, 147–156; sociomental self, 147–156

Sensation, 19–21, 42, 71–73 (*see also* cognitive, mental)

Serialization, 89–94, 103, 121, 141 (*see also* rituals)

Sex (biological) and gender (*see* gender)

Sexuality and social connectedness, 23, 34, 107, 123–125, 129, 134, 150–151

Sexual orientation and social connectedness, 24, 45, 62, 83, 105, 107, 150, 154

Shakespeare, William, 113

Shibutani, Tamotsu, 23, 42, 115, 149

Shilling, Chris, 70

Simmel, Georg, 5, 7, 40, 42, 61, 75, 148, 149, 150

Simulteneity (*see also* time, technology), 14

Singer, Jerome L., 195n. 2

Smith, Bessie, 71

Smith, Kate, 114

Soap opera (*see also under* specific shows, characters, and actors), actors, 92–96, 194n. 4; and social connectedness, 91–96; characters, ix, 16, 57–59, 93–95; online communities and Web sites, 5, 34, 44, 57–59, 77, 83, 119–122, 141, 143, 183; press, 17–18, 93, 140; programs (in general), 18, 34, 92–95, 140

Socially structured mind (*see* mind, similarity; *see also* mental model, like-mindedness, one-ness, cognitive)

Social tie, 3, 39, 73, 97, 161; weak ties, 158–159

Societal cohesion and complexity, 127–128, 146, 155–156, 158–162

Societal integration, 139, 145–146, 156, 159–162

Sociomental (*see also* mental, cognitive), bond, 2, 13, 16–17, 31–32, 39–41, 50–54, 61–62, 66–78, 79–80, 82, 85–89, 90–100, 101–126, 157–162;

community (*see* community of the mind) connection, connectedness, 2, 5, 8, 9, 11, 12, 16, 17, 19, 20, 30, 31, 36–37, 39–41, 42–78, 79–100, 101–126, 127–162, 163–171, 181–185; self (*see* self and identity); space (*see* space, sociomental)

Socioeconomic class (*see* class, socioeconomic)

Socrates, 136

Solzhenitsyn, Alexander, 31

Somers, Suzanne, 110

Sorority, 54, 111–112

Space, as neighborhood, 33–37, 93, 120; cyberspace, 8, 30, 33, 59, 85–86, 121, 126, 134, 181–185; distance, ix, 1–2, 6, 8, 10, 12–19, 31, 34, 42, 61, 69, 79, 84–86, 100, 102–103, 115, 123, 134–135, 160–161; literal, 7, 31, 34–36, 40, 47, 61, 79, 97, 112, 119, 126; mental environment, 20, 31, 33, 36, 118, 123, 139; presence in, 13–15, 31–32, 35, 89, 123–126, 139, 191n. 29; proximity in, 8, 31–33, 119; sociomental, 30–37, 63–64, 89–90, 103, 119; tangibility of, 19, 31–31, 89, 112; topology, 30–31

Speed Racer, 65

Sperry, Roger, 21

Sports and social connectedness, 17, 53–54, 90–96, 140; athletes (*see* athletes, *see* under specific athlete); online community, 5, 106, 121, 143; sporting events, 46, 70–72, 92–96; teams, connectedness to, 17, 54, 74, 104 (*see also* under specific teams)

Springsteen, Bruce, 61, 110

Stahl, Lesley, 47

Star Wars, 65

Status characteristics, 23, 52, 53, 54

Stereotypes (see others, typified)

Stevenson, Robert Louis, 48–49

Stone, Allequere, 33, 37, 43

Stone, Christopher, 52

Strategic informant sampling (snowball sampling), 163–164 (*see also* methodology)

Strength of connections, 2, 5, 7, 39, 51 54–55, 59, 79, 84, 85, 89–100, 101–126, 157–158

Stress in modern life, 6, 106–107, 127–128, 132, 141, 152

Stuart, Mary, 95

Subcultures (*see* culture)

Sudnow, David, 192 n. 7

Symbols, 9, 26, 39, 53–55, 64–66, 76, 80–84, 94, 124, 129

Synchronization, quasi-synchronization, 67–73, 89, 114

Talk and conversation, 18, 27, 28–29, 39, 53, 74, 80, 84–89, 96, 111–112, 134, 138

Tangibility of connections (see space, tangibility in)

Technology (*see also* media, mediator, Internet, online, computer, simultaneity, telephone, telegraph, postal system), and social change, 4, 6, 8–19, 65, 127–162; communication, 8–19, 32, 39, 40, 49–52, 81, 83, 85–89, 115, 122, 127–162, 147; impact of, 2, 8–19, 37, 127–162; medical, medicine, 19, 23, 50, 66; transportation, 8, 13, 136–137, 147

Telegraph, 14

Telephone, 14–16, 18, 34, 61, 85–89, 122, 123, 126, 136, 146, 160; answering machines, 15–16, 63, 143; caller ID, 143; "pals," 2

TenHouten, Warren, 189n. 11

Terrorism, terrorist groups, 22, 72–73, 76

Thayer, Lee, 24, 53, 195n. 4

Thomas, Clarence, 71

Thought collective, 22–23, 28

Thought style, 22, 25, 29, 64, 130–132, (*see also* mental model, mental perspective)

Time (*see also* simultaneity, synchronization), 6, 8, 10, 12, 13, 19, 27, 37, 41, 43, 62, 67–73, 88, 92, 96, 161

Tonnies, Ferdinand, 39–40

Totems, 80

Transportation (*see* technology, transportation)

Turkle, Sherry, 125, 150–151

Types and typification (*see* categorization; stereotypes; others, particular and typified)

Twain, Mark, 146

Twain, Shania, 58

Viewers for Quality Television, 104

Waiters, 50

Walters, Barbara, 110

Walther, Joseph B., 18, 43, 59, 103, 191n. 29, 192n. 6, 195n. 21, 196n. 12

Walther, Slovacek and Tidwell, 18, 59, 95, 191n. 29, 192n. 6

Walton, Jess, 72

Warner, W. Lloyd, 48

Weber, Max, 41

"Web" of connections, 31, 76, 149–152, 158–160, 193n. 28

Web sites (*see* media, Web sites; *see also* online, Internet)

Wellman and Gulia, 121, 124, 160, 195n. 17

Wellman, Barry, 111, 121, 124, 160, 195n. 17

Westrum, Ron, 136

Whorf, Benjamin, 22, 29

Winnicott, D.W., 117–118

Women's Liberation movement, 12

Work and occupations and social connectedness, 4–5, 7, 8, 12, 14, 16, 23, 53, 54, 55, 58, 61, 62, 73, 86, 90, 95, 96, 106, 123, 128, 147 (*see also* under specific occupation)

Worldview (*see* thought style)

Writers, connections to (*see* authors, connections to; *see also* under specific writer or author)

The Young and the Restless, 93

Zadeh, Lofti, 27

Zahn, Paula, 58

Zelig, 21

Zerubavel, Eviatar, x, 21–28, 50, 70, 129, 149, 153–156, 189n. 12, 190n. 17

```
302        Chayko, Mary,
Cha           1960-

           Connecting.
```

DATE			